The Writer of Modern Life

Edited by Michael W. Jennings

Translated by Howard Eiland, Edmund Jephcott,
Rodney Livingston, and Harry Zohn

The Writer of Modern Life

Essays on Charles Baudelaire

DISCARDED

Walter Benjamin

The Belknap Press of Harvard University Press
Cambridge, Masschusetts, and London, England 2006

Additional copyright notices appear on page 307, which constitutes
an extension of the copyright page.

Library of Congress Cataloging-in-Publication Data
Benjamin, Walter, 1892–1940.
    [Essays. English. Selections]
    The writer of modern life : essays on Charles Baudelaire /
    Walter Benjamin ; edited by Michael W. Jennings.
        p. cm.
    Selected essays from Walter Benjamin's *Gesammelte Schriften.*
    Includes bibliographical references and index.
    ISBN-13: 978-0-674-02287-4 (alk. paper)
    ISBN-10: 0-674-02287-4 (alk. paper)
        1. Baudelaire, Charles, 1821–1867—Criticism and interpretation.
    2. Baudelaire, Charles, 1821–1867—Influence.   I. Jennings, Michael
    William.   II. Title.

PQ2191.Z5B39713   2006
841'.8—dc22   2006043584

Contents

The Writer of Modern Life

Introduction

By Michael W. Jennings

Walter Benjamin's essays on Charles Baudelaire from the 1930s accomplished nothing less than a wholesale reinvention of the great French poet as the representative writer of urban capitalist modernity.[1] Before Benjamin's radical reorientation of our image of the poet, Baudelaire had usually been considered in purely aesthetic terms—as a late Romantic or as a forerunner of the French Symbolists. For Benjamin, however, Baudelaire's greatness consisted precisely in his *representativeness:* in the manner in which his poetry—often against its express intent—laid open the structure and mechanisms of his age. Benjamin was hardly alone among his contemporaries, of course, in his estimation of Baudelaire as the first fully modern writer. In England, Baudelaire was a touchstone for T. S. Eliot, who translated Baudelaire into English and produced an important essay on Baudelaire's relation to modernity.[2] In Germany, the great lyric poet Stefan George was an important link between Baudelaire and modern German writing; George's translation of *Les Fleurs du mal* is still in many ways unsurpassed.[3] Yet Eliot and George saw in Baudelaire a writer very different from the one discovered by Benjamin.[4] For Eliot, Baudelaire was the key to adequate spiritual comprehension of modernity, an important predecessor in

Eliot's own quest to find a path informed by religion through the modern wasteland; for George, Baudelaire's poetry opened onto a vast, wholly aestheticized landscape that was proof against the indignities of the modern world. What is at stake in this comparison of Benjamin and his contemporaries is more than merely Benjamin's leftism versus the conservative—or, in the case of George, proto-fascist—politics of the other poets. If Eliot's Baudelaire was a key voice in the spiritual constitution of modernity, and George's Baudelaire the beacon of all genuinely modern aesthetic production, Benjamin made Baudelaire a complex object: a largely apolitical writer whose poetry we must nevertheless comprehend before we can formulate any responsible cultural politics of modernity. Benjamin resolutely refuses to attribute a single productive social or political insight to Baudelaire himself; the achievement of Benjamin's essays is their ability to expose *Les Fleurs du mal* as uniquely, scathingly, terrifyingly *symptomatic* of Baudelaire's era—and ours.[5]

In late 1914 or early 1915, when Walter Benjamin was all of twenty-two, he began translating individual poems from Baudelaire's great lyric cycle *Les Fleurs du mal;* he returned intermittently to the poems until the early 1920s, when his translation work became intensive. In 1923, *Tableaux parisiens: Deutsche Übertragung mit einem Vorwort über die Aufgabe des Übersetzers von Walter Benjamin* (Tableaux parisiens: German Translation with a Foreword Concerning the Task of the Translator, by Walter Benjamin), which included a full translation of the central section of *Les Fleurs du mal,* appeared in a luxury edition of five hundred.[6] Benjamin had submitted some early translations to Ernst Blass, editor of the journal *Die Argonauten,* in 1920, and it was Blass who introduced him to the publisher Richard Weissbach, who eventually brought out the slender volume. To Benjamin's great disappointment, neither the introduction—Benjamin's now-famous essay "The Task of the Translator"—nor the translations themselves met with interest either from the educated public or from critics.[7] On March 15, 1922, as part of an effort to publicize his book, Benjamin took part in an evening program dedicated to Baudelaire at the Reuss und Pollack bookshop on

Berlin's Kurfürstendamm, delivering a talk on the poet and reading from his own translations. Although he appears to have spoken from memory or perhaps from notes, the two brief texts included here under the title "Baudelaire" (II and III) are probably preliminary versions of his remarks.

Both of these texts focus on binary relations within Baudelaire's works and "view of things." Much of "Baudelaire III" fixes on the chiastic relations between the terms *spleen* and *idéal* in *Les Fleurs du mal*. Some of the most memorable poetry in the volume is to be found in the cycle of poems called "Spleen":

> Pluviôse, irrité contre la ville entière,
> De son urne à grands flots verse un froid ténébreux
> Aux pâles habitants du voisin cimetière
> Et la mortalité sur les faubourgs brumeux.

> [February, peeved at Paris, pours
> a gloomy torrent on the pale lessees
> of the graveyard next door and a mortal chill
> on tenants of the foggy suburbs too.]
>
> ("Spleen et idéal," LXXV: "Spleen I")

> Je suis comme le roi d'un pays pluvieux,
> Riche, mais impuissant, jeune et pourtant très-vieux,
> Qui, de ses précepteurs méprisant les courbettes,
> S'ennuie avec ses chiens comme avec d'autres bêtes.

> [I'm like the king of a rainy country, rich
> but helpless, decrepit though still a young man
> who scorns his fawning tutors, wastes his time
> on dogs and other animals, and has no fun.]
>
> ("Spleen et idéal," LXXVII: "Spleen III")[8]

Benjamin argues that the spleen we see projected here onto the cityscape and the weather is never merely a generalized melancholy— not merely the state of being splenetic—but has its source in "that fatally foundering, doomed flight toward the ideal," while the ideal itself rises from a ground of spleen: "it is the images of melancholy that kindle the spirit most brightly." This reversal, Benjamin is at pains to point out, takes place neither in the realm of the emotions nor in that of morals, but rather in that of perception. "What speaks to us in his poetry is not the reprehensible confusion of [moral] judgment but the permissible reversal of perception." The poem "Correspondances," with its invocation of the figure of synaesthesia, remains the primary evidence for such a claim; but others, such as the lovely poem "L'Invitation au voyage," also ring changes on the notion of perceptual reversal:

> Mon enfant, ma soeur,
> Songe à la douceur
> D'aller là-bas vivre ensemble!
> Aimer à loisir,
> Aimer et mourir
> Au pays qui te ressemble!
> Les soleils mouillés
> De ces ciels brouillés
> Pour mon esprit ont les charmes
> Si mystérieux
> De tes trâitres yeux,
> Brillant à travers leurs larmes.
>
> Là, tout n'est qu'ordre et beauté,
> Luxe, calme et volupté.
>
> [Imagine the magic
> of living together
> there, with all the time in the world
> for loving each other,
> for loving and dying
> where even the landscape resembles you.
> The suns dissolved

in overcast skies
have the same mysterious charm for me
as your wayward eyes
through crystal tears,
my sister, my child!
All is order there, and elegance,
pleasure, peace, and opulence.][9]

If the central motifs of this reading are still grounded in the categories through which Baudelaire had traditionally been received, the other little essay, "Baudelaire II," breaks new ground and indeed anticipates some of the most important motifs of Benjamin's work in the 1930s. In that piece, Baudelaire emerges as a privileged reader of a special body of photographic work: time itself is portrayed as a photographer capturing the "essence of things" on a photographic plate. These plates, of course, are negatives, and "no one can deduce from the negative . . . the true essence of things as they really are." In a remarkable attempt to evoke the originality of the poet's vision, Benjamin attributes to Baudelaire not the ability to develop such a negative, but rather a "presentiment of its real picture"—that is, a vision of it in its negative state. In "Baudelaire II," his earliest reading of the poet, Benjamin attempts to account for a number of aspects of his vision—such as Baudelaire's insight deep into the nature of things, in a poem such as "Le Soleil":

Quand, ainsi qu'un poète, il descend dans les villes,
Il ennoblit le sort des choses les plus viles,
Et s'introduit en roi, sans bruit et sans valets,
Dans tous les hôpitaux et dans tous les palais.

[When, with a poet's will, the sun descends
into the cities like a king incognito,
impartially visiting palace and hospital,
the fate of all things vile is glorified.]

Or, to take another example, Baudelaire's figuration of history as a multiple exposure in "Le Cygne":

> Andromaque, je pense à vous! Ce petit fleuve,
> Pauvre et triste miroir où jadis resplendit
> L'immense majesté de vos douleurs de veuve,
> Ce Simoïs menteur qui par vos pleurs grandit,
>
> A fécondé soudain ma mèmoire fertile,
> Comme je traversais le nouveau Carrousel.
>
> [Andromache, I think of you!
> That stream, the sometime witness to your widowhood's
> enormous majesty of mourning—that
> mimic Simois salted by your tears
> suddenly inundates my memory
> as I cross the new Place du Carrousel.]

Or, to take yet another example, Baudelaire's fundamental sense of the negative—as the transient and always irreversible—in "Une Charogne":

> Oui! Telle que vous serez, ô la reine des grâces,
>   Après les derniers sacraments,
> Quand vous irez, sous l'herbe et les floraisons grasses,
>   Moisir parmi les ossements.
>
> Alors, ô ma beauté! Dites à la vermine
>   Qui vous mangera de baisers,
> Qui j'ai gardé la forme et l'essence divine
>   De mes amours décomposés!
>
> [Yes, you will come to this, my queen,
> after the sacraments,
> when you rot underground among
> the bones already there.
> But as their kisses eat you up,

my Beauty, tell the worms
I've kept the sacred essence, saved
the form of my rotted loves!]¹⁰

And Benjamin finds in Baudelaire a capability analogous to the one he attributes to Kafka in his great essay of 1934: an intimate knowledge of humanity's "mythical prehistory."¹¹ It is no doubt this knowledge of primordial good and evil that opens the "true nature" of the photographic negative to Baudelaire's "infinite mental efforts."

The centrality of the photographic metaphor, and indeed of the figure of the photographic negative, in Benjamin's first critical engagement with Baudelaire is anything but an accident. By late 1921, Benjamin was moving in the orbit of the "G Group," a cenacle of avant-garde artists centered in Berlin. The great Hungarian artist László Moholy-Nagy was part of the earliest formations of the group, and Benjamin came to know him as early as the autumn of 1921. Moholy's theories of artistic production—and especially his important essay "Production-Reproduction," published in the avant-garde journal *De Stijl* in July 1922—would preoccupy Benjamin for years to come; but in 1921 and 1922, it is clear that Moholy's photographic *practice*, which then consisted of experimentation with the photogram (a cameraless photograph that, to the uninitiated, appears to be a negative), played a role in Benjamin's first interpretation of Baudelaire. From the very beginnings of his critical engagement with Baudelaire's work, then, Benjamin was considering Baudelaire's poetry in conjunction with key categories of modernity and especially of the technologized cultural production that is characteristic of urban commodity capitalism.

After Benjamin's bookstore talk in 1922, Baudelaire became a subterranean presence in his work for the next thirteen years. This was a time of radical change in the orientation and practice of Benjamin's criticism. In the years prior to 1924 and the completion of *The Origin of German Trauerspiel,* his great study of the German Baroque play of mourning, Benjamin had been intent on a reevaluation of German Romanticism, and the development of a theory of criticism with deep roots in that very body of work. During those years, Benjamin had written precisely one essay on twentieth-century literature, an unpublished piece on Paul Scheerbart, author of utopian science fiction. Beginning in 1924, however, he turned his attention and his energies in precipitously new directions: toward contemporary European culture, Marxist politics, and a career as a journalist and wide-ranging cultural critic. By 1926 Benjamin was embarked on a program of study and writing that would, he hoped, make him Germany's most widely respected voice on the modernist and avant-garde cultural production of France and the Soviet Union. His frequent visits to Paris inspired a series of brilliant essays on Paul Valéry, André Gide, Julien Green, and Marcel Proust, as well as influential presentations and analyses of the French historical avant-garde. The essay "Surrealism: The Last Snapshot of the European Intelligentsia" (1929) presents the provisional results of his analysis of French modernism. Baudelaire, as the progenitor of French modernism, of course haunts this work, but Benjamin consistently avoided direct engagement with the poet in this period.

Reflection on Baudelaire reentered his writing in the late 1920s as Benjamin began to collect material and ideas for *The Arcades Project* (*Das Passagen-Werk*), his great history of the emergence of urban commodity capitalism in Paris around 1850. The study took its working title from the proliferation of mercantile galleries, or arcades, in mid-nineteenth-century Paris. Benjamin fastens on these structures as an organizing metaphor because they are at once a historically specific artifact and a particularly concentrated symbol of the mercantile capitalism of the period—indeed, "a world in miniature." The arcades are both street and interior, market and amusement palace, and thus reflect the ambiguity Benjamin finds characteristic of the bourgeois experience of that era. He locates the decisive historical shift to the modern era, then, not so much in large-scale modifications in the societal totality but rather in changes in concrete societal artifacts and in the way they are experienced and understood. As he put it in a draft version of the conclusion to the essay, the creations and forms of life determined by commodity production "present themselves as a phantasmagoria. . . . The world that is dominated by these phantasmagorias is—in a key word found for it by Baudelaire—the 'Modern.'"[12]

Benjamin worked on this enormous project until the end of his life, never bringing it to completion; in the years of his exile from fascist Germany after 1933, much of the work was supported by stipends from the Institute for Social Research. In 1935, Fritz Pollack, the co-director of the institute, suggested that Benjamin produce an exposé of the project that could be shown to potential sponsors. The text "Paris, the Capital of the Nineteenth Century" (included in this volume) was in fact that exposé; it thus represents Benjamin's first attempt to describe the scope and focus of *The Arcades Project*. Baudelaire would, at this stage of the project, have played a key, though not central role: the utopian socialist Charles Fourier, the photographer Louis Jacques Daguerre, the caricaturist Grandville (Jean Ignace Isidore Gérard), the constitutional monarch Louis Philippe, and the city planner Baron Georges Eugène Haussmann would have appeared alongside Baudelaire in leading roles in the drama of modernity played out amid the arcades, panoramas, world exhibitions, and barricades of Paris. The pages given over to Baudelaire are perhaps the densest in the essay: Benjamin presents, in dizzying abbreviature, a number of the central motifs of his critique of modernity: the flâneur who strolls through the urban crowd as prosthetic vehicle of a new vision; the department store as phantasmagoric space of display and consumption; the commercialization and final alienation of the intelligentsia; the prostitute as concatenated image—of death and woman, "seller and sold in one"; the gradual denaturing of art as it is subsumed by commodification and fashion; and the replacement of experience by the new concept of information. These are among the central categories that will inform the great essays on Baudelaire to come.

As Benjamin continued to amass material for his study of the arcades, and to develop a theory adequate to that material, his friends at the Institute for Social Research became increasingly eager to see some part of the project in print. In 1937, at the urging of Max

Horkheimer, the institute's director, Benjamin reconceptualized the project as a study of Baudelaire that would draw on the central concerns of *The Arcades Project* as a whole.[13] He produced a detailed outline that organized excerpts from his notes under section and chapter headings.[14] The book project, which bore the working title *Charles Baudelaire: A Lyric Poet in the Era of High Capitalism,* would have had three parts: (1) "Baudelaire as Allegorist"; (2) "The Paris of the Second Empire in Baudelaire"; and (3) "The Commodity as Poetic Object." Working feverishly throughout the summer and fall of 1938 in Skovsbostrand, Denmark, where he was a guest of his friend the great German dramatist Bertolt Brecht, Benjamin completed the middle third of the Baudelaire book and submitted this text as an essay entitled "The Paris of the Second Empire in Baudelaire" to the *Zeitschrift für Sozialforschung* (Journal for Social Research) in New York.

Benjamin's first major work on Baudelaire is one of the greatest essays of literary criticism from the twentieth century; it is also one of the most demanding of its reader, requiring not merely inordinate contributions of imagination and analysis, but a thorough knowledge of Benjamin's other work. The essay begins, disconcertingly, not with a consideration of Baudelaire's poetry, or even of Baudelaire himself, but with the evocation of a particular "intellectual physiognomy": that of the conspiratorial face of the *bohème.* For Benjamin, the bohemians were not primarily artistes starving in garrets—think of Rodolfo and Mimi in Puccini's *La Bohème*—but a motley collection of amateur and professional conspirators who imagined the overthrow of the regime of Napoleon III, France's self-elected emperor. In the opening pages of the essay, Benjamin establishes relays between the tactics employed by these figures and the *aesthetic* strategies that characterize Baudelaire's poetic production. If "surprising proclamations and mystery-mongering, sudden sallies, and impenetrable irony were part of the *raison d'état* of the Second Empire," Benjamin says, Baudelaire's poetry is likewise driven by "the enigmatic stuff of allegory" and "the mystery-mongering of the conspirator." This physiognomic evocation of Baudelaire leads not to a read-

ing of a poem where such a physiognomy flashes up at the reader—
one might think of "Satan's Litanies," with its evocation of a "Prince
of exiles, exiled Prince who, wronged / yet rises ever stronger from
defeat, / Satan, take pity on my sore distress!"[15]—but rather to an
analysis of the poem "Ragpicker's Wine," chosen because of its own
evocation of the milieu in which the conspirators operated, a series
of cheap taverns outside the city gates. This montage of various aspects of one intellectual physiognomy within the spaces in which it
arises is central to Benjamin's method in his work on Baudelaire. In
the figure of the ragpicker we find a highly charged concatenation:
"From the littérateur to the professional conspirator, everyone who
belonged to the *bohème* could recognize a bit of himself in the
ragpicker. Each person was in a more or less blunted state of revolt
against society and faced a more or less precarious future." As this
quotation from "The Paris of the Second Empire" suggests, the ragpicker was a recognizable social type. Yet the ragpicker is also a figure
for Baudelaire, for the poet who draws on the detritus of the society through which he moves, seizing that which seems useful in part
because society has found it useless. And finally, the ragpicker is
a figure for Benjamin himself, for the critic who assembles his critical montage from inconspicuous images wrested forcefully from
the seeming coherence of Baudelaire's poems. Here and throughout
Benjamin's writings on Baudelaire, we find a powerful identification
with the poet: with his social isolation, with the relative failure of his
work, and in particular with the fathomless melancholy that suffuses
every page.

Benjamin concludes this first constellation by contrasting Baudelaire with Pierre Dupont, an avowed social poet, whose work strives
for a direct, indeed simple and tendentious engagement with the political events of the day. In contrasting Baudelaire with Dupont,
Benjamin reveals a "profound duplicity" at the heart of Baudelaire's
poetry—which, he contends, is less a statement of support for the
cause of the oppressed, than a violent unveiling of their illusions. As
Benjamin wrote in his notes to the essay, "It would be an almost
complete waste of time to attempt to draw the position of a Baude-

laire into the network of the most advanced positions in the struggle for human liberation. From the outset, it seems more promising to investigate his machinations where he was undoubtedly at home: in the enemy camp. . . . Baudelaire was a secret agent—an agent of the secret discontent of his class with its own rule."[16] Although this is not the place for a full analysis of the theoretical stances that dictated Benjamin's construction of "The Paris of the Second Empire in Baudelaire," a few remarks may suggest a line of approach. By the late 1930s Benjamin was convinced that traditional historiography, with its reliance upon the kind of storytelling that suggests the inevitable process and outcome of historical change, "is meant to cover up the revolutionary moments in the occurrence of history. . . . The places where tradition breaks off—hence its peaks and crags, which offer footing to one who would cross over them—it misses."[17] Benjamin's essay is thus composed of a series of vivid images torn from their "natural" or "original" context and integrated into a text based on principles of montage.[18] And he did so from the conviction that these images, often based on seemingly inconsequential details of large historical structures, have been ignored as the dominant class ascribes truth value to its own, ideologically inspired version of history. In order to uncover what Benjamin calls "true history" or "primal history," he proposes "to extract, to cite, what has remained inconspicuously buried beneath—being, as it was, of so little help to the powerful."[19] How, though, are we to understand the *relationships* between the images in Benjamin's text? Far from the "lack of mediation" or "billiard-ball determinism" attributed to Benjamin's practice by Theodor Adorno and Fredric Jameson, Benjamin counts on the "expressive" capacity of his images.[20] "The economic conditions under which society exists are expressed in the superstructure—precisely as, with the sleeper, an overfull stomach finds not its reflection but its expression in the contents of dreams, which, from a causal point of view, it may be said to 'condition.'"[21] Benjamin thus seeks to create a textual space in which a speculative, intuitive, and analytical intelligence can move, reading images and the relays between them in such a way that the *present* meaning of "what has been comes together in a flash." This is what Benjamin calls the dialectical image. And "The Paris of the Second Empire in Baudelaire" is the finest, most fully realized example of the critical practice informed by the theory of the dialectical image.[22]

In the central section of "Paris of the Second Empire in Baudelaire," titled "The Flâneur," Benjamin turns to an extended consideration of the reciprocally generative relations between certain artistic genres and societal forms. In the crowded streets of the urban metropolis, the individual is not merely absorbed into the masses: all traces of individual existence are in fact effaced. And popular literary and artistic forms such as physiologies (literary and artistic exemplifications of physiognomic types) and panoramas (representations of "typical" tableaux in Paris) arose, Benjamin argues, precisely in order to quell the deep-seated unease that characterized this situation: through their "harmlessness" they suggested a "perfect bonhomie" devoid of all resistance to the social order of the day, and in so doing contributed to the "phantasmagoria of Parisian life."

The concept of phantasmagoria is pervasive in Benjamin's late writings on Baudelaire. Originally an eighteenth-century illusionistic optical device by which shadows of moving figures were projected onto a wall or screen, phantasmagoria, as Benjamin sees it, stands squarely in a tradition beginning with Karl Marx. In a famous chapter of *Capital* called "The Fetishism of Commodities and the Secret Thereof," Marx suggests that the commodities that flow through the capitalist system of production and exchange take on the qualities of the religious fetish: that is, extrasensory capacities are attributed to them such that, when they function within extensive networks, commodities work to suppress the human rational capacity and appeal instead to the emotions, much as a religious fetish appeals to and organizes an irrational belief structure. The important Hungarian-German philosopher Georg Lukács built on this concept in a book of 1923, *History and Class Consciousness;* there, Lukács argued that the cumulative effect of these networks of fetishized commodities is that of a "second nature," an environment so suggestively "real" that we move through it as if it were given and natural when in fact it is a socioeconomic construct. For Benjamin, "phantasmagoria" is widely coextensive with the term "second nature"; the term "phantasmagoria" simply emphasizes the powerfully illusory quality of this environment, a quality that has a debilitating effect upon the human ability to come to rational decisions—and in fact to understand our own world. Physiologies are in this sense deeply complicit with phantasmagoria, in that they fraudulently suggest we are in possession of a knowledge that we do not in fact have. As Benjamin says in "The Paris of the Second Empire," physiologies "assured people that everyone could—unencumbered by any factual knowledge—make out the profession, character, background, and lifestyle of passers-by."

The "soothing little remedies" offered by physiologies could only be a temporary check on the character of life under modern conditions. Benjamin suggests that another genre developed, one "concerned with the disquieting and threatening aspects of urban life." This genre was the detective story. If, in the dreamlike space of the urban phantasmagoria, the denizens of the city were nonetheless confronted with a series of shocks and an attendant sense of unease, the detective story, with its reliance on ratiocination, provided an apparent solution, one that "allows the intellect to break through this emotion-laden atmosphere."[23] Baudelaire himself, Benjamin believed, was incapable of producing detective stories. "The structure of his drives" blocked any rational structures in the poet: "Baudelaire was too good a reader of the Marquis de Sade to be able to compete with Poe."

If Baudelaire's poetry is neither symptomatic of social conditions (as were the physiologies) nor capable of providing procedures for dealing with them (as did the detective story), what exactly is the relationship of that poetry to modernity? Benjamin champions Baudelaire precisely because his work claims a particular historical responsibility: in allowing itself to be marked by the ruptures and aporias of modern life, it reveals the brokenness and falseness of modern experience. At the heart of Benjamin's reading is thus a theory of shock, developed on the basis of a now-famous reading of the poem

"A une passante" (To a Passer-By). The speaker of the poem, moving through the "deafening" street amid the crowd, suddenly spies a woman walking along and "with imposing hand / Gathering up a scalloped hem." The speaker is transfixed, his body twitches, wholly overcome by the power of the image. Yet, Benjamin argues, the spasms that run through the body are not caused by "the excitement of a man in whom an image has taken possession of every fiber of his being"; their cause is instead the powerful, isolated shock "with which an imperious desire suddenly overcomes a lonely man."

This notion of a shock-driven poetic capability was a significant departure from the understanding of artistic creation prevalent in Benjamin's day and in fact still powerfully present today. The poet is, on this view, not a genius who "rises above" his age and distills its essence for posterity. For Benjamin, the greatness of Baudelaire consists instead in his absolute *susceptibility* to the worst excrescences of modern life: Baudelaire was in possession not of genius, but of an extraordinarily "sensitive disposition" that enabled him to perceive, through a painful empathy, the character of an age. And for Benjamin, the "character of the age" consisted in its thoroughgoing commodification. Baudelaire was not simply *aware of* the processes of commodification from which the phantasmagoria constructs itself; he in fact *embodied* those processes in an emphatic manner. When he takes his work to market, the poet surrenders himself *as a commodity* to "the intoxification of the commodity immersed in a surging stream of customers." The poet's role as producer and purveyor of commodities opens him to a special "empathy with inorganic things." And this, in turn, "was one of his sources of inspiration." Baudelaire's poetry is thus riven by its images of a history that is nothing less than a "permanent catastrophe." This is the sense in which Baudelaire was the "secret agent" of the destruction of his own class.

Approaching the conclusion to "The Paris of the Second Empire in Baudelaire," in the section entitled "Modernity," Benjamin makes a case for Baudelaire as the characteristic writer of modern life; he seeks to reveal Baudelaire's heroism. "The hero is the true subject of modernity. In other words, it takes a heroic constitution to live modernity." Baudelaire as the modern hero, then, is more than the flâneur who strolls the streets of Paris with an empathetic openness, and more than the commoditized purveyor of aesthetic commodities. He is the modern individual who has, piece by piece, been stripped of the possessions and security of bourgeois life and forced to take refuge in the street. As the harried denizen of the warren of streets leading away from the elegance of the *grands boulevards,* Baudelaire is rendered defenseless against the shocks of modern life. His heroism thus consists in his constant willingness to have the character of his age mark and scar his body. "The resistance that modernity offers to the natural productive élan of an individual is out of all proportion to his strength. It is understandable if a person becomes exhausted and takes refuge in death." Heroism thus assumes the form of a mourning for a loss that has not yet occurred but always threatens—a Baudelairean notion that Benjamin places at the very center of his reading.

The pathos that infuses this section of the essay arises from Walter Benjamin's intense identification with Baudelaire's situation. The most prominent features of Baudelaire's biography—the penniless poet condemned to a lack of recognition at first equivalent to an inner exile, and then, at the end of his life, to self-imposed exile in Belgium—conform closely to those of Benjamin himself, the greatest critic of his era yet someone who, as he put it, could find no place on earth where he could both earn a minimum amount and subsist on a minimum amount. The temptation of suicide's release was never far from Benjamin's thoughts in the period of his exile, and his imputation of "exhaustion" to Baudelaire was certainly a powerful projective act.

Yet the character of life under modern conditions is not portrayed as irredeemably damned. "The Paris of the Second Empire in Baudelaire" suggests, if subtly and intermittently, that Baudelaire's poetry might hold the key to an understanding of that apparently unchangeable history—history as "one-way street," as Benjamin called an important text from 1928—as the "object of a conquest."[24] Even though the modern hero and the age that spawned him are "destined for doom," there nonetheless exists a retrospective and wholly subterranean hope that modernity might harbor the elements of its own redemption. The question thus arises as to "whether [modernity] itself will ever be able to become antiquity." If Victor Hugo saw in modern Paris so many palpable remainders of the ancient world that he could speak of "Parisian antiquity," Baudelaire, says Benjamin, insists instead that modernity is bound to the classical through a shared *decrepitude,* by a "mourning for what was and lack of hope for what is to come." Those aspects of the modern city made to appear "truly new" under capitalism soon reveal themselves as outdated. "Modernity has changed most of all, and the antiquity it was supposed to contain really presents a picture of the obsolete." As early as 1929, in his essay on Surrealism, Benjamin had expressed his conviction that meaningful social change might arise from the "revolutionary energies" of that which is obsolete. This conviction was founded on the contention that the mechanisms of the capitalist process reveal themselves fully only in their waste products—in that which no longer serves a purpose and is thus free from the mechanisms of ideological control so pervasive elsewhere. It is the *experience* of such obsolete artifacts, and through them of the coercive illusions of capitalism, that might give rise to political action as a corrective. Baudelaire's spleen—that is, his profound disgust at things as they were—is only the most evident emotional sign of this state of affairs.

The most effective and revelatory potentials discussed in "The Paris of the Second Empire in Baudelaire," however, are those attributed to Baudelaire's language itself. "His prosody is like the map of a big city in which one can move about inconspicuously, shielded by blocks of houses, gateways, courtyards. On this map, words are given clearly designated positions before the outbreak of a revolt." But how might such tactically situated words actually give rise to revolution? Part of Benjamin's complex answer to this question lies in a reconception of the notion of allegory he had developed in his great book on the Baroque play of mourning, *The Origin of German Trauerspiel*

(1928). There, Benjamin had argued that these works of art, long neglected because of their apparently grave aesthetic flaws, in fact bore within them a particularly responsible historical index of their age. They gave access not so much to a hidden knowledge of the Baroque as to the insight that *all* knowledge of a given system is subjective and illusory. "Related as [knowledge] is to the depths of the subjective, it is basically only knowledge of evil. It is 'nonsense' in the profound sense in which Kierkegaard conceived the word. This knowledge, the triumph of subjectivity and the onset of an arbitrary rule over things, is the origin of all allegorical contemplation." In the allegorical mode of representation, dominant in Trauerspiel and prevalent, Benjamin argues, in Baudelaire, "any person, any object, any relationship can mean absolutely anything else. With this possibility a destructive but just verdict is passed on the profane world: it is characterized as a world in which the detail is of no great importance."[25] Allegory, in its brokenness, is the aesthetic form that bears the most responsible relationship to a history that is a permanent catastrophe. In claiming that Baudelaire's prosody is like a map, Benjamin argues that it is less the words themselves than their *placement* in the map of a text that gives rise to their potential revolutionary power. This relational character of poetic language, its deployment of such stratagems as spacing and displacement, its "calculated disharmony between the image and object," mark Baudelaire as an allegorist. And within the linguistic spaces so opened, Benjamin saw that experience of the utter meaninglessness of the modern world might arise—that, in other words, the phantasmagoria might be broken down and exposed for what it is. As Benjamin put it in *Central Park*, the collection of reflections upon which he was working while writing "The Paris of the Second Empire": "To interrupt the course of the world— that was Baudelaire's deepest intention."

With clouds of war hanging over Europe—clouds dispersed only temporarily by the infamous Munich Accords—Benjamin submitted his completed essay to the *Journal for Social Research* in late September 1938. He wrote to Theodor Adorno that the completion of the essay had been "a race against the war; and despite the fear that choked me, I experienced a feeling of triumph on the day I brought the 'Flâneur'—which had been planned for almost fifteen years—safely under a roof (even if only the fragile one of a manuscript!)"[26] In mid-November Benjamin received what was arguably the most crushing rejection of his career: the news, conveyed in an extensive critique by Adorno, that the Institute for Social Research would not publish "The Paris of the Second Empire in Baudelaire."[27] It is hardly surprising that it took Benjamin almost a month to answer; Adorno's letter had plunged him into a deep depression from which he emerged only in the spring of 1939. Sensing in advance that his local arguments would have little effect, Benjamin concluded his reply with the plea that a wider audience—and history—be allowed to judge his work. The plea fell on deaf ears. He was asked to rework the central section of his essay along lines acceptable to Adorno and Horkheimer.

While still at work on "The Paris of the Second Empire," Benjamin had begun to collect extended passages of interpretation and theoretical reflection under the working title "Central Park." The title remains enigmatic: it certainly refers to New York's Central Park, thus serving as a kind of beacon for a hoped-for escape from Europe, but also simply designates a parking place for "central" reflections that had no home, as yet, in the larger Baudelaire project, which still bore the working title *Charles Baudelaire: A Lyric Poet in the Age of High Capitalism*. The fragments in "Central Park" touch on a remarkable range of topics: on Baudelaire's sexuality as an expression of bourgeois impotence; on the critique of progress, which Benjamin apostrophized as the fundamental tenet of bourgeois liberalism; on Baudelaire, Jugendstil, and the threat of an increasing technologization; and, predominantly, on the problems addressed in the two still unwritten sections of the Baudelaire book: the ones on allegory ("Baudelaire as Allegorist") and phantasmagoria ("The Commodity as Poetic Object").[28]

The institute's rejection of "The Paris of the Second Empire in Baudelaire," though, forced Benjamin to turn away from further work on the Baudelaire book project in order to revise the essay's central section, "The Flâneur," for submission to the institute's journal. From February through July of 1939, Benjamin worked steadily toward an essay that could be published in New York. That essay, "On Some Motifs in Baudelaire," takes up many of the problems—and solutions—evident in "The Paris of the Second Empire in Baudelaire." But it does so within a context very different from that of the earlier piece, which was a general consideration of Baudelaire's place in his era. In the later essay, he examines Baudelaire's work from the perspective of its reception in the twentieth century. "If conditions for a positive reception of lyric poetry have become less favorable, it is reasonable to assume that only in rare instances does lyric poetry accord with the experience of its readers. This may be due to a change in the structure of their experience." Benjamin goes on to posit the nature of this change; he discriminates—in a formulation now given very wide currency—between long experience *(Erfahrung)* and isolated experience *(Erlebnis)*. Long experience is presented as a coherent body of knowledge and wisdom that is not merely retainable in human memory but transmissible from generation to generation. Benjamin's essay "The Storyteller," with its rather nostalgic evocation of a precapitalist era, adduces oral literature as the privileged form of such transmission within traditional societies. Isolated experience, on the other hand, emerges in "On Some Motifs in Baudelaire" as a form of experience bound to the shocks experienced by the individual strolling amid the urban masses; isolated experience, far from being retainable or transmissible, is in fact parried by consciousness and leaves a trace in the unconscious. Of particular interest to Benjamin, though, is the case in which this defensive mechanism fails—that is, the case in which the shock is *not* parried by consciousness, but instead penetrates and deforms it. These unparried shocks give rise, for Benjamin, to the central images of Baudelaire's poetry.

The middle sections of "On Some Motifs in Baudelaire" turn to the social form in which urban shock is most prevalent: the crowd. Benjamin here expands upon his earlier analysis of "A une passante," and adds to it a brilliant reading of Poe's tale "The Man of the

Crowd." What most clearly separates "On Some Motifs in Baudelaire" from the earlier essay, though, is not this expansion of earlier ideas, but rather their insertion into a context suggested by the history of media. Drawing on his pathbreaking work in the theory of media, "The Work of Art in the Age of Its Technological Reproducibility," Benjamin argues that the isolation of the individual—the bourgeois retreat from the urban masses into the comfort of privacy and domesticity—"brings those enjoying it closer to mechanization." The looming chaos of the streets, with its hurtling cars and jostling humans, is controlled technologically, by advances as simple as traffic signals. Technology constitutes not just a prosthetic extension of the human sensory capacity, enabling a complex series of reactions, but a veritable training school for the human sensorium that enables its subsistence in the modern world.

Benjamin understands the greatness of Baudelaire's poetry as a paradoxical capacity. Its imagery is produced, on the one hand, by Baudelaire's submission to the shock experience of modern life in its full force; the reaction may be splenetic, but it is also heroic. This splenetic dimension, however, stands in tension with Baudelaire's *idéal:* the capacity to fix in language "days of recollection [*Eingedenken*], not marked by any immediate experience [*Erlebnis*]." This particular form of sensitivity—to beauty, to the comfort of ritual, to the longing for a coherent and comprehensible experience—is articulated, for Benjamin, in two sonnets, "Correspondances" and "La Vie antérieure." This, too, is part of Baudelaire's heroism: the attempt to capture an experience "which seeks to establish itself in crisis-proof form." Some commentators have viewed Benjamin's discussion of this recollection of the ideal as exemplifying a nostalgia that permeates his late work: that same bourgeois nostalgia for an existence which would be proof against the humiliations and deeply disturbing shocks of a penurious life on the urban streets. But if such a nostalgia exists in Benjamin's work on Baudelaire, it does so only as a faint undercurrent. Baudelaire's evocation of a life of plenitude—of "luxe, calme et volupté"—is instead for Benjamin in large part a *repoussoir,* a perspective device that allows Baudelaire "to fathom the full meaning of the breakdown which he, as a modern man, was witnessing."

The bracketing of the nostalgic dimension of Benjamin's reading is essential if the reader is to receive the full force of Benjamin's final characterization of Baudelaire's poetry as fully modern. In the final sections of "On Some Motifs in Baudelaire," Benjamin argues that Baudelaire's status as the representative poet of urban capitalist modernity rests upon the ability of his work to mount an attack on what he calls "auratic" art. The term "aura" first appears in Benjamin's 1929 essay "Little History of Photography," but the most fully developed definition is to be found in his "Work of Art" essay: "What, then, is aura? A strange tissue of space and time: the unique appearance of a distance, however near it may be. To follow with the eye— while resting on a summer afternoon—a mountain range on the horizon or a branch that casts its shadow on the beholder is to breathe the aura of those mountains, of that branch."[29] A work of art may be said to have an aura if it claims a unique status based less on its quality, use value, or worth per se than on its figurative distance from the beholder. I say "figurative," since, as the definition intimates, this distance is not primarily a space between painting and spectator or between text and reader but a psychological inapproachability—an authority—claimed on the basis of the work's position within a tradition. The distance that intrudes between work and viewer is most often, then, a temporal distance: auratic texts are sanctioned by their inclusion in a time-tested canon. For Benjamin, integration into the Western tradition is coterminous with an integration into cultic practices: "Originally, the embeddedness of an artwork in the context of tradition found expression in a cult. As we know, the earliest artworks originated in the service of rituals. . . . In other words: *the unique value of the "authentic" work of art always has its basis in ritual.*"[30] This is in effect a description of the inevitable fetishization of the work of art, less through the process of its creation than through the process of its transmission. If the work of art remains a fetish, a distanced and distancing object that exerts an irrational and incontrovertible power, it attains a cultural status that lends it a sacrosanct inviolability. It also remains in the hands of a privileged few. The auratic work exerts claims to power that parallel and reinforce the larger claims to political power of the class for whom such objects are most meaningful: the bourgeoisie. The theoretical defense of auratic art was and is central to the maintenance of their power. It is not just that auratic art, with its ritually certified representational strategies, poses no threat to the dominant class, but that the sense of authenticity, authority, and permanence projected by the auratic work of art represents an important cultural substantiation of the claims to power of the dominant class.

Benjamin credits Baudelaire, to be sure, with deep insight into the phenomenon of the aura. Yet Baudelaire's lyric poetry is great not because of this insight, but precisely because it is "marked by the disintegration of the aura." If auratic art, in its plenitude, assumes human capacities and seems to return our gaze, art marked by the loss of the aura is broken and mute, its gaze stunted or turned inward. It arises in a social situation, conditioned by technology, in which humans in public spaces *cannot* return the gaze of others. "Before the development of buses, railroads, and trams in the nineteenth century, people had never been in situations where they had to look at one another for long minutes or even hours without speaking to one another." Such a passenger, and such a poet, are unlikely to surrender to "distance and to faraway things." Baudelaire's poetry, in its fixing of the shock effect of movement through the urban crowd, breaks through the "magic of distance" as it "steps too close" and shatters the illusions—of the aura and, by extension, of a system of power.

In late 1863 Baudelaire published an essay called "The Painter of Modern Life" in three installments in the newspaper *Figaro*. The reader who returns to Baudelaire's essay after making the acquaintance of the essays in the present volume will find that Benjamin's task—the depiction of the manner in which Baudelaire and his work are representative of modernity in a way achieved by no other writer—was less the invention of a new Baudelaire than the assertion of the centrality of a number of aspects of Baudelaire's work that had been neglected or misunderstood. When Baudelaire writes, "By 'modernity' I mean the ephemeral, the fugitive, the contingent, the half of art whose other half is the eternal and the immutable," we encounter the physiognomy of Benjamin's poet riven by the splenetic and the ideal.[31] "The Painter of Modern Life" is in fact shot through with themes highlighted in Benjamin's essays: the increasing importance of fashion; the replacement of permanence and solidity with transience and fragmentation; the loss of status of the modern artist—the descent from a state of genius to one of "convalescence";[32] the importance of such seemingly marginal figures as the dandy and the flâneur; the isolation and alienation of the modern individual in the urban crowd, where "the spectator is a prince who everywhere rejoices in his incognito";[33] and even the sounding of the theme of phantasmagoria. In fact, the central insight of "On Some Motifs in Baudelaire"—the understanding of the development of the poetic image from a basis in shock—is present in suggestive form in "The Painter of Modern Life": "I am prepared to . . . assert that inspiration has something in common with a convulsion, and that every sublime thought is accompanied by a more or less violent nervous shock which has its repercussions in the very core of the brain."[34]

The true originality of Benjamin's reading of Baudelaire consists, then, not so much in the working-through of these and other motifs for which his essays are known. It consists in the rethinking of Baudelaire's representativeness in light of his claim in "The Painter of Modern Life" that his work *makes present* the character of an age: "The pleasure which we derive from the representation of the present is due not only to the beauty with which it can be invested, but also to its essential quality of being present."[35] An adequate reading of Baudelaire's work must then banish forever the "ghostly attraction" of the past and restore to it the "light and movement of life."[36]

Every line that Walter Benjamin wrote about Baudelaire is an attempt to banish that ghost, and to bring the poet's work to bear upon the present. Long before he turned to the concentrated work on Baudelaire that he pursued in the 1930s, Benjamin had written: "What is at stake is not to portray literary works in the context of their age, but to represent the age that perceives them—our age—in the age during which they arose. It is this that makes literature into an organon of history; and to achieve this, and not to reduce literature to the material of history, is the task of the literary historian."[37] Walter Benjamin's essays on Charles Baudelaire and his era are perhaps the most profound and troubling representation we have of the capitalist modernity of the early twentieth century.

Baudelaire

II

An image to characterize Baudelaire's way of looking at the world. Let us compare time to a photographer—earthly time to a photographer who photographs the essence of things. But because of the nature of earthly time and its apparatus, the photographer manages only to register the negative of that essence on his photographic plates. No one can read these plates; no one can deduce from the negative, on which time records the objects, the true essence of things as they really are. Moreover, the elixir that might act as a developing agent is unknown. And there is Baudelaire: he doesn't possess the vital fluid either—the fluid in which these plates would have to be immersed so as to obtain the true picture. But he, he alone, is able to read the plates, thanks to infinite mental efforts. He alone is able to extract from the negatives of essence a presentiment of its real picture. And from this presentiment speaks the negative of essence in all his poems.

Underlying Baudelaire's writings is the old idea that knowledge is guilt. His soul is that of Adam, to whom Eve (the world) once upon a time offered the apple, from which he ate. Thereupon the spirit expelled him from the garden. Knowledge of the world had not been enough for him; he wanted to know its good and evil sides as well.

And the possibility of this question, which he was never able to answer, is something he bought at the price of eternal remorse [*Remord*]. His soul has this mythical prehistory, of which he knows, and thanks to which he knows more than others about redemption. He teaches us above all to understand the literal meaning of the word "knowledge" in the story of Eden.

Baudelaire as *littérateur*. This is the only vantage point from which to discuss his relationship with Jeanne Duval. For him as a *littérateur*, the hedonistic and hieratic nature of the prostitute's existence came to life.

III

The ambiguity of "Fair is foul, and foul is fair." The witches mean it in the sense of mixing things up, and in this sense it can be understood only morally. But applied to the objects of Baudelaire's poetry it means not mixing but reversing—that is to say, it is to be imagined not in the sphere of morality but in that of perception. What speaks to us in his poetry is not the reprehensible confusion of [moral] judgment but the permissible reversal of perception.

A school of writers who praise recent French poetry, but would be at a loss to distinguish clearly between *la morgue* and Laforgue.

The significance of the life legend Baudelaire imagined for himself.

Eckart von Sydow, *Die Kultur der Dekadenz* [The Culture of Decadence], Dresden: Sybillen-Verlag, 1921.

Hans Havemann, *Der Verworfene* [The Reprobate], Zweemann-Verlag.

The Souffleur, II, 3, p. 1 / *Nouveaux prétextes* by Gide, Paris 1911.

Spleen et idéal. Because of the abundance of connotations in this title, it is not translatable. Each of the two words on its own contains a double meaning. Both *spleen* and *idéal* are not just spiritual essences but also an intended effect upon them, as is expressed in

[Stefan] George's translation *Trübsinn und Vergeistigung* [Melancholy and Spiritualization]. But they do not express only that intended effect; in particular, the sense of a radiant and triumphant spirituality—such as is evoked in the sonnet "L'Aube spirituelle," among many others—is not rendered adequately by *Vergeistigung*. *Spleen*, too, even when understood merely as intended effect, not as archetypal image, is more than *Trübsinn*. Or rather, it is *Trübsinn* only in the final analysis: first and foremost, it is that fatally foundering, doomed flight toward the ideal, which ultimately—with the despairing cry of Icarus—comes crashing down into the ocean of its own melancholy. In both the oldest and the most recent foreign word in his language, Baudelaire indicates the share of time and eternity in these two extreme realms of the spirit. And doesn't this ambiguous title also imply that archetypal image and intended effect are mysteriously intertwined? Doesn't the title mean that it is the melancholic above all whose gaze is fixed on the ideal, and that it is the images of melancholy that kindle the spiritual most brightly?

Fragment written in 1921–1922; unpublished in Benjamin's lifetime. Translated by Rodney Livingstone.

Paris, the Capital
of the Nineteenth Century

The waters are blue, the plants pink; the evening is sweet to look on;
One goes for a walk; the *grandes dames* go for a walk; behind them stroll the
petites dames.
—NGUYEN TRONG HIEP, *PARIS, CAPITALE DE LA FRANCE: RECUEIL DE VERS*
(HANOI, 1897), POEM 25

I. Fourier, or the Arcades

The magic columns of these palaces
Show to the amateur on all sides,
In the objects their porticos display,
That industry is the rival of the arts.
—*NOUVEAUX TABLEAUX DE PARIS* (PARIS, 1828), VOL. 1, P. 27

Most of the Paris arcades come into being in the decade and a half
after 1822. The first condition for their emergence is the boom in the
textile trade. *Magasins de nouveautés,* the first establishments to keep
large stocks of merchandise on the premises, make their appearance.[1]
They are the forerunners of department stores. This was the period
of which Balzac wrote: "The great poem of display chants its stanzas of color from the Church of the Madeleine to the Porte Saint-
Denis."[2] The arcades are a center of commerce in luxury items. In
fitting them out, art enters the service of the merchant. Contemporaries never tire of admiring them, and for a long time they remain a drawing point for foreigners. An *Illustrated Guide to Paris*
says: "These arcades, a recent invention of industrial luxury, are
glass-roofed, marble-paneled corridors extending through whole
blocks of buildings, whose owners have joined together for such en-

terprises. Lining both sides of these corridors, which get their light from above, are the most elegant shops, so that the *passage* is a city, a world in miniature." The arcades are the scene of the first gas lighting.

The second condition for the emergence of the arcades is the beginning of iron construction. The Empire saw in this technology a contribution to the revival of architecture in the classical Greek sense. The architectural theorist Boetticher expresses the general view of the matter when he says that, "with regard to the art forms of the new system, the formal principle of the Hellenic mode" must come to prevail.[3] Empire is the style of revolutionary terrorism, for which the state is an end in itself. Just as Napoleon failed to understand the functional nature of the state as an instrument of domination by the bourgeois class, so the architects of his time failed to understand the functional nature of iron, with which the constructive principle begins its domination of architecture. These architects design supports resembling Pompeian columns, and factories that imitate residential houses, just as later the first railroad stations will be modeled on chalets. "Construction plays the role of the subconscious."[4] Nevertheless, the concept of engineer, which dates from the revolutionary wars, starts to make headway, and the rivalry begins between builder and decorator, Ecole Polytechnique and Ecole des Beaux-Arts.

For the first time in the history of architecture, an artificial building material appears: iron. It serves as the basis for a development whose tempo accelerates in the course of the century. This development enters a decisive new phase when it becomes apparent that the locomotive—on which experiments had been conducted since the end of the 1820s—is compatible only with iron tracks. The rail becomes the first prefabricated iron component, the precursor of the girder. Iron is avoided in home construction but used in arcades, exhibition halls, train stations—buildings that serve transitory purposes. At the same time, the range of architectural applications for glass expands, although the social prerequisites for its widened application as building material will come to the fore only a hundred years later. In Scheerbart's *Glasarchitektur* (1914), it still appears in the context of utopia.[5]

Each epoch dreams the one to follow.
—MICHELET, "AVENIR! AVENIR!"[6]

Corresponding to the form of the new means of production, which in the beginning is still ruled by the form of the old (Marx), are images in the collective consciousness in which the new is permeated with the old. These images are wish images; in them the collective seeks both to overcome and to transfigure the immaturity of the social product and the inadequacies in the social organization of production. At the same time, what emerges in these wish images is the resolute effort to distance oneself from all that is antiquated—which includes, however, the recent past. These tendencies deflect the imagination (which is given impetus by the new) back upon the primal past. In the dream in which each epoch entertains images of its successor, the latter appears wedded to elements of primal history [*Urgeschichte*]—that is, to elements of a classless society. And the experiences of such a society—as stored in the unconscious of the collective—engender, through interpenetration with what is new, the utopia that has left its trace in a thousand configurations of life, from enduring edifices to passing fashions.

These relations are discernible in the utopia conceived by Fourier.[7] Its secret cue is the advent of machines. But this fact is not directly expressed in the Fourierist literature, which takes as its point of departure the amorality of the business world and the false morality enlisted in its service. The phalanstery is designed to restore human beings to relationships in which morality becomes superfluous. The highly complicated organization of the phalanstery appears as machinery. The meshing of the passions, the intricate collaboration of *passions mécanistes* with the *passion cabaliste,* is a primitive contrivance formed—on analogy with the machine—from materials of psychology. This machinery made of men produces the land of milk and honey, the primeval wish symbol that Fourier's utopia has filled with new life.

Fourier saw, in the arcades, the architectural canon of the phalanstery. Their reactionary metamorphosis with him is characteristic: whereas they originally serve commercial ends, they become, for him, places of habitation. The phalanstery becomes a city of arcades. Fourier establishes, in the Empire's austere world of forms, the colorful idyll of Biedermeier. Its brilliance persists, however faded, up through Zola, who takes up Fourier's ideas in his book *Travail,* just as he bids farewell to the arcades in his *Thérèse Raquin.*[8]—Marx came to the defense of Fourier in his critique of Carl Grün, emphasizing the former's "colossal conception of man."[9] He also directed attention to Fourier's humor. In fact, Jean Paul, in his *Levana,* is as closely allied to Fourier the pedagogue as Scheerbart, in his *Glass Architecture,* is to Fourier the utopian.[10]

II. Daguerre, or the Panoramas

Sun, look out for yourself!
—A. J. WIERTZ, *OEUVRES LITTÉRAIRES* (PARIS, 1870), P. 374

Just as architecture, with the first appearance of iron construction, begins to outgrow art, so does painting, in its turn, with the first appearance of the panoramas.[11] The high point in the diffusion of panoramas coincides with the introduction of arcades. One sought tirelessly, through technical devices, to make panoramas the scenes of a perfect imitation of nature. An attempt was made to reproduce the changing daylight in the landscape, the rising of the moon, the rush of waterfalls. David counsels his pupils to draw from nature as it is shown in panoramas.[12] In their attempt to produce deceptively lifelike changes in represented nature, the panoramas prepare the way not only for photography but for [silent] film and sound film.

Contemporary with the panoramas is a panoramic literature. *Le Livre des cent-et-un* [The Book of a Hundred-and-One], *Les Fran-*

çais peints par eux-mêmes [The French Painted by Themselves], *Le Diable à Paris* [The Devil in Paris], and *La Grande Ville* [The Big City] belong to this. These books prepare the belletristic collaboration for which Girardin, in the 1830s, will create a home in the feuilleton.[13] They consist of individual sketches, whose anecdotal form corresponds to the panoramas' plastically arranged foreground, and whose informational base corresponds to their painted background. This literature is also socially panoramic. For the last time, the worker appears, isolated from his class, as part of the setting in an idyll.

Announcing an upheaval in the relation of art to technology, panoramas are at the same time an expression of a new attitude toward life. The city dweller, whose political supremacy over the provinces is attested many times in the course of the century, attempts to bring the countryside into town. In the panoramas, the city opens out, becoming landscape—as it will do later, in subtler fashion, for the flâneurs. Daguerre is a student of the panorama painter Prévost, whose establishment is located in the Passage des Panoramas.[14] Description of the panoramas of Prévost and Daguerre. In 1839 Daguerre's panorama burns down. In the same year, he announces the invention of the daguerreotype.

Arago presents photography in a speech to the National Assembly.[15] He assigns it a place in the history of technology and prophesies its scientific applications. On the other side, artists begin to debate its artistic value. Photography leads to the extinction of the great profession of portrait miniaturist. This happens not just for economic reasons. The early photograph was artistically superior to the miniature portrait. The technical grounds for this advantage lie in the long exposure time, which requires of a subject the highest concentration; the social grounds for it lie in the fact that the first photographers belonged to the avant-garde, from which most of their clientele came. Nadar's superiority to his colleagues is shown by his attempt to take photographs in the Paris sewer system: for the first time, the lens was deemed capable of making discoveries.[16] Its importance becomes still greater as, in view of the new technological and social reality, the subjective strain in pictorial and graphic information is called into question.

The world exhibition of 1855 offers for the first time a special display called "Photography." In the same year, Wiertz publishes his great article on photography, in which he defines its task as the philosophical enlightenment of painting.[17] This "enlightenment" is understood, as his own paintings show, in a political sense. Wiertz can be characterized as the first to demand, if not actually foresee, the use of photographic montage for political agitation. With the increasing scope of communications and transport, the informational value of painting diminishes. In reaction to photography, painting begins to stress the elements of color in the picture. By the time Impressionism yields to Cubism, painting has created for itself a broader domain into which, for the time being, photography cannot follow. For its part, photography greatly extends the sphere of commodity exchange, from midcentury onward, by flooding the market with countless images of figures, landscapes, and events which had previously been available either not at all or only as pictures for individual customers. To increase turnover, it renewed its subject matter through modish variations in camera technique—innovations that will determine the subsequent history of photography.

III. Grandville, or the World Exhibitions

Yes, when all the world from Paris to China
Pays heed to your doctrine, O divine Saint-Simon,
The glorious Golden Age will be reborn.
Rivers will flow with chocolate and tea,
Sheep roasted whole will frisk on the plain,
And sautéed pike will swim in the Seine.
Fricasseed spinach will grow on the ground,
Garnished with crushed fried croutons;
The trees will bring forth apple compotes,
And farmers will harvest boots and coats.

It will snow wine, it will rain chickens,
And ducks cooked with turnips will fall from the sky.
—LANGLÉ AND VANDERBURCH, *LOUIS-BRONZE ET LE SAINT-SIMONIEN*
(THÉÂTRE DU PALAIS-ROYAL, FEBRUARY 27, 1832)[18]

World exhibitions are places of pilgrimage to the commodity fetish. "Europe is off to view the merchandise," says [Hippolyte] Taine in 1855.[19] The world exhibitions are preceded by national exhibitions of industry, the first of which takes place on the Champ de Mars in 1798. It arises from the wish "to entertain the working classes, and it becomes for them a festival of emancipation."[20] The worker occupies the foreground, as customer. The framework of the entertainment industry has not yet taken shape; the popular festival provides this. Chaptal's speech on industry opens the 1798 exhibition.[21]—The Saint-Simonians, who envision the industrialization of the earth, take up the idea of world exhibitions. Chevalier, the first authority in the new field, is a student of Enfantin and editor of the Saint-Simonian newspaper *Le Globe*.[22] The Saint-Simonians anticipated the development of the global economy, but not the class struggle. Next to their active participation in industrial and commercial enterprises around the middle of the century stands their helplessness on all questions concerning the proletariat.

World exhibitions glorify the exchange value of the commodity. They create a framework in which its use value recedes into the background. They open a phantasmagoria which a person enters in order to be distracted. The entertainment industry makes this easier by elevating the person to the level of the commodity. He surrenders to its manipulations while enjoying his alienation from himself and others.—The enthronement of the commodity, with its luster of distraction, is the secret theme of Grandville's art.[23] This is consistent with the split between utopian and cynical elements in his work. Its ingenuity in representing inanimate objects corresponds to what Marx calls the "theological niceties" of the commodity.[24] They are manifest clearly in the *spécialité*—a category of goods which appears at this time in the luxuries industry. Under Grandville's pencil, the whole of nature is transformed into specialties. He presents them in the same spirit in which the advertisement (the term *réclame* also originates at this point) begins to present its articles. He ends in madness.

Fashion: "Madam Death! Madam Death!"
—LEOPARDI, "DIALOGUE BETWEEN FASHION AND DEATH"[25]

World exhibitions propagate the universe of commodities. Grandville's fantasies confer a commodity character on the universe. They modernize it. Saturn's ring becomes a cast-iron balcony on which the inhabitants of Saturn take the evening air.[26] The literary counterpart of this graphic utopia is found in the books of the Fourierist naturalist Toussenel.[27]—Fashion prescribes the ritual according to which the commodity fetish demands to be worshiped. Grandville extends the authority of fashion to objects of everyday use, as well as to the cosmos. In taking it to an extreme, he reveals its nature. Fashion stands in opposition to the organic. It couples the living body to the inorganic world. To the living, it defends the rights of the corpse. The fetishism that succumbs to the sex appeal of the inorganic is its vital nerve. The cult of the commodity presses such fetishism into its service.

For the Paris world exhibition of 1867, Victor Hugo issues a manifesto: "To the Peoples of Europe." Earlier, and more unequivocally, their interests had been championed by delegations of French workers, of which the first had been sent to the London world exhibition of 1851 and the second, numbering 750 delegates, to that of 1862. The latter delegation was of indirect importance for Marx's founding of the International Workingmen's Association.[28]—The phantasmagoria of capitalist culture attains its most radiant unfolding in the world exhibition of 1867. The Second Empire is at the height of its power. Paris is acknowledged as the capital of luxury and fashion. Offenbach sets the rhythm of Parisian life.[29] The operetta is the ironic utopia of an enduring reign of capital.

IV. Louis Philippe, or the Interior

The head. . .
On the night table, like a ranunculus,
Rests.
—BAUDELAIRE, "UNE MARTYRE"[30]

Under Louis Philippe,[31] the private individual makes his entrance on the stage of history. The expansion of the democratic apparatus through a new electoral law coincides with the parliamentary corruption organized by Guizot.[32] Under cover of this corruption, the ruling class makes history; that is, it pursues its affairs. It furthers railway construction in order to improve its stock holdings. It promotes the reign of Louis Philippe as that of the private individual managing his affairs. With the July Revolution, the bourgeoisie realized the goals of 1789 (Marx).

For the private individual, the place of dwelling is for the first time opposed to the place of work. The former constitutes itself as the interior. Its complement is the office. The private individual, who in the office has to deal with reality, needs the domestic interior to sustain him in his illusions. This necessity is all the more pressing since he has no intention of allowing his commercial considerations to impinge on social ones. In the formation of his private environment, both are kept out. From this arise the phantasmagorias of the interior—which, for the private man, represents the universe. In the interior, he brings together the far away and the long ago. His living room is a box in the theater of the world.

Excursus on Jugendstil.[33] The shattering of the interior occurs via Jugendstil around the turn of the century. Of course, according to its own ideology, the Jugendstil movement seems to bring with it the consummation of the interior. The transfiguration of the solitary soul appears to be its goal. Individualism is its theory. With van de Velde, the house becomes an expression of the personality. Ornament is to this house what the signature is to a painting. But the real meaning of Jugendstil is not expressed in this ideology. It represents the last attempted sortie of an art besieged in its ivory tower by technology. This attempt mobilizes all the reserves of inwardness. They find their expression in the mediumistic language of the line, in the flower as symbol of a naked vegetal nature confronted by the technologically armed world. The new elements of iron construction—girder forms—preoccupy Jugendstil. In ornament, it endeavors to win back these forms for art. Concrete presents it with new possibilities for plastic creation in architecture. Around this time, the real gravitational center of living space shifts to the office. The irreal center makes its place in the home. The consequences of Jugendstil are depicted in Ibsen's *Master Builder*:[34] the attempt by the individual, on the strength of his inwardness, to vie with technology leads to his downfall.

I believe . . . in my soul: the Thing.
—LÉON DEUBEL, *OEUVRES* (PARIS, 1929), P. 193

The interior is the asylum of art. The collector is the true resident of the interior. He makes his concern the transfiguration of things. To him falls the Sisyphean task of divesting things of their commodity character by taking possession of them. But he bestows on them only connoisseur value, rather than use value. The collector dreams his way not only into a distant or bygone world but also into a better one—one in which, to be sure, human beings are no better provided with what they need than in the everyday world, but in which things are freed from the drudgery of being useful.

The interior is not just the universe but also the étui of the private individual. To dwell means to leave traces. In the interior, these are accentuated. Coverlets and antimacassars, cases and containers are devised in abundance; in these, the traces of the most ordinary objects of use are imprinted. In just the same way, the traces of the inhabitant are imprinted in the interior. Enter the detective story, which pursues these traces. Poe, in his "Philosophy of Furniture" as well as in his detective fiction, shows himself to be the first physiognomist of the domestic interior. The criminals in early detective novels are neither gentlemen nor apaches,[35] but private citizens of the middle class.

V. Baudelaire, or the Streets of Paris

Everything becomes an allegory for me.
—BAUDELAIRE, "LE CYGNE"[36]

Baudelaire's genius, which is nourished on melancholy, is an allegorical genius. For the first time, with Baudelaire, Paris becomes the subject of lyric poetry. This poetry is no hymn to the homeland; rather, the gaze of the allegorist, as it falls on the city, is the gaze of the alienated man. It is the gaze of the flâneur, whose way of life still conceals behind a mitigating nimbus the coming desolation of the big-city dweller. The flâneur still stands on the threshold—of the metropolis as of the middle class. Neither has him in its power yet. In neither is he at home. He seeks refuge in the crowd. Early contributions to a physiognomics of the crowd are found in Engels and Poe.[37] The crowd is the veil through which the familiar city beckons to the flâneur as phantasmagoria—now a landscape, now a room. Both become elements of the department store, which makes use of flânerie itself to sell goods. The department store is the last promenade for the flâneur.

In the flâneur, the intelligentsia sets foot in the marketplace—ostensibly to look around, but in truth to find a buyer. In this intermediate stage, in which it still has patrons but is already beginning to familiarize itself with the market, it appears as the *bohème*. To the uncertainty of its economic position corresponds the uncertainty of its political function. The latter is manifest most clearly in the professional conspirators, who all belong to the *bohème*. Their initial field of activity is the army; later it becomes the petty bourgeoisie, occasionally the proletariat. Nevertheless, this group views the true leaders of the proletariat as its adversary. The *Communist Manifesto* brings their political existence to an end. Baudelaire's poetry draws its strength from the rebellious pathos of this group. He sides with the asocial. He realizes his only sexual communion with a whore.

Easy the way that leads into Avernus.
—VIRGIL, THE AENEID[38]

It is the unique provision of Baudelaire's poetry that the image of woman and the image of death intermingle in a third: that of Paris. The Paris of his poems is a sunken city, and more submarine than subterranean. The chthonic elements of the city—its topographic formations, the old abandoned bed of the Seine—have evidently found in him a mold. Decisive for Baudelaire in the "death-fraught idyll" of the city, however, is a social, a modern substrate. The modern is a principal accent of his poetry. As spleen, it fractures the ideal ("Spleen et idéal").[39] But precisely modernity is always citing primal history. Here, this occurs through the ambiguity peculiar to the social relations and products of this epoch. Ambiguity is the appearance of dialectic in images, the law of dialectics at a standstill. This standstill is utopia and the dialectical image, therefore, dream image. Such an image is afforded by the commodity per se: as fetish. Such an image is presented by the arcades, which are house no less than street. Such an image is the prostitute—seller and sold in one.

I travel in order to get to know my geography.
—NOTE OF A MADMAN, IN MARCEL RÉJA, L'ART CHEZ LES FOUS (PARIS, 1907), P. 131

The last poem of Les Fleurs du Mal: "Le Voyage." "Death, old admiral, up anchor now." The last journey of the flâneur: death. Its destination: the new. "Deep in the Unknown to find the new!"[40] Newness is a quality independent of the use value of the commodity. It is the origin of the semblance that belongs inalienably to images produced by the collective unconscious. It is the quintessence of that false consciousness whose indefatigable agent is fashion. This semblance of the new is reflected, like one mirror in another, in the semblance of the ever recurrent. The product of this reflection is the phantasmagoria of "cultural history," in which the bourgeoisie enjoys its false consciousness to the full. The art that begins to doubt its task and ceases to be "inseparable from . . . utility" (Baudelaire)[41] must make novelty into its highest value. The *arbiter novarum rerum* for such an art becomes the snob. He is to art what the dandy is to fashion.— Just as in the seventeenth century it is allegory that becomes the canon of dialectical images, in the nineteenth century it is novelty. Newspapers flourish, along with *magasins de nouveautés*. The press organizes the market in spiritual values, in which at first there is a boom. Nonconformists rebel against consigning art to the marketplace. They rally round the banner of *l'art pour l'art*.[42] From this watchword derives the conception of the "total work of art"—the *Gesamtkunstwerk*—which would seal art off from the developments of technology. The solemn rite with which it is celebrated is the pendant to the distraction that transfigures the commodity. Both abstract from the social existence of human beings. Baudelaire succumbs to the rage for Wagner.[43]

VI. Haussmann, or the Barricades

I venerate the Beautiful, the Good, and all things great;
Beautiful nature, on which great art rests—
How it enchants the ear and charms the eye!
I love spring in blossom: women and roses.
—BARON HAUSSMANN, *CONFESSION D'UN LION DEVENU VIEUX*[44]

The flowery realm of decorations,
The charm of landscape, of architecture,
And all the effect of scenery rest
Solely on the law of perspective.
—FRANZ BÖHLE, *THEATER-CATECHISMUS* (MUNICH), P. 74

Haussmann's ideal in city planning consisted of long perspectives down broad straight thoroughfares. Such an ideal corresponds to the tendency—common in the nineteenth century—to ennoble technological necessities through artistic ends. The institutions of the bourgeoisie's worldly and spiritual dominance were to find their apotheosis within the framework of the boulevards. Before their completion, boulevards were draped across with canvas and unveiled like monuments.—Haussmann's activity is linked to Napoleonic imperialism. Louis Napoleon promotes investment capital, and Paris experiences a rash of speculation.[45] Trading on the stock exchange displaces the forms of gambling handed down from feudal society. The phantasmagorias of space to which the flâneur devotes himself find a counterpart in the phantasmagorias of time to which the gambler is addicted. Gambling converts time into a narcotic. [Paul] Lafargue explains gambling as an imitation in miniature of the mysteries of economic fluctuation.[46] The expropriations carried out under Haussmann call forth a wave of fraudulent speculation. The rulings of the Court of Cassation, which are inspired by the bourgeois and Orleanist opposition, increase the financial risks of Haussmannization.[47]

Haussmann tries to shore up his dictatorship by placing Paris under an emergency regime. In 1864, in a speech before the National Assembly, he vents his hatred of the rootless urban population, which keeps increasing as a result of his projects. Rising rents drive the proletariat into the suburbs. The *quartiers* of Paris in this way lose their distinctive physiognomy. The "red belt" forms.[48] Haussmann gave himself the title of "demolition artist," *artiste démolisseur.* He viewed his work as a calling, and emphasizes this in his memoirs. Meanwhile he estranges the Parisians from their city. They no longer feel at home there, and start to become conscious of the inhuman character of the metropolis. Maxime Du Camp's monumental work *Paris* owes its inception to this consciousness.[49] The *Jérémiades d'un Haussmannisé* give it the form of a biblical lament.[50]

The true goal of Haussmann's projects was to secure the city against civil war. He wanted to make the erection of barricades in Paris impossible for all time. With the same end in mind, Louis Philippe had already introduced wooden paving. Nonetheless, barricades played a role in the February Revolution.[51] Engels studies the tactics of barricade fighting.[52] Haussmann seeks to neutralize these tactics on two fronts. Widening the streets is designed to make the erection of barricades impossible, and new streets are to furnish the shortest route between the barracks and the workers' districts. Contemporaries christen the operation "strategic embellishment."

Reveal to these depraved,
O Republic, by foiling their plots,
Your great Medusa face
Ringed by red lightning.
—WORKERS' SONG FROM ABOUT 1850, IN ADOLF STAHR, *ZWEI MONATE IN PARIS* (OLDENBURG, 1851), VOL. 2, P. 199[53]

The barricade is resurrected during the Commune.[54] It is stronger and better secured than ever. It stretches across the great boulevards, often reaching a height of two stories, and shields the trenches behind it. Just as the *Communist Manifesto* ends the age of professional conspirators, so the Commune puts an end to the phantasmagoria holding sway over the early years of the proletariat. It dispels the illusion that the task of the proletarian revolution is to complete the work of 1789 hand in hand with the bourgeoisie. This illusion dominates the period 1831–1871, from the Lyons uprising to the Commune. The bourgeoisie never shared in this error. Its battle against the social rights of the proletariat dates back to the great Revolution, and converges with the philanthropic movement that gives it cover and that is in its heyday under Napoleon III. Under his reign, this movement's monumental work appears: Le Play's *Ouvriers européens.*[55] Side by side with the concealed position of philanthropy, the bourgeoisie has always maintained openly the position of class warfare.[56] As early as 1831, in the *Journal des Débats,* it acknowledges that "every manufacturer lives in his factory like a plantation owner among his slaves." If it is the misfortune of the workers' rebellions of old that no theory of revolution directs their course, it is also this absence of theory that, from another perspective, makes possible their spontaneous energy and the enthusiasm with which they set about establishing a new society. This enthusiasm, which reaches its peak in the Commune, wins over to the working class at times the best elements of the bourgeoisie, but leads it in the end to succumb to their worst elements. Rimbaud and Courbet declare their support for the Commune.[57] The burning of Paris is the worthy conclusion to Haussmann's work of destruction.[58]

My good father had been in Paris.
—KARL GUTZKOW, *BRIEFE AUS PARIS* (LEIPZIG, 1842), VOL. 1, P. 58

Balzac was the first to speak of the ruins of the bourgeoisie.[59] But it was Surrealism that first opened our eyes to them. The development of the forces of production shattered the wish symbols of the previous century, even before the monuments representing them had collapsed. In the nineteenth century this development worked to emancipate the forms of construction from art, just as in the sixteenth century the sciences freed themselves from philosophy. A start is made with architecture as engineered construction. Then comes the reproduction of nature as photography. The creation of fantasy prepares to become practical as commercial art. Literature submits to montage in the feuilleton. All these products are on the point of entering the market as commodities. But they linger on the threshold. From this epoch derive the arcades and *intérieurs*, the exhibition halls and panoramas. They are residues of a dream world. The realization of dream elements, in the course of waking up, is the paradigm of dialectical thinking. Thus, dialectical thinking is the organ of historical awakening. Every epoch, in fact, not only dreams the one to follow but, in dreaming, precipitates its awakening. It bears its end within itself and unfolds it—as Hegel already noticed—by cunning. With the destabilizing of the market economy, we begin to recognize the monuments of the bourgeoisie as ruins even before they have crumbled.

Written May 1935; unpublished in Benjamin's lifetime. *Gesammelte Schriften*, V, 45–59. Translated by Howard Eiland.

The Paris of the Second Empire in Baudelaire

Une capitale n'est pas absolument nécessaire à l'homme.
—SENANCOUR[1]

I. The Bohème

The *bohème* appears in a suggestive context in the writings of Marx. In this category he includes the professional conspirators he talks about in his detailed note on the memoirs of the police agent de La Hodde—a piece that appeared in the *Neue Rheinische Zeitung* in 1850.[2] To evoke the physiognomy of Baudelaire means to speak of the way in which he resembles this political type. Marx outlines this type as follows:

> The development of proletarian conspiracies produced a need for a division of labor. Their members were divided into *conspirateurs d'occasion* [occasional conspirators]—that is, workers who carried on conspiracies only in addition to their other employment, who merely attended the meetings and kept themselves in readiness to appear at the assembly point upon orders from the leader—and professional conspirators, who devoted themselves entirely to the conspiracy and made a living from it. . . . The social position of this class determined its whole character. . . . Their uncertain existence, which in specific cases depended more on chance than on their activities;

their irregular life, whose only fixed stations were the taverns of the wine dealers (the gathering places of the conspirators); and their inevitable acquaintance with all sorts of dubious people place them in that social sphere which in Paris is called *la bohème*."[3]

In passing, it should be noted that Napoleon III himself began his rise in a milieu related to the one described above. It is well known that one of the tools of his presidential period was the Society of the Tenth of December, whose cadres, according to Marx, were supplied by "the whole indeterminate, disintegrated, fluctuating mass which the French call the *bohème*."[4] As emperor, Napoleon continued to develop his conspiratorial habits. Surprising proclamations and mystery-mongering, sudden sallies, and impenetrable irony were part of the *raison d'état* of the Second Empire. The same traits are found in Baudelaire's theoretical writings. He usually presents his views apodictically. Discussion is not his style; he avoids it even when the glaring contradictions in the theses he continually appropriates require discussion. He dedicated his "Salon de 1846" to all "bourgeois"; he appears as their advocate, and his manner is not that of an *advocatus diaboli*. Later—for example, in his invectives against the school of *bon sens*—he attacks the "'honnête' bourgeoise" and the notary (the person such a woman holds in respect), as if he were the most rabid *bohémien*.[5] Around 1850 he proclaimed that art could not be separated from utility; a few years thereafter he championed *l'art pour l'art* [art for art's sake].[6] In all this, he was no more concerned with playing a mediating role for his public than Napoleon III was when he switched, almost overnight and behind the French parliament's back, from protective tariffs to free trade. These traits, at any rate, make it understandable that exponents of official criticism—above all, Jules Lemaître—perceived very little of the theoretical energy latent in Baudelaire's prose.[7]

Marx continues his description of the *conspirateurs de profession* as follows:

For them, the only condition for revolution is the effective organization of their conspiracy. . . . They embrace inventions which are supposed to perform revolutionary miracles: fire bombs, destructive machines with magical effects, riots that are to be the more miraculous and surprising the less rational their foundation. Occupying themselves with such projects, they have no other aim but the immediate one of overthrowing the existing government, and they profoundly despise the more theoretical enlightenment of the workers regarding their class interests. Hence their anger—not proletarian but plebeian—at the *habits noirs* [black coats], the more or less educated people who represent that side of the movement and of whom they can never become entirely independent, since these are the official representatives of the party.[8]

Ultimately, Baudelaire's political insights do not go beyond those of these professional conspirators. Whether he bestows his sympathies on clerical reaction or on the Revolution of 1848, their expression remains unmediated and their foundation fragile. The image he presented in the February days—brandishing a rifle on some Paris street corner and shouting "Down with General Aupick!"—is a case in point.[9] He could, in any case, have adopted Flaubert's statement, "Of all of politics, I understand only one thing: revolt." It could then have been understood in the sense of the final passage in a note which has come down to us together with his sketches on Belgium: "I say 'Long live the revolution!' as I would say 'Long live destruction! Long live penance! Long live chastisement! Long live death!' I would be happy not only as a victim; it would not displease me to play the hangman as well—so as to feel the revolution from both sides! All of us have the republican spirit in our blood, just as we have syphilis in our bones. We have a democratic and syphilitic infection."[10]

What Baudelaire thus expresses could be called the metaphysics of the *provocateur*. In Belgium, where he wrote this note, he was for a while regarded as a French police spy. Actually, such arrangements were hardly considered strange; on December 20, 1855, Baudelaire wrote to his mother with reference to the literary men who were working as agents for the police: "My name will never appear in their shameful registers."[11] What earned Baudelaire such a reputation in Belgium can hardly have been only his manifest hostility toward Hugo, who was proscribed in France but acclaimed in Belgium.[12] His devastating irony contributed to the origin of that rumor; he may have taken pleasure in spreading it himself. The seeds of the *culte de la blague,* which reappears in Georges Sorel and has become an integral part of fascist propaganda, are first found in Baudelaire.[13] The spirit in which Céline wrote his *Bagatelles pour un massacre,* and its very title, go back directly to a diary entry by Baudelaire: "A fine conspiracy could be organized for the purpose of exterminating the Jewish race."[14] The Blanquist Rigault, who ended his conspiratory career as police chief of the Paris Commune, seems to have had the same macabre sense of humor frequently mentioned in documents about Baudelaire.[15] In Charles Prolès' *Hommes de la Révolution de 1871,* we read that "Rigault, despite his extreme cold-bloodedness, was also something of a coarse jokester. That was an integral part of him, down to his fanaticism."[16] Even the terrorist pipe-dream which Marx encountered among the *conspirateurs* has its counterpart in Baudelaire. "If I ever regain the vigor and energy which I had on a few occasions," he wrote to his mother on December 23, 1865, "I will vent my anger in terrifying books. I want to turn the whole human race against me. The delight this would give me would console me for everything."[17] This grim rage—*la rogne*—was the emotion which a half-century of barricade fights had nurtured in Parisian professional conspirators.

"It is they," writes Marx about these conspirators, "who erect the first barricades and command them."[18] The barricade was indeed at the center of the conspiratorial movement. It had revolutionary tradition on its side. More than four thousand barricades had studded the city during the July Revolution.[19] When Fourier looked for an example of *travail non salarié mais passionné,* he found none that was more obvious than the building of barricades.[20] In his novel *Les Misérables,* Hugo gives an impressive picture of those barricades, while leaving the people who manned them in the shadows. "Everywhere an invisible police force within the rebellion was on guard. It maintained order—that is, the night. . . . Eyes that might have looked down on these towering shadows from above would have encountered here and there an indistinct glow revealing broken, irregular outlines, profiles of strange constructions. In these ruins something resembling lights moved. In these places stood the barricades."[21] In the fragmentary "Address to Paris" which was to have concluded *Les Fleurs du mal,* Baudelaire does not say farewell to the city without invoking its barricades; he remembers its "magic cobblestones which rise up to form fortresses."[22] These stones, to be sure, are "magic" because Baudelaire's poem says nothing about the hands which set them in motion. But this very pathos is probably indebted to Blanquism, for the Blanquist Tridon cries out in a similar vein: "O force, reine des barricades, toi qui brille dans l'éclair et dans l'émeute, . . . c'est vers toi que les prisonniers tendent leurs mains enchaînées."[23] After the demise of the Commune, the proletariat groped its way behind the barricades as a mortally wounded animal withdraws to its lair. The fact that the workers, who had been trained in barricade fighting, did not favor the open battle which was bound to block Thiers's path was partly to blame for their defeat.[24] As a recent historian of the Commune writes, these workers "preferred battle in their own quarters to an encounter in the open field, . . . and if it had to be, they preferred to die behind a barricade built of cobblestones from a Paris street."[25]

In those days Blanqui, the most important of the Paris barricade chiefs, sat in his last prison, the Fort du Taureau.[26] He and his associates, claimed Marx in his analysis of the June Insurrection, were "the true leaders of the proletarian party."[27] It is hardly possible to overestimate the revolutionary prestige which Blanqui possessed at that time and preserved up to his death. Before Lenin, there was no one else who had a clearer profile among the proletariat. His features were engraved in Baudelaire's mind. Baudelaire's manuscripts include a page that bears a sketch of Blanqui's head, in addition to other improvised drawings.—The concepts Marx uses in his depiction of the conspiratorial milieu in Paris clearly bring out Blanqui's ambiguous position in it. There are good reasons for the traditional view of Blanqui as a putschist. In this view he constitutes the type of politician who, as Marx said, regards it as his task "to anticipate the revolutionary developmental process, bring it artificially to a head, and improvise a revolution without the conditions for one."[28] If, by contrast, we look at existing descriptions of Blanqui, he seems to resemble one of the *habits noirs* who were the hated rivals of those professional conspirators. An eyewitness has given the following description of Blanqui's Club des Halles:

> If one wishes to get an accurate idea of the impression made at the outset by Blanqui's revolutionary club, in comparison with the two clubs which the Party of Order then had, one should imagine an audience watching the Comédie Française present a play by Racine or Corneille and should contrast this audience with the crowd that fills a circus in which acrobats are performing breakneck feats. A member of Blanqui's club was, as it were, in a chapel devoted to the orthodox rites of conspiracy. The doors were open to all, but only the initiates came back. After a wearisome litany by the oppressed, . . . the priest of this place arose. His pretext was that he was going to give a résumé of the complaints of his clients, of the people represented by the half-dozen presumptuous and irritated blockheads who had just been heard from. In reality, he gave an analysis of the situation. His outward appearance was distinguished; his clothes were immaculate. He had a finely formed head, and his facial expression was calm. Only the wild flashing of his eyes sometimes portended trouble; his eyes were narrow, small, and penetrating, and usually they looked kind rather than hard. His speech was measured, fatherly, and distinct—next to the oratorical style of Thiers, the least declamatory I have heard.[29]

In this account, Blanqui appears as a doctrinaire. The *signalement* [description] of the *habit noir* is accurate even in its smallest details. It was well known that "the old man" was in the habit of wearing black gloves while lecturing.[30] But the measured seriousness and the impenetrability which were part of Blanqui's makeup appear different in the light of a statement by Marx. With reference to these professional conspirators, he writes: "They are the alchemists of the revolution and fully share the disintegration of ideas, the narrow-mindedness, and the obsessions of the earlier alchemists."[31] This almost automatically yields the image of Baudelaire: the enigmatic stuff of allegory in one, the mystery-mongering of the conspirator in the other.

As is to be expected, Marx makes deprecatory remarks about the taverns in which the low conspirators felt at home. The miasma that prevailed there was familiar to Baudelaire. This was the atmosphere that gave rise to the great poem entitled "Le Vin des chiffonniers" [The Ragpickers' Wine], which can be dated to the middle of the century. At that time, motifs which appear in this poem were being publicly discussed. One thing under discussion was the tax on wine. The Constituent Assembly of the Republic had promised its repeal, the same promise that had been made in 1830. In his *Klassenkämpfe in Frankreich* [Class Struggles in France], Marx showed how the repeal of this tax represented both a demand by the urban proletariat and a concurrent demand by the peasants. The tax was equally high on everyday wines and on the finest wines, and it decreased consumption "by setting up *octrois* [toll houses] at the gates of all cities with more than four thousand inhabitants and changing every town into a foreign country with protective tariffs on French wine."[32] "Through the wine tax," wrote Marx, "the peasants tested the bouquet of the government." But this tax also harmed the city-dwellers and forced them to go to taverns outside the city limits in their search for cheap wine. There the tax-free wine which was called *le vin de la barrière* was dispensed. If one can believe H.-A. Frégier, section head at police headquarters, workers who imbibed that wine displayed their enjoyment—full of pride and defiance—as the only enjoyment granted them.

"There are women who do not hesitate to follow their husbands to the *barrière* [town gate] with their children who are old enough to work. . . . Afterward they start their way home half-drunk and act more drunk than they are, so that everyone may notice that they have drunk quite a bit. Sometimes the children follow their parents' example."[33] "One thing is certain," wrote a contemporary observer. "The wine of the *barrières* has saved the governmental structure from quite a few blows."[34] The wine gave the disinherited access to dreams of future revenge and future glory. Thus, in "The Ragpickers' Wine":

> On voit un chiffonnier qui vient, hochant la tête,
> Buttant, et se cognant aux murs comme un poète,
> Et, sans prendre souci des mouchards, ses sujets,
> Epanche tout son coeur en glorieux projets.
>
> Il prête des serments, dicte des lois sublimes,
> Terrasse les méchants, relève les victimes,
> Et sous le firmament comme un dais suspendu
> S'enivre des splendeurs de sa propre vertu.[35]
>
> [One sees a ragpicker coming—shaking his head,
> Stumbling, and colliding against walls like a poet;
> And, heedless of police informers, his humble subjects,
> He pours out his heart in glorious devisings.
>
> He swears solemn oaths, dispenses laws sublime,
> Lays low the wicked, raises up the victims,
> And under a sky suspended like a canopy
> Becomes intoxicated on the splendors of his own virtue.]

When the new industrial processes gave refuse a certain value, ragpickers appeared in the cities in larger numbers. They worked for middlemen and constituted a sort of cottage industry located in the streets. The ragpicker fascinated his epoch. The eyes of the first investigators of pauperism were fixed on him with the mute question: Where does the limit of human misery lie? In his book *Des Classes dangereuses de la population,* Frégier devotes six pages to the ragpicker. Le Play gives the budget of a Paris ragpicker and his family for the period 1849–1850, presumably the time when Baudelaire's poem was written.[36]

A ragpicker cannot, of course, be considered a member of the *bohème.* But from the littérateur to the professional conspirator, everyone who belonged to the *bohème* could recognize a bit of himself in the ragpicker. Each person was in a more or less blunted state of revolt against society and faced a more or less precarious future. At the proper time, he was able to sympathize with those who were shaking the foundations of this society. The ragpicker was not alone in his dream. He was accompanied by comrades; they, too, reeked of wine casks, and they, too, had turned gray in battles. His moustache drooped like an old flag. On his rounds he encountered the mouchards, the police informers whom he dominated in his dreams.[37] Social motifs from everyday Parisian life had already appeared in Sainte-Beuve, where they had been captured by lyric poetry but were not necessarily understood. Penury and alcohol combined in the mind of the cultured man of leisure in a way that differed substantially from the combination in the mind of a Baudelaire.

> Dans ce cabriolet de classe j'examine
> L'homme qui me conduit, qui n'est plus que machine,
> Hideux, à barbe épaisse, à longs cheveux collés;
> Vice, et vin, et sommeil chargent ses yeux soûlés.
>
> Comment l'homme peut-il ainsi tomber? pensais-je,
> Et je me reculais à l'autre coin du siège.[38]
>
> [In this fine cab I examine
> The man who is driving me,
> Who is no more than a machine,

Hideous, with a thick beard and long, dirty hair.
Vice, wine, and sleep make his drunken eyes heavy.
How can man deteriorate that way? So I thought,
And I drew back to the other corner of the seat.]

This is the beginning of the poem; what follows is an edifying interpretation. Sainte-Beuve asks himself whether his own soul is not almost as neglected as the soul of the coachman.

The litany entitled "Abel et Cain" shows the basis for Baudelaire's view of the disinherited, which was freer and more reasonable
than Sainte-Beuve's. The poem turns the contest between the biblical
brothers into one between eternally irreconcilable races.

> Race d'Abel, dors, bois et mange;
> Dieu te sourit complaisamment.
>
> Race de Caïn, dans la fange
> Rampe et meurs misérablement.[39]
>
> [Race of Abel, sleep, drink, and eat;
> God smiles on you indulgently.
> Race of Cain, in the mire
> Grovel and die miserably.]

The poem consists of sixteen distichs; every second distich begins the
same way. Cain, the ancestor of the disinherited, appears as the
founder of a race, and this race can be none other than the proletariat. In 1838, Granier de Cassagnac published his *Histoire des classes
ouvrières et des classes bourgeoises*.[40] This work claimed to trace the
origin of the proletarians: they form a class of subhumans which
sprang from the crossing of robbers with prostitutes. Did Baudelaire
know these speculations? Quite possibly. What is certain is that Marx,
who hailed Granier de Cassagnac as "the thinker" of Bonapartist reaction, had encountered them. In his book *Capital*, he parried this
racial theory by developing the concept of a "peculiar race of com-
modity-owners,"[41] by which he meant the proletariat. The race de-

scended from Cain appears in Baudelaire in precisely this sense, though admittedly he would not have been able to define it. It is the race of those who possess no commodity but their labor power.

Baudelaire's poem is part of the cycle entitled "Révolte."[42] Its three parts are blasphemous in tone. Baudelaire's satanism must not be taken too seriously. If it has some significance, it is as the only attitude in which Baudelaire was able to sustain a nonconformist position for any length of time. The last poem in the cycle, "Les Litanies de Satan" [Satanic Litanies], is, by virtue of its theological content, the *miserere* of an ophiolatrous liturgy. Satan appears with his Luciferian halo as the keeper of profound knowledge, as an instructor in Promethean skills, as the patron saint of the stubborn and unyielding. Between the lines flashes the dark head of Blanqui. "Toi qui fais au proscrit ce regard calme et haut / Qui damne tout un peuple autour d'un échafaud."[43] ["You who give the outlaw that calm, proud look / Which can damn an entire multitude gathered around a scaffold."] This Satan, whom the chain of invocations also terms the "father confessor . . . of the conspirator," is different from the infernal intriguer who is called Satan Trismegistos the Demon in the poems, and appears in the prose pieces as His Highness, whose subterranean dwelling lies in the vicinity of the boulevard. Lemaître has pointed out the dichotomy which makes the devil "in one place the author of all evil and in others the great vanquished, the great victim."[44] It is merely a different view of the problem if one asks what impelled Baudelaire to give a radical theological form to his radical rejection of those in power.

After the defeat of the proletariat in the June struggles, the protest against bourgeois ideas of order and respectability was waged more effectively by the ruling classes than by the oppressed.[45] Those who espoused freedom and justice saw Napoleon III not as the soldier-king that he wanted to be, following in his uncle's footsteps, but as a confidence man favored by fortune. This is how he is portrayed in *Les Châtiments.*[46] The *bohème dorée,* for its part, viewed his sumptuous feasts and the splendor with which he surrounded himself as a realization of their dreams of a "free" life. The memoirs of Count

Viel-Castel, in which he described the emperor's surroundings, make a Mimi and a Schaunard appear quite respectable and philistine by comparison.[47] Among the upper classes, cynicism was part of the accepted style; in the lower classes, a rebellious argumentativeness was the norm. In his *Eloa,* Vigny had, in the tradition of Byron, paid homage to Lucifer (the fallen angel) in the gnostic sense.[48] Barthélemy, on the other hand, in his *Némésis,* had associated satanism with the ruling classes; he had a *Messe des agios* celebrated and a psalm about annuities sung.[49] Baudelaire was thoroughly familiar with this dual aspect of Satan. To him, Satan spoke not only for the upper crust but for the lower classes as well. Marx could hardly have wished for a better reader of the following lines from *Der achtzehnte Brumaire:* "When the Puritans complained at the Council of Constance about the wicked lives of the popes, . . . Cardinal Pierre d'Ailly thundered at them: 'Only the devil incarnate can save the Catholic Church, and you demand angels!' Thus, the French bourgeoisie cried after the coup d'état: 'Only the head of the Society of the Tenth of December can save bourgeois society! Only theft can save property, perjury religion, bastardy the family, and disorder order.'"[50] Even in his rebellious hours, Baudelaire, an admirer of the Jesuits, did not wish to renounce this savior completely and forever. His verses hold in reserve what his prose did not deny itself; this is why Satan appears in them. From Satan they derive their subtle power to avoid forswearing all loyalty to that which understanding and humaneness rebelled against—even though such loyalty may be expressed in desperate protests. Almost always the confession of piousness comes from Baudelaire like a battle cry. He will not give up his Satan. Satan is the real stake in the struggle which Baudelaire had to carry on with his unbelief. It is a matter not of sacraments and prayers, but of the Luciferian privilege of blaspheming the Satan to whom one has fallen prey.

Baudelaire intended his friendship with Pierre Dupont to indicate that he was a social poet.[51] The critical writings of Barbey d'Aurevilly contain a sketch of that author: "In this talent and this mind, Cain has the upper hand over the gentle Abel—the brutal, starved, envious, wild Cain who has gone to the cities to consume the sediment of rancor which has accumulated in them and participate in the false ideas which triumph there."[52] This characterization expresses exactly what gave Baudelaire solidarity with Dupont. Like Cain, Dupont had "gone to the cities" and turned away from the idyllic. "He has absolutely no connection with poems as our fathers conceived of them, . . . even with simple romances."[53] Dupont sensed the approaching crisis of lyric poetry as the rift between city and country grew wider. One of his verses contains an awkward admission of this: Dupont says that the poet "lends his ear alternately to the forests and to the masses." The masses rewarded him for his attention: around 1848 Dupont was the talk of the town. As the achievements of the Revolution were being lost one after another, Dupont wrote his "Chant du vote" [Song of Suffrage]. There are few things in the political literature of those days that can rival its refrain. It is a leaf in that laurel crown which Karl Marx claimed for the "threateningly dark brows"[54] of the June fighters.

> Fais voir, en déjouant la ruse,
> O République! à ces pervers,
> Ta grande face de Méduse
> Au milieu de rouges éclairs![55]

> [In foiling their plots, show
> To these evildoers, O Republic,
> your great Medusa face
> Ringed by red lightning!]

The introduction which Baudelaire contributed to a collection of Dupont's poetry in 1851 was an act of literary strategy. It contains the following remarkable statement: "The puerile utopia of the school of *l'art pour l'art* excluded morality and often even passion, and this necessarily made it sterile." And with an obvious reference to Auguste Barbier, he goes on to say: "When a poet appeared who, despite occasional ineptitude, almost always proved to be great, and who in flaming language proclaimed the sacredness of the 1830 insurrection and sang the misery of England and Ireland, . . . the question was settled once and for all, and henceforth art was inseparable from both morality and utility."[56] This has nothing of the profound duplicity which animates Baudelaire's own poetry. His verse supported the oppressed, though it espoused not only their cause but their illusions as well. It had an ear for the songs of the revolution and also for the "higher voice" which spoke from the drumroll of the executions. When Bonaparte came to power through a coup d'état, Baudelaire was momentarily enraged. "Then he looked at events from a 'providential point of view' and submitted like a monk."[57] "Theocracy and communism"[58] were, to him, not convictions but insinuations which vied for his attention; the one was not as seraphic and the other not as Luciferian as he probably thought. It did not take long for Baudelaire to abandon his revolutionary manifesto, and a number of years later he wrote: "Dupont owed his first poems to the grace and feminine delicacy of his nature. Fortunately, the revolutionary activity which in those days carried almost everyone away did not entirely deflect him from his *natural* course."[59] Baudelaire's abrupt break with *l'art pour l'art* was of value to him only as an attitude. It permitted him to announce the latitude which was at his disposal as a man of letters. In this he was ahead of the writers of his time, including the greatest. This makes it evident in what respects he was above the literary activity which surrounded him.

For a century and a half, the literary life of the day had been centered around journals. Toward the end of the third decade of the century, this began to change. The feuilleton provided a market for *belles-lettres* in the daily newspaper. The introduction of this cultural section epitomized the changes which the July Revolution had wrought in the press.[60] During the restoration period, single copies of newspapers could not be sold; people had to subscribe to obtain a paper. Anyone who could not pay the high price of eighty francs for a year's subscription had to go to a café, where often several people stood around reading one copy. In 1824, there were 47,000 newspaper subscribers in Paris; in 1836, there were 70,000; and in 1846, there were 200,000. Girardin's paper, *La Presse*, played a decisive part in this rise.[61] It brought about three important innovations: a lower subscription price of forty francs, advertisements, and the serial novel. At the same time, short, abrupt news items began to compete with detailed reports. These news items caught on because they could be employed commercially. The so-called *réclame* paved the way for them; this was an apparently independent notice which was actually paid for by a publisher and which appeared in the editorial section of the newspaper, referring to a book that had been advertised the day before or in the same issue. As early as 1839, Sainte-Beuve complained about the demoralizing effect of the *réclame:* "How could they damn a product [in a critical review] when the same product was described two inches below as being a wonder of the age? The attraction of the ever larger type-size in which advertisements were printed gained the upper hand; they constituted a magnetic mountain which deflected the compass."[62] The *réclame* marked the beginning of a development which culminated with the stock-exchange notices that appeared in the journals and were paid for by interested persons. It is virtually impossible to write a history of information separately from a history of the corruption of the press.

These informative items required little space. They, and not the political editorials or the serialized novels, enabled a newspaper to have a different look every day—an appearance that was cleverly varied when the pages were made up and constituted part of the paper's attractiveness. These items had to be constantly replenished. City gossip, theatrical intrigues, and "things worth knowing" were their most popular sources. Their intrinsic cheap elegance, a quality that became so characteristic of the feuilleton section, was in evidence from the beginning. In her *Letters from Paris,* Madame de Girardin welcomed photography as follows: "At present, much attention is being paid to Monsieur Daguerre's invention, and nothing is more comical than the serious elucidations of it that our salon scholars are providing. Monsieur Daguerre need not worry; no one is going to steal his secret from him. . . . Truly, his invention is wonderful; but people do not understand it—there have been too many explanations of it."[63] The feuilleton style was not accepted immediately or everywhere. In 1860 and 1868, the two volumes of Baron Gaston de Flotte's *Bévues parisiennes* appeared in Marseilles and Paris.[64] They set about combating the carelessness with which historical information was given, particularly in the feuilleton section of the Parisian press.—The news fillers originated in cafés, over apéritifs. "The custom of taking an apéritif . . . arose with the boulevard press. When there were only the large, serious papers, . . . cocktail hours were unknown. The cocktail hour is the logical consequence of the 'Paris timetable' and of city gossip."[65] Through coffeehouse life, editors became accustomed to the rhythm of the news service even before its machinery had been developed. When the electric telegraph came into use toward the end of the Second Empire, the boulevards lost their monopoly. News of accidents and crimes could now be obtained from all over the world.

The assimilation of a man of letters to the society in which he lived took place on the boulevard, in the following way. On the boulevard, he kept himself in readiness for the next incident, witticism, or rumor. There he unfolded the full drapery of his connections with colleagues and men-about-town, and he was as much dependent on their results as the cocottes were on their disguises.[66] On the boulevards he spent his hours of idleness, which he displayed before people as part of his working hours. He behaved as if he had learned from Marx that the value of a commodity is determined by the worktime needed from society to produce it. In view of the protracted periods of idleness which in the eyes of the public were necessary for the realization of his own labor power, its value became almost fantastic. This high valuation was not limited to the public. The high payments for feuilletons at that time indicate that they were grounded in social conditions. There was in fact a connection between the decrease in the cost of newspaper subscriptions, the increase in advertising, and the growing importance of the feuilleton section.

"In the light of the new arrangements [the lowering of subscription rates], newspapers had to live on advertising revenues. . . . In order to obtain as many advertisements as possible, the quarter-page which had become a poster had to be seen by as many subscribers as possible. It was necessary to have a lure which was directed at all regardless of their private opinion and which replaced politics with curiosity. . . . Once the point of departure existed (the subscription rate of 40 francs), there was an almost inevitable progression from advertisements to serialized novels."[67] This very fact explains the large fees paid for such contributions. In 1845, Dumas signed a contract with *Le Constitutionnel* and *La Presse* guaranteeing him a minimum annual payment of 63,000 francs for supplying at least eighteen installments a year.[68] For his *Mystères de Paris,* Eugène Sue received an advance of 100,000 francs.[69] Lamartine's income has been estimated at 5 million francs for the period from 1838 to 1851. He received 600,000 francs for his *Histoire des Girondins,* which first appeared in the feuilleton section.[70] The generous fees paid for everyday literary merchandise necessarily led to abuses. When publishers acquired manuscripts, they occasionally reserved the right to print them under the name of a writer of their choice. This was predicated on the fact that some successful novelists were not fussy about the use of their names. Some details about this can be found in a lampoon entitled *Fabrique de romans: Maison Alexandre Dumas et Cie.*[71] The *Revue des Deux Mondes* commented at that time: "Who knows the titles of all the books written by Monsieur Dumas? Does he know them himself? Unless he keeps a ledger with a 'Debit' and a 'Credit' side, he surely has forgotten more than one of his legitimate, illegitimate, or adopted children."[72] It was said that Dumas employed a whole army of poor writers in his cellars. As late as 1855, ten years after this commentary by the great review, a small organ of the *bohème* printed the following picturesque scene from the life of a successful novelist whom the author calls de Sanctis: "When he arrived home, Monsieur de Sanctis carefully locked the door . . . and opened a small door hidden behind his books. He found himself in a rather dirty, poorly lit little room. There sat a man with disheveled hair who looked sullen but obsequious and had a long goose-quill in his hand. Even from a distance, it was apparent he was a born novelist, though he was only a former ministry-employee who had learned the art of Balzac from reading *Le Constitutionnel*. He is the real author of *The Chamber of Skulls;* he is the novelist."[73] During the Second Republic, the French parliament tried to combat the proliferation of the feuilleton; each installment of a serial novel was taxed one centime. After a short time this regulation was rescinded, since the reactionary press laws which curtailed freedom of opinion enhanced the value of the feuilleton.

The generous remuneration for feuilletons coupled with their large market helped the writers who supplied them to build great reputations. It was natural for an individual to exploit his reputation together with his financial resources; a political career opened up for him almost automatically. This led to new forms of corruption, which were more consequential than the misuse of well-known writers' names. Once the political ambition of a writer had been aroused, it was natural for the regime to show him the right road. In 1846 Salvandy, the minister of colonies, invited Alexandre Dumas to take a trip to Tunis at government expense—estimated at 10,000 francs—to publicize the colonies.[74] The expedition was unsuccessful, cost a lot of money, and ended with a brief inquest in the Chamber of Deputies. Sue had more luck; on the strength of the success of his *Mystères de Paris,* he not only increased the number of *Le Constitutionnel*'s subscribers from 3,600 to 20,000, but was elected a deputy in 1850 with the votes of 130,000 Parisian workingmen. It was not much of a gain for the proletarian voters; Marx called his election "a sentimentally belittling commentary"[75] on the seats previously won. If literature was able to open a political career to favored writers, this career in turn may be used for a critical evaluation of their writings. Lamartine constitutes a case in point.

Lamartine's decisive successes, the *Méditations* and the *Harmonies,* hark back to a time when France's peasants were still able to enjoy the fruits of their agricultural labors. In a naive poem addressed to Alphonse Karr, the poet equated his creativity with that of a vineyard owner:[76]

> Tout homme avec fierté peut vendre sa sueur!
> Je vends ma grappe en fruit comme tu vends ta fleur,
> Heureux quand son nectar, sous mon pied qui la foule,
> Dans mes tonneaux nombreux en ruisseaux d'ambre coule,
> Produisant à son maître ivre de sa cherté,
> Beaucoup d'or pour payer beaucoup de liberté![77]

> [Every man can sell his sweat with pride!
> I sell my bunch of grapes as you sell your flowers,
> Happy when its nectar, under my foot which tramples it,
> Flows into my many casks in amber streams,
> Producing for its master, who is intoxicated by its high price,
> A lot of gold to pay for a lot of freedom!]

These lines, in which Lamartine praises his prosperity as rustic and boasts of the fees which his produce obtains on the market, are revealing if one reads them less from the viewpoint of morality[78] than as an expression of Lamartine's class feeling—that of a peasant with a plot of land. This is part of the history of Lamartine's poetry. By the 1840s, the situation of the smallholder peasant had become critical. He was in debt; his plot "no longer lay in the so-called fatherland—it lay in the register of mortgages."[79] This meant the decline of rural optimism, the basis of the transfiguring view of nature which is characteristic of Lamartine's poetry. "But while the newly created small holding—in its harmony with society, its dependence on the forces of nature, and its subjection to the authority which protected it from above—was inherently religious, the small holding ruined by debts, at odds with society and authority, and driven beyond its own limits is inherently irreligious. Heaven was quite a nice supplement to the newly acquired strip of land, especially because heaven controls the weather; it becomes an insult when it is forced on people as a substitute for a plot of land."[80] Lamartine's poems had been cloud formations in that very heaven. As Sainte-Beuve wrote in 1830, "The poetry of André Chénier . . . is, so to speak, the landscape over which Lamartine has spread the heavens."[81] This heaven collapsed forever in 1848, when the French peasants voted for Bonaparte as president. Lamartine had helped to prepare the way for that vote.[82] On Lamartine's role in the revolution, Sainte-Beuve commented: "He probably never thought he was destined to become the Orpheus who would guide and moderate that invasion of barbarians with his golden lyre."[83] Baudelaire dryly calls him "a bit whorish, a bit prostituted."[84]

Virtually no one had a keener eye for the problematic sides of this splendid figure than Baudelaire. This may be due to the fact that he himself had always felt little splendor attaching to his own person. Porché believes it looks as though Baudelaire had no choice about where he could place his manuscripts.[85] Ernest Raynaud writes: "Baudelaire had to be prepared for unethical practices. He was dealing with publishers who counted on the vanity of sophisticated people, amateurs, and beginners, and who accepted manuscripts only if a subscription was purchased."[86] Baudelaire's actions were in keeping with this state of affairs. He offered the same manuscript to several papers at the same time and authorized reprints without indicating them as such. From his early period on, he viewed the literary market without any illusions. In 1846 he wrote: "No matter how beautiful a house may be, it is primarily, and before one dwells on its beauty, so-and-so many meters high and so-and-so many meters long. In the same way, literature, which constitutes the most inestimable substance, is primarily a matter of filling up lines; and a literary architect whose mere name does not guarantee a profit must sell at any price."[87] Until his dying day, Baudelaire had little status in the literary marketplace. It has been calculated that he earned no more than 15,000 francs from all his writings.

"Balzac is ruining himself with coffee; Musset is dulling himself by drinking absinthe. . . . Murger is dying in a sanatorium, as is now Baudelaire. And not one of these writers has been a socialist!"[88]

Thus wrote Sainte-Beuve's private secretary, Jules Troubat. Baudelaire surely deserved the recognition intended by the last sentence. But this does not mean that he lacked insight into the true situation of a man of letters. He often confronted the writer, first and foremost himself, with the figure of the whore. His sonnet to the venal muse—"La Muse vénale"—speaks of this. His great introductory poem "Au Lecteur" presents the poet in the unflattering position of someone who takes cold cash for his confessions. One of his earliest poems, which figures among those excluded from *Les Fleurs du mal,* is addressed to a streetwalker. This is its second stanza:

> Pour avoir des souliers, elle a vendu son âme;
> Mais le bon Dieu rirait si, près de cette infâme,
> Je tranchais du Tartufe et singeais la hauteur,
> Moi qui vends ma pensée et qui veux être auteur.[89]

> [In order to have shoes, she has sold her soul;
> But the Good Lord would laugh if, in the presence of that
>   vile woman,
> I played the hypocrite and acted lofty—
> I who sell my thought and wish to be an author.]

The last stanza, "Cette bohème-là, c'est mon tout" ["That bohemian woman—she means everything to me"], casually includes this creature in the brotherhood of the *bohème.* Baudelaire knew the true situation of the man of letters: he goes to the marketplace as a flâneur—ostensibly to look around, but in truth to find a buyer.

II. The Flâneur

Once a writer had entered the marketplace, he looked around as if in a panorama.[90] A special literary genre has captured the writer's first attempts to orient himself. This is the genre of panoramic literature. It was no accident that *Le Livre des cent-et-un, Les Français peints par eux-mêmes, Le Diable à Paris,* and *La Grande Ville* were popular in the capital city at the same time as the panoramas.[91] These works consist of individual sketches which, as it were, reproduce the dynamic foreground of those panoramas with their anecdotal form and the sweeping background of the panoramas with their store of information. Numerous authors contributed to the volumes. Thus, these anthologies are products of the same collective belletristic endeavor for which Girardin had provided an outlet in the feuilleton. They were the salon attire of a literature which was basically designed to be sold on the street. In this literature, the inconspicuous, paperback, pocket-size volumes called "physiologies" had pride of place. They investigated the human types that a person taking a look at the marketplace might encounter. From the itinerant street vendor of the boulevards to the dandy in the opera-house foyer, there was not a figure of Paris life that was not sketched by a *physiologue*. The great flowering of the genre came in the early 1840s—the period that marked the *haute école* of the feuilleton. Baudelaire's generation went through it. The fact that it meant little to Baudelaire himself indicates the early age at which he went his own way.

In 1841 there were seventy-six new physiologies.[92] After that year the genre declined, and it disappeared together with the reign of the Citizen King, Louis Philippe. It was a petty-bourgeois genre from the ground up. Monnier, its master, was a philistine endowed with an uncommon capacity for self-observation.[93] Nowhere did these physiologies break through the most limited horizon. After each human type had been covered, the physiology of the city had its turn. There appeared *Paris la nuit, Paris à table, Paris dans l'eau, Paris à cheval, Paris pittoresque, Paris marié.*[94] When this vein, too, was exhausted, a "physiology" of the nations was attempted. Nor was the "physiology" of animals neglected, for animals have always been an innocuous subject. Innocuousness was of the essence. In his studies on the history of caricature, Eduard Fuchs points out that the beginning of the physiologies coincided with the so-called September Laws, the tightened censorship of 1836.[95] These laws summarily forced out of politics an array of capable artists with a background in satire. If that could be done in the graphic arts, the government's maneuver was bound to be all the more successful in literature, for there was no political energy there that could compare with that of a Daumier. Reaction, then, was the principle "which explains the colossal parade of bourgeois life that . . . began in France. . . . Everything passed in review. . . . Days of celebration and days of mourning, work and play, conjugal customs and bachelors' practices, the family, the home, children, school, society, the theater, character types, professions."[96]

The leisurely quality of these descriptions fits the style of the flâneur who goes botanizing on the asphalt. But even in those days it was impossible to stroll about everywhere in the city. Before Haussmann, wide pavements were rare; the narrow ones afforded little protection from vehicles.[97] Flânerie could hardly have assumed the importance it did without the arcades. "These arcades, a recent invention of industrial luxury," says an illustrated guide to Paris of 1852, "are glass-roofed, marble-paneled corridors extending through whole blocks of buildings, whose owners have joined together for such enterprises. Lining both sides of these corridors, which get their light from above, are the most elegant shops, so that the *passage* is a city, a world in miniature." It is in this world that the flâneur is at home; he provides the arcade—"the favorite venue of strollers and smokers, the haunt of all sorts of little *métiers*"[98]—with its chronicler and philosopher. As for himself, the arcade provides him with an unfailing remedy for the kind of boredom that easily arises under the baleful eye of a sated reactionary regime. In the words of Guys as quoted by Baudelaire, "Anyone who is capable of being bored in a crowd is a blockhead. I repeat: a blockhead, and a contemptible one."[99] The arcades are something between a street and an *intérieur*. If one can say that the physiologies employ an artistic device, it is the proven device of the feuilleton—namely, the transformation of the boulevard into an *intérieur*. The street becomes a dwelling place for the flâneur; he is as much at home among house façades as a citizen is within his four walls. To him, a shiny enameled shop sign is at least as good a wall ornament as an oil painting is to a bourgeois in his living room. Buildings' walls are the desk against which he presses his notebooks; newsstands are his libraries; and café terraces are the balconies from which he looks down on his household after his work is done. That life in all its variety and inexhaustible wealth of permutations can thrive only among the gray cobblestones and against the gray background of despotism was the political secret of the literature to which the physiologies belonged.

These writings were socially dubious, as well. The long series of eccentric or appealingly simple or severe figures which the physiologies presented to the public in character sketches had one thing in common: they were harmless and perfectly affable. Such a view of one's fellow man was so remote from experience that there were bound to be uncommonly weighty motives for it. The reason was an uneasiness of a special sort. People had to adapt themselves to a new and rather strange situation, one that is peculiar to big cities. Simmel has provided an excellent formulation of what was involved here.[100] "Someone who sees without hearing is much more uneasy than someone who hears without seeing. In this, there is something characteristic of the sociology of the big city. Interpersonal relationships in big cities are distinguished by a marked preponderance of visual activity over aural activity. The main reason for this is the public means of transportation. Before the development of buses, railroads, and trams in the nineteenth century, people had never been in situations where they had to look at one another for long minutes or even hours without speaking to one another."[101] These new situations were, as Simmel recognized, not pleasant. In his *Eugene Aram,* Bulwer-Lytton orchestrated his description of big-city dwellers with a reference to Goethe's remark that each person, the most worthy as well as the most despicable, carries around a secret which would make him hateful to everyone else if it became known.[102] The physiologies were just the thing to brush such disquieting notions aside as insignificant. They constituted, so to speak, the blinkers of the "narrow-minded city animal" that Marx wrote about.[103] A description of the proletarian in Foucaud's *Physiologie de l'industrie française* shows what a thoroughly limited vision these physiologies offered when the need arose: "Quiet enjoyment is almost exhausting for a workingman. The house in which he lives may be surrounded by greenery under a cloudless sky; it may be fragrant with flowers and enlivened by the chirping of birds. But if a worker is idle, he will remain inaccessible to the charms of solitude. On the other hand, if a loud noise or a whistle from a distant factory happens to hit his ear, if he so much as hears the monotonous clattering of the machines in a factory, his face immediately brightens. He no longer senses the choice fragrance of flowers. The smoke from the tall factory chimney, the booming blows on the anvil, make him tremble with joy. He remembers the happy days of his labors, which were guided by the spirit of the inventor."[104] The entrepreneur who read this description may have gone to bed more relaxed than usual.

It was indeed the most obvious thing to give people a friendly picture of one another. Thus, the physiologies helped fashion the phantasmagoria of Parisian life in their own way. But their method could not get them very far. People knew one another as debtors and creditors, salesmen and customers, employers and employees, and above all as competitors. In the long run, it seemed quite unlikely that they could be made to believe their associates were harmless oddballs. So these writings soon developed another view of the matter which was much more bracing. They went back to the physiognomists of the eighteenth century, although they had little to do with the more solid endeavors of those earlier authors. In Lavater and Gall there was, in addition to speculative and visionary impulses, genuine empiricism.[105] The physiologies eroded the reputation of this empiricism without adding anything of their own. They assured people that everyone could—unencumbered by any factual knowledge—make out the profession, character, background, and lifestyle of passers-by. The physiologies present this ability as a gift which a good fairy lays in the cradle of the big-city dweller. With such certainties, Balzac, more than anyone else, was in his element. They encouraged his predilection for unqualified statements. "Genius," he wrote, "is so visible in a person that even the least educated man walking around in Paris will, when he comes across a great artist, know immediately what he has found."[106] Delvau, Baudelaire's friend and the most interesting among the minor masters of the feuilleton, claimed that he could di-vide the Parisian public according to its various strata as easily as a geologist distinguishes the layers in rocks. If that sort of thing could be done, then life in the big city was surely not as disquieting as it probably seemed to people. And the following questions by Baudelaire were just empty phrases: "What are the dangers of the forest and the prairie, compared with the daily shocks and conflicts of civilization? Whether a man grabs his victim on a boulevard or stabs his quarry in unknown woods—does he not remain both here and there the most perfect of all beasts of prey?"[107]

For this victim, Baudelaire uses the term *dupe*. The word refers to someone who is cheated or fooled, and such a person is the antithesis of a connoisseur of human nature. The more alien a big city becomes, the more knowledge of human nature—so it was thought—one needs to operate in it. In actuality, the intensified struggle for survival led an individual to make an imperious proclamation of his interests. When it is a matter of evaluating a person's behavior, intimate familiarity with these interests will often be much more useful than familiarity with his character. The ability the flâneur prides himself on is, therefore, more likely to be one of the idols Bacon already located in the marketplace. Baudelaire hardly paid homage to this idol. His belief in original sin made him immune to belief in a knowledge of human nature. He sided with de Maistre, who had combined a study of dogma with a study of Bacon.[108]

The soothing little remedies that the physiologists offered for sale were soon outmoded. On the other hand, the literature concerned with the disquieting and threatening aspects of urban life was destined for a great future. This literature, too, dealt with the masses, but its method was different from that of the physiologies. It cared little about the definition of types; rather, it investigated the functions which are peculiar to the masses in a big city. One of these claimed particular attention; it had been emphasized in a police report as early as the turn of the nineteenth century. "It is almost impossible," wrote a Parisian secret agent in 1798, "to maintain good behavior in a thickly populated area where an individual is, so to speak, unknown to everyone else and thus does not have to blush in front of anyone."[109] Here the masses appear as the asylum that shields an asocial person from his persecutors. Of all the menacing aspects of the masses, this one became apparent first. It lies at the origin of the detective story.

In times of terror, when everyone is something of a conspirator, everybody will be in the position of having to play detective. Flânerie gives the individual the best prospects of doing so. Baudelaire wrote: "An observer is a *prince* who is everywhere in possession of his incognito."[110] If the flâneur is thus turned into an unwilling detective, it does him a lot of good socially, for it legitimates his idleness. His indolence is only apparent, for behind this indolence there is the watchfulness of an observer who does not take his eyes off a miscreant. Thus, the detective sees rather wide areas opening up to his self-esteem. He develops reactions that are in keeping with the tempo of a big city. He catches things in flight; this enables him to dream that he is like an artist. Everyone praises the swift crayon of the graphic artist. Balzac claims that artistry as such is linked to quick grasp.[111]— Forensic knowledge coupled with the pleasant nonchalance of the flâneur: this is the essence of Dumas' *Mohicans de Paris*. The hero of this book decides to go in search of adventure by following a scrap of paper which he has given to the wind as a plaything. No matter what traces the flâneur may follow, every one of them will lead him to a crime. This is an indication of how the detective story, regardless of its sober calculations, also participates in the phantasmagoria of Parisian life. It does not yet glorify the criminal, though it does glorify his adversaries and, above all, the hunting grounds where they pursue him. Messac has shown how writers have attempted to bring in echoes of Cooper.[112] The most interesting thing about Cooper's influence is that it is not concealed but displayed. In the aforementioned *Mohicans de Paris,* this display is in the very title; the author promises readers that he will open a primeval forest and a prairie for them in Paris. The woodcut used as a frontispiece in the third volume shows a street overgrown with trees and shrubs that was little frequented in those days; the caption under this picture reads: "The primeval forest on the rue d'Enfer." The publisher's brochure for this volume limns the connection with a magnificent phrase which reveals the author's enthusiasm for himself: "'Paris' and 'Mohicans': . . . these two names clash like the *qui vive* of two gigantic unknowns. An abyss separates the two; across it flashes a spark of that electric light which has its source in Alexandre Dumas." Even earlier, Féval had involved a redskin in the adventures of a metropolis.[113] While riding in a fiacre, this man, whose name is Tovah, manages to scalp his four white companions so stealthily that the coachman suspects nothing. *Les Mystères de Paris* refers to Cooper in its opening pages, promising that its heroes from the Parisian underworld "are no less removed from civilization than the savages who are so splendidly depicted by Cooper." But it is Balzac who, above all, never tires of referring to Cooper as his model. "The poetry of terror that pervades the American woods, with their clashes between tribes on the warpath—this poetry which stood Cooper in such good stead attaches in the same way to the smallest details of Parisian life. The pedestrians, the shops, the hired coaches, a man leaning against a window—all this was of the same burning interest to the members of Peyrade's bodyguard as a tree stump, a beaver's den, a rock, a buffalo skin, a motionless canoe, or a floating leaf was to the reader of a novel by Cooper."[114] Balzac's intrigue is rich in forms that fall somewhere between tales of Indians and detective stories. At an early date, there were objections to his "Mohicans in spencer jackets" and "Hurons in frock coats."[115] On the other hand, Hippolyte Babou, who was close to Baudelaire, wrote retrospectively in 1857: "When Balzac breaks through walls to give free rein to observation, people listen at the doors. . . . In short, they behave, as our prudish English neighbors phrase it, like *police detectives*."[116]

The detective story, whose interest lies in its logical structure (which the crime story as such need not have), appeared in France for the first time when Poe's stories "The Mystery of Marie Roget," "The Murders in the Rue Morgue," and "The Purloined Letter" were translated. With his translations of these models, Baudelaire adopted the genre. Poe's work was definitely absorbed in his own, and Baudelaire emphasizes this fact by stating his solidarity with the method in which the individual genres that Poe embraced harmonize. Poe was one of the greatest technicians of modern literature. As Valéry pointed out,[117] he was the first to attempt the scientific story, the modern cosmogony, and the description of pathological phenomena. These genres he regarded as exact products of a method for which he claimed universal validity. Baudelaire sided with him on this point, and in Poe's spirit he wrote: "The time is approaching when it will be understood that a literature which refuses to proceed in brotherly concord with science and philosophy is a murderous and suicidal literature."[118] The detective story, the most momentous of Poe's technical achievements, belonged to a literature that satisfied Baudelaire's postulate. Its analysis constitutes part of the analysis of Baudelaire's own work, despite the fact that Baudelaire wrote no stories of this type. *Les Fleurs du mal* incorporates three of its decisive elements as *disjecta membra:* the victim and the scene of the crime ("Une Martyre"), the murderer ("Le Vin de l'assassin"), and the masses ("Le Crépuscule du soir"). The fourth element is lacking—the one that permits the intellect to break through this emotion-laden atmosphere. Baudelaire wrote no detective story because, given the structure of his drives, it was impossible for him to identify with the detective. In him, the calculating, constructive element was on the side of the asocial and had become an integral part of cruelty. Baudelaire was too good a reader of the Marquis de Sade to be able to compete with Poe.[119]

The original social content of the detective story focused on the obliteration of the individual's traces in the big-city crowd. Poe concerns himself with this motif in detail in "The Mystery of Marie Roget," the longest of his detective stories. At the same time, this story is the prototype for the way journalistic information is used in solving crimes. Poe's detective, the Chevalier Dupin, here works not with personal observation but with reports from the daily press. The critical analysis of these reports constitutes the scaffolding in the story. Among other things, the time of the crime has to be established. One paper, *Le Commercial,* expresses the view that Marie Roget, the murdered woman, was done away with immediately after she left her mother's apartment. Poe writes:

> "It is impossible . . . that a person so well known to thousands as this young woman was, should have passed three blocks without some one having seen her." This is the way of thinking of a man long resident in Paris—a public man—and one whose walks to and fro in the city have been mostly limited to the vicinity of the public offices. . . . He passes to and fro, at regular intervals, within a confined periphery abounding in individuals who are led to observation of his person through interest in the kindred nature of his occupation with their own. But the walks of Marie may, in general, be supposed discursive. In this particular instance it will be understood as most probable that she proceeded upon a route of more than average diversity from her accustomed ones. The parallel which we imagine to have existed in the mind of *Le Commercial* would only be sustained in the event of the two individuals traversing the whole city. In this case, granting the personal acquaintances to be equal, the chances would be also equal that an equal number of personal *rencontres* would be made. For my own part, I should hold it not only as possible, but as far more than probable, that Marie might have proceeded, at any given period, by any one of the many routes between her own residence and that of her aunt, without meeting a single individual whom she knew, or by whom she was known. In viewing this question in its full and proper light, we must hold steadily in mind the great disproportion between the personal acquaintances of even the most noted individual in Paris, and the entire population of Paris itself.

If one disregards the context which gives rise to these reflections in Poe, the detective loses his competence but the problem does not lose its validity. A variation of it forms the basis of one of the most famous poems in *Les Fleurs du mal,* the sonnet entitled "A une passante" [To a Passer-By].

La rue assourdissante autour de moi hurlait.
Longue, mince, en grand deuil, douleur majestueuse,
Une femme passa, d'une main fastueuse
Soulevant, balançant le feston et l'ourlet;

Agile et noble, avec sa jambe de statue.
Moi, je buvais, crispé comme un extravagant,
Dans son oeil, ciel livide où germe l'ouragan,
La douceur qui fascine et le plaisir qui tue.

Un éclair . . . puis la nuit!—Fugitive beauté
Dont le regard m'a fait soudainement renaître,
Ne te verrai-je plus que dans l'éternité?
Ailleurs, bien loin d'ici! trop tard! *jamais* peut-être!
Car j'ignore où tu fuis, tu ne sais où je vais,
O toi que j'eusse aimée, ô toi qui le savais![120]

[The street around me roared, deafening.
Tall, slender, in deep mourning, majestic in her grief,
A woman passed—with imposing hand
Gathering up a scalloped hem—
Agile and noble, her leg like a statue's.
And as for me, twitching like one possessed, I drank
From her eyes—livid sky brewing a storm—
The sweetness that fascinates and the pleasure that kills.

A lightning flash . . . then night!—Fugitive beauty,
Whose gaze has suddenly given me new life,
Will I see you again before the close of eternity?

Elsewhere, very far from here! Too late! Perhaps *never!*
For where you're off to I'll never know, nor do you know
    where I'm going—
O you whom I could have loved, O you who knew it too!]

This sonnet presents the crowd not as the refuge of a criminal but as the refuge of love which flees from the poet. One may say that it deals with the function of the crowd not in the life of the citizen but in the life of the eroticist. At first glance this function appears to be a negative one, but it is not. Far from eluding the eroticist in the crowd, the apparition which fascinates him is brought to him by this very crowd. The delight of the city-dweller is not so much love at first sight as love at last sight. The word "jamais" marks the high point of the encounter, when the poet's passion seems to be frustrated but in reality bursts out of him like a flame. He is seared by this flame, but no phoenix arises from it. The rebirth in the first tercet reveals a view of the event which in the light of the preceding stanza seems very problematic. What makes his body twitch spasmodically is not the excitement of a man in whom an image has taken possession of every fiber of his being; it partakes more of the shock with which an imperious desire suddenly overcomes a lonely man. The phrase "comme un extravagant" almost expresses this; the poet's emphasis on the fact that the female apparition is in mourning is not designed to conceal it. In reality, there is a profound gulf between the quatrains which present the occurrence and the tercets which transfigure it. When Thibaudet says that these verses "could only have been written in a big city,"[121] he does not penetrate beneath their surface. The inner form of these verses is revealed in the fact that they depict love itself as being stigmatized by the big city.[122]

Since the days of Louis Philippe, the bourgeoisie has endeavored to compensate itself for the fact that private life leaves no traces in the big city. It seeks such compensation within its four walls—as if it were striving, as a matter of honor, to prevent the traces, if not of its days on earth then at least of its possessions and requisites of daily life, from disappearing forever. The bourgeoisie unabashedly makes impressions of a host of objects. For slippers and pocket watches, thermometers and egg cups, cutlery and umbrellas, it tries to get covers and cases. It prefers velvet and plush covers, which preserve the impression of every touch. For the Makart style, the style of the end of the Second Empire, a dwelling becomes a kind of casing.[123] This style views it as a case for a person and embeds him in it, together with all his appurtenances, tending his traces as nature tends dead fauna embedded in granite. One must note that there are two sides to this process. The real or sentimental value of the objects thus preserved is emphasized. They are removed from the profane gaze of nonowners; in particular, their outlines are blurred in a characteristic way. It is no accident that resistance to controls, something that becomes second nature to asocial persons, displays a resurgence in the propertied bourgeoisie.—In such customs, one can see the dialectical illustration of a text which appeared in many installments in the *Journal Officiel*.[124] As early as 1836, Balzac wrote in *Modeste Mignon*: "Poor women of France! You would probably like to remain unknown, so that you can carry on your little romances. But how can you manage this in a civilization which registers the departures and arrivals of coaches in public places, counts letters and stamps them when they are posted and again when they are delivered, assigns numbers to houses, and will soon have the whole country, down to the smallest plot of land, in its registers?"[125] Since the French Revolution, an extensive network of controls had been bringing bourgeois life ever more tightly into its meshes. The numbering of houses in the big cities may be used to document the progressive standardization. Napoleon's administration had made such numbering obligatory for Paris in 1805. In proletarian neighborhoods, to be sure, this simple police measure had encountered resistance. As late as 1864, the following was reported about Saint-Antoine, the carpenters' neighborhood: "If one asks an inhabitant of this suburb what his address is, he will always give the name of his house and not its cold, official number."[126] In the long run, of course, such resistance was of no avail against the government's effort to establish a multifarious web of registrations—a means of compensating for the elimination of traces that takes place when people disappear into the masses of the big cities. Baudelaire found this effort as much of an encroachment as did any criminal. Trying to evade his creditors, he went to cafés or reading circles. Sometimes he had two domiciles at the same time—but on days when the rent was due, he often spent the night at a third place with friends. So he roamed about in the city, which had long since ceased to be home for the flâneur. Every bed in which he lay became a "lit 'hasardeux'"[127] for him. Crépet has counted fourteen Paris addresses for Baudelaire in the years 1842 to 1858.

Technical measures had to come to the aid of the administrative control process. In the early days of the process of identification, whose current standard derives from the Bertillon method, the identity of a person was established through his signature.[128] The invention of photography was a turning point in the history of this process. It was no less significant for criminology than the invention of the printing press was for literature. Photography made it possible for the first time to preserve permanent and unmistakable traces of a human being. The detective story came into being when this most decisive of all conquests of a person's incognito had been accomplished. Since that time, there has been no end to the efforts to capture [*dingfest machen*] a man in his speech and actions.

Poe's famous tale "The Man of the Crowd" is something like an X-ray of a detective story. It does away with all the drapery that a crime represents. Only the armature remains: the pursuer, the crowd, and an unknown man who manages to walk through London in such a way that he always remains in the middle of the crowd. This unknown man is the flâneur. That is how Baudelaire understood him when, in his essay on Guys, he called the flâneur "l'homme des foules" [the man of the crowd]. But Poe's description of this figure is devoid of the connivance which Baudelaire's notion included. To Poe, the flâneur was, above all, someone who does not feel comfortable in his own company. This is why he seeks out the crowd; the reason he hides in it is probably close at hand. Poe purposely blurs the difference between the asocial person and the flâneur. The harder a man is to find, the more suspicious he becomes. Refraining from a prolonged pursuit, the narrator quietly sums up his insight as follows: "'This old man is the embodiment and the spirit of crime,' I said to myself. 'He refuses to be alone. *He is the man of the crowd.*'"

The author does not demand the reader's interest in this man alone; his description of the crowd will claim at least as much interest, for documentary as well as artistic reasons. In both respects, the crowd stands out. The first thing that strikes one is the rapt attention with which the narrator follows the spectacle of the crowd. This same spectacle is followed, in a well-known story by E. T. A. Hoffmann, by the "cousin at his corner window."[129] But this man, who is in his own home, views the crowd with great circumspection, whereas the man who stares through the window of a coffeehouse has a penetrating gaze. In the difference between the two observation posts lies the difference between Berlin and London. On the one hand, there is the man of leisure. He sits in his alcove as in a box at the theater; when he wants to take a closer look at the marketplace, he has opera glasses at hand. On the other hand, there is the anonymous consumer who enters a café and will shortly leave it again, attracted by the magnet of the mass which constantly has him in its range. On the one side, there is a multiplicity of little genre pictures which together constitute an album of colored engravings; on the other side, there is a view which could inspire a great etcher: an enormous crowd in which no one is either quite transparent or quite opaque to everyone else. A German petty bourgeois is subject to very narrow limits, yet Hoffmann by nature belonged to the family of the Poes and Baudelaires. In the biographical notes to the original edition of his last writings, we read: "Hoffmann was never especially fond of nature. He valued people—communication with them, observations about them, merely seeing them—more than anything else. If he went for a walk in summer, something that he did every day toward evening in fine weather, there was hardly a wine tavern or a confectioner's shop that he did not look in on, to see whether anyone was inside and who might be there."[130] At a later date, when Dickens went traveling, he repeatedly complained about the lack of street noises, which were indispensable to him for his work. "I cannot express how much I want these [the streets]," he wrote in 1846 from Lausanne while he was working on *Dombey and Son.* "It seems as if they supplied something to my brain, which it cannot bear, when busy, to lose. For a week or a fortnight I can write prodigiously in a retired place, . . . and a day in London sets me up again and starts me. But the toil and labor of writing, day after day, without that magic lantern, is *immense*. . . . *My* figures seem disposed to stagnate without crowds about them."[131] Among the many things that Baudelaire criticized about Brussels, a city he hated, was something that filled him with particular rage: "No shopwindows. Strolling— something that nations with imagination love—is impossible in Brussels. There is nothing to see, and the streets are unusable."[132] Baudelaire loved solitude, but he wanted it in a crowd.

Poe, in the course of his story, lets darkness fall. He lingers over the city by gaslight. The appearance of the street as an *intérieur* in which the phantasmagoria of the flâneur is concentrated is hard to separate from the gas lighting. The first gas lamps burned in the arcades. The attempt to use them under the open sky was made in Baudelaire's childhood: candelabra-shaped lights were installed on the Place Vendôme. Under Napoleon III, the number of gas lamps in Paris grew rapidly.[133] This way of increasing safety in the city made the crowds feel at home in the open streets even at night, and removed the starry sky from the ambience of the big city more effectively than tall buildings had ever done. "I draw the curtain over the sun; now it has been put to bed, as is proper. Henceforth I shall see no other light but that of the gas flame."[134] The moon and the stars are no longer worth mentioning.

In the heyday of the Second Empire, the shops in the main streets did not close before ten o'clock at night. It was the great age of *noctambulisme*. In the chapter of his *Heures parisiennes* which is devoted to the second hour after midnight, Delvau wrote: "A person may take a rest from time to time; he is permitted stops and resting places. But he has no right to sleep."[135] On Lake Geneva, Dickens nostalgically remembered Genoa, where two miles of lighted streets had enabled him to roam about at night. Later, when flânerie went out of style with the extinction of the arcades and gaslight was no longer considered fashionable, a last flâneur strolling sadly through the empty Passage Colbert had the impression that the flickering of the gas lamps indicated merely the flame's own fear that the gas bill would not be paid at the end of the month.[136] This is when

Stevenson wrote his plaint about the disappearance of the gas lamps. He muses particularly on the rhythm with which lamplighters would go through the streets and light one lamp after another. From the outset, this rhythm contrasted with the uniformity of the dusk, but now the contrast becomes brutally shocking with the spectacle of entire cities suddenly being illuminated by electric light. "Such a light as this should shine only on murders and public crime, or along the corridors of lunatic asylums, a horror to heighten horror."[137] There is some indication that only in its late stages did people take an idyllic view of gaslight such as the one presented by Stevenson, who wrote its obituary. The above-mentioned story by Poe is a good case in point. There can hardly be a more uncanny description of this light: "The rays of the gas lamps, feeble at first in their struggle with the dying day, had now at length gained ascendancy, and threw over every thing a fitful and garish lustre. All was dark yet splendid—as that ebony to which has been likened the style of Tertullian."[138] "Inside a house," wrote Poe elsewhere, "gas is definitely inadmissible. Its flickering, harsh light offends the eye."

The London crowd seems as gloomy and confused as the light in which it moves. This is true not only of the rabble that crawls "out of its dens" at night. The clerks of higher rank are described by Poe as follows: "They had all slightly bald heads, from which the right ears, long used to pen-holding, had an odd habit of standing off on end. I observed that they always removed or settled their hats with both hands, and wore watches, with short gold chains of a substantial and ancient pattern." In his description, Poe did not aim at any direct observation. The uniformities to which the petty bourgeois are subjected by virtue of being part of the crowd are exaggerated; their appearance is not far from being uniform. Even more astonishing is the description of the way the crowd moves.

By far the greater number of those who went by had a satisfied business-like demeanor, and seemed to be thinking only of making their way through the press. Their brows were knit, and their eyes rolled quickly; when pushed against by fellow-wayfarers they evinced no symptom of impatience, but adjusted their clothes and hurried on. Others, still a numerous class, were restless in their movements, had flushed faces, and talked and gesticulated to themselves, as if feeling in solitude on account of the very denseness of the company around. When impeded in their progress, these people suddenly ceased muttering, but redoubled their gesticulations, and awaited, with an absent and overdone smile upon the lips, the course of the persons impeding them. If jostled, they bowed profusely to the jostlers, and appeared overwhelmed with confusion.[139]

One might think he was speaking of half-drunken wretches. Actually, they were "noblemen, merchants, attorneys, tradesmen, stock-jobbers."[140] Something other than a psychology of the classes is involved here.[141]

There is a lithograph by Senefelder which represents a gambling club.[142] Not one of the individuals depicted is pursuing the game in the customary fashion. Each man is dominated by his affect: one shows unrestrained joy; another, distrust of his partner; a third, dull despair; a fourth evinces belligerence; another is preparing to take leave of the world. In its extravagance, this lithograph is reminiscent of Poe. Poe's subject, to be sure, is greater, and his means are in keeping with this. His masterly stroke in the above description is that he does not show the hopeless isolation of men within their private concerns through the variety of their behavior, as does Senefelder, but expresses this isolation in absurd uniformities of dress or conduct. The servility with which those pushed even go on to apologize shows where the devices Poe employs here come from. They derive from the repertoire of clowns, and Poe uses them in a fashion similar to that later employed by clowns. In the performance of a clown, there is an obvious reference to economic mechanisms. With his abrupt movements, he imitates both the machines which push the material and the economic boom which pushes the merchandise. The segments of the crowd described by Poe enact a similar mimesis of the "feverish . . . pace of material production," along with the forms of business that go with it. What the fun fair, which turned the average man into a clown, later accomplished with its bumper cars and related amusements is anticipated in Poe's description. The people in his story behave as if they can no longer express themselves through anything but reflex actions. These goings-on seem even more dehumanized because Poe talks only about people. If the crowd becomes jammed up, this is not because it is being impeded by vehicular traffic—there is no mention of vehicles anywhere—but because it is being blocked by other crowds. In a mass of this nature, flânerie could never flourish.

In Baudelaire's Paris, things had not yet come to such a pass. Ferries were still crossing the Seine at points where later there would be bridges. In the year of Baudelaire's death, an entrepreneur could still cater to the comfort of the well-to-do with a fleet of five hundred sedan chairs circulating about the city. Arcades, where the flâneur would not be exposed to the sight of carriages—which scorned to recognize pedestrians as rivals—were enjoying undiminished popularity. There was the pedestrian who wedged himself into the crowd, but there was also the flâneur who demanded elbow room and was unwilling to forgo the life of a gentleman of leisure. He goes his leisurely way as a personality; in this manner he protests against the division of labor which makes people into specialists. He protests no less against their industriousness. Around 1840 it was briefly fashionable to take turtles for a walk in the arcades. The flâneurs liked to have the turtles set the pace for them. If they had had their way, progress would have been obliged to accommodate itself to this pace. But this attitude did not prevail. Taylor—who popularized the catchphrase "Down with dawdling!"—carried the day.[143] Some people sought to anticipate coming developments while there was still time. Rattier wrote in 1857 in his utopia *Paris n'existe pas:* "The flâneur whom we used to encounter on the sidewalks and in front of shopwindows, this nonentity, this constant rubberneck, this inconsequential type who was always in search of cheap emotions and knew about nothing but cobblestones, fiacres, and gas lamps, . . . has now become a farmer, a vintner, a linen manufacturer, a sugar refiner, a steel magnate."[144]

On his peregrinations, at a late hour, the man of the crowd winds up in a department store where there still are many customers. He moves about like someone who knows his way around the place. Were there multilevel department stores in Poe's day? No matter; Poe lets the restless man spend an "hour and a half, or thereabouts" in this bazaar. "He entered shop after shop, priced nothing, spoke no word, and looked at all objects with a wild and vacant stare." If the arcade is the classical form of the *intérieur*—and this is the way the street presents itself to the flâneur—the department store is the form of the *intérieur*'s decay. The department store is the last promenade for the flâneur. If in the beginning the street had become an *intérieur* for him, now this *intérieur* turned into a street, and he roamed through the labyrinth of commodities as he had once roamed through the labyrinth of the city. A magnificent touch in Poe's story is that it not only contains the earliest description of the flâneur but also prefigures his end.

Jules Laforgue said that Baudelaire was the first to speak of Paris "as someone condemned to live in the capital day after day."[145] He might have said that Baudelaire was also the first to speak of the opiate that afforded relief to men so condemned, and only to them. The crowd is not only the newest asylum of outlaws; it is also the latest narcotic for people who have been abandoned. The flâneur is someone abandoned in the crowd. He is thus in the same situation as the commodity. He is unaware of this special situation, but this does not diminish its effect on him; it permeates him blissfully, like a narcotic that can compensate him for many humiliations. The intoxication to which the flâneur surrenders is the intoxication of the commodity immersed in a surging stream of customers.

If there were such a thing as a commodity-soul (a notion that Marx occasionally mentions in jest),[146] it would be the most empathetic ever encountered in the realm of souls, for it would be bound to see every individual as a buyer in whose hand and house it wants to nestle. Empathy is the nature of the intoxication to which the flâneur abandons himself in the crowd. "The poet enjoys the incomparable privilege of being himself and someone else, as he sees fit. Like those roving souls in search of a body, he enters another person whenever he wishes. For him alone, all is open; and if certain places seem closed to him, it is because in his view they are not worth visiting."[147] The commodity itself is the speaker here. Yes, the last words give a rather accurate idea of what the commodity whispers to a poor wretch who passes a shopwindow containing beautiful and expensive things. These objects are not interested in this person; they do not empathize with him. In the important prose poem "Les Foules," we hear the voice—speaking in different words—of the fetish itself, which Baudelaire's sensitive disposition resonated with so powerfully: that empathy with inorganic things which was one of his sources of inspiration.[148]

Baudelaire was a connoisseur of narcotics, yet one of their most important social effects probably escaped him. It consists in the charm displayed by addicts under the influence of drugs. Commodities derive the same effect from the crowd that surges around and intoxicates them. The concentration of customers which makes up the market, which in turn makes the commodity a commodity, enhances its attractiveness to the average buyer. When Baudelaire speaks of "the religious intoxication of great cities,"[149] the commodity is probably the unnamed subject of this state. And the "holy prostitution of the soul," next to which "what people call love is quite small, quite limited, and quite feeble,"[150] really can be nothing other than the prostitution of the commodity's soul—if the comparison with love retains its meaning. Baudelaire speaks of "cette sainte prostitution de l'âme qui se donne tout entière, poésie et charité, à l'imprévu qui se montre, à l'inconnu qui passe."[151] It is this very *poésie* and this very *charité* which prostitutes claim for themselves. They tried the secrets of the free market; in this respect, commodities had no advantage over them. Some of the commodity's charms were based on the market, and each of these turned into a means of power. As such, they were noted by Baudelaire in his "Crépuscule du soir":

A travers les lueurs que tourmente le vent
La Prostitution s'allume dans les rues;
Comme une fourmilière elle ouvre ses issues;
Partout elle se fraye un occulte chemin,
Ainsi que l'ennemi qui tente un coup de main;
Elle remue au sein de la cité de fange
Comme un ver qui dérobe à l'Homme ce qu'il mange.[152]

[Through the flickering light tormented by the wind
Prostitution flares up in the streets;
Like an anthill it opens its outlets;
Everywhere it follows a devious path,
Like an enemy bent on a surprise attack;
It stirs at the heart of the city of mire
Like a worm that takes its food from Man.]

Only the mass of inhabitants permits prostitution to spread over large parts of the city. And only the mass enables the sexual object to become intoxicated with the hundred stimuli which that object produces.

Not everyone found the spectacle offered by the crowds in big-city streets intoxicating. Long before Baudelaire wrote his prose poem "Les Foules," Friedrich Engels had undertaken to describe the bustle in the streets of London.

A city such as London, where a man might wander for hours at a time without reaching the beginning of the end, without meeting the slightest hint which could lead to the inference that there is open country within reach, is a strange thing. This colossal centralization, this heaping together of two and a half million human beings in one place, has multiplied the power of this two and a half million a hundredfold. . . . But the sacrifices which all this has cost become apparent later. After roaming the streets of the capital for a day or two, making headway with difficulty through the human turmoil and the endless lines of vehicles, after visiting the slums of the metropolis, one realizes for the first time that these Londoners have been forced to sacrifice the best qualities of their human nature, in order to bring about all the marvels of civilization which crowd their city. . . . The very turmoil of the streets has something repulsive about it, something against which human nature rebels. The hundreds of thousands of people from every class and rank crowding past each other—are they not all human beings with the same qualities and powers, and with the same interest in being happy? . . . And still they crowd by one another as though they had nothing in common, nothing to do with one another, and their only agreement is the tacit one that each keep to his own side of the pavement, so as not to delay the opposing stream of the crowd, while no man thinks to honor another with so much as a glance. The brutal indifference, the unfeeling isolation of each within his private concerns, becomes the more repellent and offensive the more these individuals are crowded together in a limited space.[153]

The flâneur only seems to break through this "unfeeling isolation of each within his private concerns," by filling the hollow space created in him by such isolation with the borrowed—and fictitious—isolations of strangers. Next to Engels' lucid description, it sounds obscure when Baudelaire writes: "The pleasure of being in a crowd is a mysterious expression of the enjoyment of the multiplication of number."[154] But this statement becomes clear if one imagines it spoken not only from the viewpoint of a person but also from that of a commodity. To be sure, insofar as a person, as labor power, is a commodity, there is no need for him to identify himself as such. The more conscious he becomes of his mode of existence, the mode imposed on him by the system of production, the more he proletarianizes himself, the more he will be gripped by the chilly breath of the commodity economy, and the less he will feel like empathizing with commodities. But things had not yet reached that point with the class of the petty bourgeoisie to which Baudelaire belonged. On the scale we are dealing with here, this class was only at the beginning of its decline. Inevitably, many of its members would one day become aware of the commodity nature of their labor power. But this day had not yet come; until then, they were permitted (if one may put it this way) to pass the time. The very fact that their share could, at best, be enjoyment, but never power, made the period which history gave them a space for passing time. Anyone who sets out to while away time seeks enjoyment. It was self-evident, however, that the more this class wanted to have its enjoyment *in* this society, the more limited this enjoyment would be. The enjoyment promised to be less limited if this class found enjoyment *of* this society possible. If it wanted to achieve virtuosity in this kind of enjoyment, it could not spurn empathizing with commodities. It had to enjoy this identification with all the pleasure and uneasiness which derived from a presentiment of its own determination as a class. Finally, it had to approach this determination with a sensitivity that perceives charm even in damaged and decaying goods. Baudelaire, who in a poem to a courtesan called her heart "bruised like a peach, ripe like her body, for the lore of love," possessed that sensitivity. This is what made possible his enjoyment of society as someone who had already half withdrawn from it.

In the attitude of someone who enjoyed in this way, he let the spectacle of the crowd act on him. The deepest fascination of this spectacle lay in the fact that, even as it intoxicated him, it did not blind him to the horrible social reality. He remained conscious of it, though only in the way in which intoxicated people are "still" aware of reality. This is why in Baudelaire the big city almost never finds expression through a direct presentation of its inhabitants. The directness and harshness with which Shelley captured London through the depiction of its people could not benefit Baudelaire's Paris.

Hell is a city much like London,
A populous and a smoky city;

There are all sorts of people undone,
And there is little or no fun done;
Small justice shown, and still less pity.[155]

For the flâneur, there is a veil over this picture. This veil is formed by the masses; it billows "in the twisting folds of the old metropolises."[156] Because of it, horrors have an enchanting effect upon him.[157] Only when this veil tears and reveals to the flâneur "one of the populous squares . . . which are empty during street fighting"[158] does he, too, get an undistorted view of the big city.

If any proof were needed of the force with which the experience of the crowd moved Baudelaire, it would be the fact that he undertook to vie with Hugo in this experience. That Hugo's strength lay here, if anywhere, was evident to Baudelaire. He praises the "caractère poétique . . . interrogatif"[159] of Hugo's work, and says that Hugo not only knows how to reproduce clear things sharply and distinctly but also reproduces with appropriate obscurity what has manifested itself only dimly and indistinctly. One of the three poems in "Tableaux parisiens" which are dedicated to Hugo begins with an invocation of the crowded city: "Teeming city, city full of dreams."[160] Another follows old women in the "teeming tableau"[161] of the city, as they move through the crowd.[162] The crowd is a new subject in lyric poetry. Someone once remarked that "the crowd was unbearable" for the innovator Sainte-Beuve, and this was said appreciatively, as something fitting and proper for a poet.[163] During his exile in Jersey, Hugo opened this subject up for poetry. On his walks along the coast, the topic took shape for him, thanks to one of the extreme antitheses that were necessary for his inspiration. In Hugo, the crowd enters literature as an object of contemplation. The surging ocean is its model, and the thinker who reflects on this eternal spectacle is the true explorer of the crowd, in which he loses himself as he loses himself in the roaring of the sea. "As the exile on his lonely cliff looks out toward the great nations destined for momentous things, he looks down into the past of their peoples. . . . He carries himself and his destiny into the fullness of events; they become alive in him and blend with the life of the natural forces—with the sea, the crumbling rocks, the shifting clouds, and the other exalted things that are part of a lonely, quiet life in communion with nature."[164] "L'océan même s'est ennuyé de lui,"[165] said Baudelaire about Hugo, touching the man brooding on the cliffs with the light-pencil of his irony. Baudelaire did not feel inclined to follow the spectacle of nature. His experience of the crowd bore the traces of the "heartache and the thousand natural shocks" which a pedestrian suffers in the bustle of a city and which keep his self-awareness all the more alert. (Basically it is this very self-awareness that he lends to the strolling commodity.) For Baudelaire, the crowd never was a stimulus to casting the plumb-line of his thought into the depths of the world. Hugo, on the other hand, writes, "Les profondeurs sont des multitudes,"[166] and thereby gives enormous scope to his thinking. The natural supernatural which affected Hugo in the form of the crowd shows itself in the forest, in the animal kingdom, and by the surging sea; in any of these places, the physiognomy of a big city can flash up for a few moments. "La Pente de la rêverie" gives a splendid idea of the promiscuity at work among the multitude of living things.

> La nuit avec la foule, en ce rêve hideux,
> Venait, s'épaississant ensemble toutes deux,
> Et, dans ces régions que nul regard ne sonde,
> Plus l'homme était nombreux,
> Plus l'ombre était profonde.[167]
>
> [In that hideous dream, night together with the crowd
> Arrived, both growing ever thicker;
> And in those regions which no gaze can fathom,
> The more numerous were the people,
> the deeper was the darkness.]

And:

> Foule sans nom! chaos! des voix, des yeux, des pas.
> Ceux qu'on n'a jamais vu, ceux qu'on ne connaît pas.

Tous les vivants!—cités bourdonnantes aux oreilles
Plus qu'un bois d'Amérique ou une ruche d'abeilles.[168]

[Nameless mob! chaos! voices, eyes, footsteps.
Those one has never seen, those one does not know.
All the living!—cities buzzing in our ears
Louder than an American forest or a hive full of bees.]

    With the crowd, nature exercises its fundamental rights over the city. But it is not nature alone which exercises its rights in this way. There is an astonishing place in *Les Misérables* where the web of the woods appears as the archetype of mass existence. "What had happened on this street would not have astonished a forest. The tree trunks and the underbrush, the weeds, the inextricably entwined branches, and the tall grasses lead an obscure kind of existence. Invisible things flit through the teeming immensity. What is below human beings perceives, through a fog, that which is above them."[169] This description contains the characteristics of Hugo's experience with the crowd. In the crowd, that which is below a person comes in contact with what holds sway above him. This promiscuity encompasses all others. In Hugo, the crowd appears as a bastard form which shapeless, superhuman powers create from those creatures that are below human beings. In the visionary strain that runs through Hugo's conception of the crowd, social reality gets its due more than it does in the "realistic" treatment which he gave the crowd in politics. For the crowd really is a spectacle of nature—if one may apply this term to social conditions. A street, a conflagration, or a traffic accident assembles people who are not defined along class lines. They present themselves as concrete gatherings, but socially they remain abstract—namely, in their isolated private concerns. Their models are the customers who, each acting in his private interest, gather at the market around their "common cause." In many cases, such gatherings have only a statistical existence. This existence conceals the really monstrous thing about them: that the concentration of private persons as such is an accident resulting from their private concerns. But if these concentrations become evident—and totalitarian states see to this by making the concentration of their citizens permanent and obligatory for all their purposes—their hybrid character is clearly manifest, particularly to those who are involved. They rationalize the accident of the market economy which brings them together in this way as "fate" in which "the race" is reunited. In doing so, they give free rein to both the herd instinct and to reflective action. The peoples who are in the foreground of the western European stage make the acquaintance of the supernatural which confronted Hugo in the crowd. Hugo, to be sure, was unable to assess the historical significance of this force. But it left its imprint on his work as a strange distortion: a set of spiritualistic protocols.

Hugo's contact with the spirit world—which, as we know, profoundly affected both his life and his writing on the Isle of Jersey—was, strange though this may seem, primarily a contact with the masses, which the poet necessarily missed in exile. For the crowd is the spirit world's mode of existence. Thus, Hugo saw himself primarily as a genius in a great assembly of geniuses who were his ancestors. In his *William Shakespeare,* he devoted one rhapsodic page after another to the procession of those aristocrats of the intellect, beginning with Moses and ending with Hugo. But they constitute only a small group in the tremendous multitude of the departed. To Hugo's chthonian mind, the *ad plures ire*[170] of the Romans was not an empty phrase.—In his last séance, the spirits of the dead came late, as messengers of the night. Hugo's Jersey notes have preserved their messages:

> Every great man works on two works: the work he creates as a living person and his spirit-work. A living man devotes himself to the first work. But in the deep still of the night, the spirit-creator—oh, horror!—awakens in him. "What?!" cries the person. "Isn't that all?" "No," replies the spirit. "Arise." The storm is raging, dogs and foxes are howling, darkness is everywhere, nature shudders and winces under the whip of God. . . . The spirit-creator sees the phantom idea. The words bris-

tle and the sentence shudders . . . The windowpanes get fogged and dull, the lamp is seized with fear. . . . Watch out, living person, man of a century, you vassal of an idea that comes from the earth. For this is madness, this is the grave, this is infinity, this is a phantom idea.[171]

The cosmic shudder induced by the experience of the invisible—the shudder that Hugo preserves here—bears no similarity to the naked terror which overcame Baudelaire in his moments of "spleen." Also, Baudelaire mustered little sympathy for Hugo's undertaking. "True civilization," he said, "does not lie in table-turning." But Hugo was not concerned with civilization. He felt truly at home in the spirit world. One could say that it was the cosmic complement of a household that comprised horror as an integral part. His intimate acquaintance with the apparitions removes much of their frightening quality. Such intimacy is not without its labored quality and brings out the threadbare nature of the apparitions. The counterparts of these nocturnal ghosts are the meaningless abstractions—the more or less ingenious embodiments—that are inscribed on the monuments of that period. In the Jersey protocols, "Drama," "Poetry," "Literature," "Thought," and many other terms of this type are often heard in conjunction with the voices of chaos.

For Hugo, the immense throngs of the spirit world are—and this may bring the riddle closer to a solution—primarily an audience. The fact that his work absorbed motifs of the talking table is less strange than the fact that he customarily produced it in front of this table. The unstinting acclaim provided by the Beyond while he was in exile gave him a foretaste of the boundless acclaim that would await him at home in his old age. When, on his seventieth birthday, the population of the capital streamed toward his house on the avenue d'Eylau, the image of the wave surging against the cliffs was realized and the message of the spirit world was fulfilled.

In the final analysis, the impenetrable obscurity of mass existence was also the source of Victor Hugo's revolutionary speculations. In

Les Châtiments, the day of liberation is described as "Le jour où nos pillards, où nos tyrans sans nombre / Comprendront que quelqu'un remue au fond de l'ombre."[172] ["The day when our pillagers, our tyrants without number, / Will understand that there is someone stirring deep in the darkness."] Could there be a reliable revolutionary judgment in keeping with this view of the suppressed masses, this view based on the crowd? Wasn't this perspective, rather, clear evidence of the limitation of such a judgment, no matter what its origin? On November 25, 1848, in a debate in the Chamber of Deputies, Hugo inveighed against Cavaignac's barbaric suppression of the June revolt.[173] But on June 20, in the discussion of the *ateliers nationaux,* he had said: "The monarchy had its idlers; the republic has its petty thieves."[174] Hugo reflected the superficial views of the day, as well as a blind faith in the future, but he also had a profound vision of the life that was forming in the womb of nature and in the womb of the people. Hugo never succeeded in fashioning a bridge between these two. He saw no need for such a bridge, and this explains the tremendous aspirations and scope of his work, and presumably also the tremendous influence of his oeuvre on his contemporaries. In the chapter of *Les Misérables* entitled "L'Argot," the two conflicting sides of his nature confront each other with impressive harshness. After a bold look into the linguistic workshop of the lower classes, the poet concludes by writing: "Since 1789, the entire nation, as a people, has unfolded in the purified individual. There is no poor man who does not have his rights, and thus his own moment in the limelight. Every poor wretch bears the honor of France inside him. The dignity of each citizen is an inner bulwark. Anyone who is free is conscientious, and everyone who has the vote rules."[175] Victor Hugo saw things the way the experience gleaned from a successful literary and political career presented them to him. He was the first great writer whose works have collective titles: *Les Misérables, Les Travailleurs de la mer.* To him the crowd meant, almost in the ancient sense, the crowd of his constituents—that is, the masses of his readers and his voters. Hugo was, in a word, no flâneur.

For the crowd that kept company with Hugo, and with which he kept company, there was no Baudelaire. But this crowd did exist for Baudelaire. Every day, the sight of it caused him to plumb the depths of his failure, and this probably was not the least of the reasons he wanted to gaze at it. The desperate pride he thus felt—in bursts, as it were—was fed by the fame of Victor Hugo. But he was probably spurred on even more strongly by Hugo's political creed, the creed of the *citoyen*.[176] The masses of the big city could not disconcert him. He recognized the urban crowds and wanted to be flesh of their flesh. Secularism, Progress, and Democracy were inscribed on the banner which he waved over their heads. This banner transfigured mass existence. It was the canopy over the threshold which separated the individual from the crowd. Baudelaire guarded this threshold, and that differentiated him from Victor Hugo. But he resembled him too, since he, like Hugo, failed to see through the social semblance [*Schein*] which is precipitated in the crowd. He therefore placed it in opposition to a model which was as uncritical as Hugo's conception of the crowd. This model was the hero. While Victor Hugo was celebrating the crowd as the hero of a modern epic, Baudelaire was seeking a refuge for the hero among the masses of the big city. Hugo placed himself in the crowd as a *citoyen;* Baudelaire divorced himself from the crowd as a hero.

III. Modernity

Baudelaire patterned his image of the artist after an image of the hero. From the beginning, each is an advocate of the other. In "Salon de 1845" he wrote: "The artist's will must be strongly developed, and always very fruitful, in order to give the stamp of uniqueness even to second-rate works. . . . The viewer enjoys the effort, and his eye drinks the sweat."[177] In his *Conseils aux jeunes littérateurs* of the following year, there is a fine formula in which the "contemplation opiniâtre de l'oeuvre de demain"[178] appears as the guarantee of inspiration. Baudelaire is familiar with the "indolence naturelle des inspirés";[179] Musset—so he says—never understood how much work it takes "to let a work of art emerge from a daydream."[180] He, on the other hand, comes before the public from the outset with his own code, precepts, and taboos. Barrès claimed that he could recognize "in every little word by Baudelaire a trace of the toil that helped him achieve such great things."[181] "Even in his nervous crises," writes Gourmont, "Baudelaire retains something healthy."[182] The most felicitous formulation is given by the symbolist Gustave Kahn when he says that "with Baudelaire, poetic work resembled physical effort."[183] Proof of this is found in his work—in a metaphor worth closer inspection.

It is the metaphor of the fencer. Baudelaire was fond of using it to present martial elements as artistic elements. When he describes Constantin Guys, whom he admired, he captures him at a moment when everyone else is asleep. How Guys stands there "bent over his table, scrutinizing the sheet of paper just as intently as he does the objects around him by day; how he uses his pencil, his pen, his brush like a rapier, spurts water from his glass to the ceiling and tries his pen on his shirt; how he pursues his work swiftly and intensely, as though afraid that his images might escape him. Thus he is combative, even when alone, and parries his own blows."[184] In the opening stanza of his poem "Le Soleil," Baudelaire portrayed himself in the throes of just such a "fantastic battle," and this is probably the only place in *Les Fleurs du mal* where he is shown at his poetic labors. The duel in which every artist is engaged and in which he "screams with fear before he is vanquished"[185] is framed as an idyll; its violence recedes into the background and its charm is manifest.

> Le long du vieux faubourg, où pendent aux masures
> Les persiennes, abri des secrètes luxures,
> Quand le soleil cruel frappe à traits redoublés
> Sur la ville et les champs, sur les toits et les blés,
> Je vais m'exercer seul à ma fantasque escrime,
> Flairant dans tous les coins les hasards de la rime,

Trébuchant sur les mots comme sur les pavés,
Heurtant parfois des vers depuis longtemps rêvés.[186]

[Through decrepit neighborhoods on the outskirts of town,
   where
Slatted shutters hang at the windows of hovels that shelter
   secret lusts;
At a time when the cruel sun beats down with redoubled
   force
On city and countryside, on rooftops and cornfields,
I go out alone to practice my fantastical fencing,
Scenting opportunities for rhyme on every streetcorner,
Stumbling over words as though they were cobblestones,
Sometimes knocking up against verses dreamed long ago.]

To give these prosodic experiences their due in prose as well was one of the intentions Baudelaire had pursued in *Le Spleen de Paris,* his poems in prose. In his dedication of this collection to Arsène Houssaye, the editor-in-chief of *La Presse,* Baudelaire expresses, in addition to this intention, what was really at the bottom of those experiences.[187] "Who among us has not dreamed, in his ambitious moments, of the miracle of a poetic prose, musical, yet without rhythm and without rhyme, supple and darting enough to adapt to the lyrical stirrings of the soul, the undulations of reverie, and the sudden leaps of consciousness? This obsessive ideal is born, above all, from the experience of giant cities, from the intersecting of their myriad relations."[188]

If one tries to imagine this rhythm and investigate this mode of work, it turns out that Baudelaire's flâneur was not a self-portrait of the poet to the extent that this might be assumed. An important trait of the real-life Baudelaire—that is, of the man committed to his work—has been omitted from this portrayal: his absentmindedness.—In the flâneur, the joy of watching prevails over all. It can concentrate on observation; the result is the amateur detective. Or it can stagnate in the rubbernecker; then the flâneur has turned into a *badaud.*[189] The revealing representations of the big city have come from neither. They are the work of those who have traversed the city absently, as it were, lost in thought or worry. The image of "fantasque escrime" ["fantastical fencing"] does justice to these individuals; Baudelaire is thinking of their condition, which is anything but the condition of the observer. In his book on Dickens, Chesterton has masterfully captured the man who roams the big city lost in thought.[190] Charles Dickens' constant peregrinations began in his childhood. "Whenever he had done drudging, he had no other resource but drifting, and he drifted over half London. He was a dreamy child, thinking mostly of his own dreary prospects. . . . He walked in darkness under the lamps of Holborn, and was crucified at Charing Cross. . . . He did not go in for 'observation,' a priggish habit; he did not look at Charing Cross to improve his mind or count the lamp-posts in Holborn to practise his arithmetic. . . . Dickens did not stamp these places on his mind; he stamped his mind on these places."[191]

In his later years, Baudelaire did not often have the opportunity to stroll through the streets of Paris. His creditors were pursuing him; the symptoms of his illness were becoming more severe; and there was strife between him and his mistress. The shocks that his worries caused him and the myriad ideas with which he parried them were reproduced by Baudelaire the poet in the feints of his prosody. Recognizing the labor that he devoted to his poems under the image of fencing means learning to comprehend them as a continual series of tiny improvisations. The variants of his poems indicate how diligently he was working and how greatly he was concerned with even the most minor of them. The expeditions on which he encountered his poetic "problem children" on the street corners of Paris were not always undertaken voluntarily. In the early years of his life as a man of letters, when he was living at the Hotel Pimodan, his friends had occasion to admire the discretion with which he banned all traces of work from his room, beginning with the top of his desk.[192] In those days, he set out to conquer the streets—in images. Later, when he abandoned one part of his bourgeois existence after another, the street increasingly became a place of refuge for him. But in flânerie, there was from the outset an awareness of the fragility of this existence. It makes a virtue out of necessity, and in this it displays the structure which is in every way characteristic of Baudelaire's conception of the hero.

The necessity which is here disguised is not only a material one; it concerns poetic production. The stereotypes in Baudelaire's experiences, the lack of mediation among his ideas, and the frozen unrest in his features indicate that he did not possess the reserves which an individual acquires from great knowledge and a comprehensive view of history. "Baudelaire had what is a great defect in a writer, a defect he was unaware of: he was ignorant. What he knew, he knew thoroughly; but he knew little. He remained unacquainted with history, physiology, archaeology, and philosophy. . . . He had little interest in the outside world; he may have been aware of it, but he certainly did not study it."[193] By way of countering this and similar criticisms,[194] one might naturally and legitimately point out that a working poet could find it necessary and useful to keep his distance from the world, and that idiosyncratic elements are essential to all productivity. But there is another side to the situation, one that favors the overtaxing of the productive person in the name of a principle: the principle of "creativity." This overtaxing is all the more dangerous because, even as it flatters the self-esteem of the productive person, it effectively protects the interests of a social order that is hostile to him. The lifestyle of the bohemian has fostered a superstition about creativeness—a superstition Marx countered with an observation that applies equally to intellectual and to manual labor. The opening sentence of his draft of the Gotha program, "Labor is the source of all wealth and all culture," is accompanied by this critical note: "The bourgeois have very good reasons for imputing supernatural creative power to labor, since the fact that labor depends on nature has a direct correlate: a man whose only property is his labor must, in all societies and civilizations, be the slave of other people who have become proprietors of the material working conditions."[195] Baudelaire owned few of the material conditions for intellectual labor. A personal library, an apartment of his own—there was nothing he did not have to do without in the course of his life, which was equally precarious in Paris and outside the city. On December 26, 1853, he wrote to his mother: "I am used to a certain measure of physical suffering. I am adept at making do with two shirts layered under torn trousers and a jacket which lets in the wind, and I am so experienced at using straw or even paper to plug up the holes in my shoes that moral suffering is almost the only kind I perceive as suffering. Yet I must admit that I have reached the point where I don't make any sudden movements or walk a lot, because I fear that I might tear my clothes even more."[196] Among the experiences which Baudelaire has transfigured in the image of the hero, experiences of this kind were the least equivocal.

Around the same time, the dispossessed person makes another appearance in the guise of the hero, this incarnation an ironic one and in a different place—namely, in the writings of Marx. Marx speaks of the ideas of Napoleon I and says: "The *idées napoléoniennes* culminate in the preponderance of the army. The army was the *point d'honneur* of small-holding farmers who were transformed into heroes." Now, however, under Napoleon III the army "is no longer the flower of farm youth, but is the swamp flower of the peasant *lumpenproletariat*. It consists largely of *remplaçants*, . . . just as the second Bonaparte is himself a *remplaçant*, a substitute for Napoleon."[197] If one turns away from this view and returns to the image of the fencing poet, one will find another image momentarily superimposed upon it: the image of the marauder, the soldier who roams through the countryside.[198] Above all, however, two of Baudelaire's famous lines, with their subtle syncope, resound more distinctly over the socially empty space that Marx mentions. They conclude the second stanza of the third poem of "Les Petites Vieilles." Proust accompanies them with the words "il semble impossible d'aller au-delà."[199]

Ah! que j'en ai suivi, de ces petites vieilles!
Une, entre autres, à l'heure où le soleil tombant

Ensanglante le ciel de blessures vermeilles,
Pensive, s'asseyait à l'écart sur un banc,

Pour entendre un de ces concerts, riches de cuivre,
Dont les soldats parfois inondent nos jardins,
Et qui, dans ces soirs d'or où l'on se sent revivre,
Versent quelque héroïsme au coeur des citadins.[200]

[Ah, how many of those little old women I have followed!
There was one who—at that hour when the setting sun
Bloodies the sky with bright red wounds—
Was sitting alone, pensive, on a park bench,

Listening to the sounds of one of those brass-band concerts
With which soldiers sometimes flood our public gardens,
And which, on those golden evenings when you feel yourself
    reviving,
Instill a bit of heroism in citizens' hearts.]

The brass bands made up of the sons of impoverished peasants, playing their melodies for the city's poor—these represent the heroism
that shyly hides its threadbare quality in the word "quelque" ["a bit
of"] and that, in this very gesture, shows itself to be genuine and the
only kind that is still produced by this society. In the hearts of its
heroes, there is no emotion that would not also find a place in the
hearts of the little people who gather round a military band.

The public gardens—the poem refers to them as "nos jardins"—
are those open to city-dwellers whose longing is directed in vain at
the large, closed parks. The people that come to these public gardens
are not entirely the crowd that swirls about the flâneur. "No matter
what party one may belong to," wrote Baudelaire in 1851, "it is impossible not to be gripped by the spectacle of this sickly population,
which swallows the dust of the factories, breathes in particles of cot-
ton, and lets its tissues be permeated by white lead, mercury, and all
the poisons needed for the production of masterpieces . . . ; the spectacle of this languishing and pining population to whom *the earth*

owes its wonders, who feel hot, crimson blood coursing through their veins, and who cast a long, sorrowful look at the sunlight and shadows of the great parks."[201] This population is the background which casts the outlines of the hero into bold relief. Baudelaire supplied his own caption for the image he presents. Beneath it he wrote the words: "La Modernité."

The hero is the true subject of *la modernité.* In other words, it takes a heroic constitution to live modernity. This was Balzac's opinion as well. Balzac and Baudelaire are opposed to Romanticism on this point. They transfigure passions and resolution; the Romantics transfigured renunciation and surrender. But the new way of looking at things is far more variegated and expressed with many more reservations in a poet than in a novelist. Two figures of speech will demonstrate this. Both introduce the reader to the hero in his modern manifestation. In Balzac, the gladiator becomes a *commis voyageur.* The great traveling salesman Gaudissart is getting ready to work the Touraine region. Balzac describes his preparations and interrupts himself to exclaim: "What an athlete! What an arena! And what weapons: he, the world, and his glib tongue!"[202] Baudelaire, on the other hand, recognizes the fencing slave in the proletarian. Of the promises which the wine gives the disinherited, the fifth stanza of the poem "L'Ame du vin" names the following:

> J'allumerai les yeux de ta femme ravie;
> A ton fils je rendrai sa force et ses couleurs
> Et serai pour ce frêle athlète de la vie
> L'huile qui raffermit les muscles des lutteurs.[203]

> [I shall brighten your delighted wife's eyes;
> To your son I'll restore strength and color,
> And for this frail athlete of life be
> The oil that fortifies wrestlers' muscles.]

What the wage-earner achieves through his daily labors is no less impressive than what helped a gladiator win applause and fame in ancient times. This image is of the stuff of Baudelaire's best insights; it derives from his reflection about his own situation. A passage from the "Salon de 1859" indicates how he wished it to be viewed. "When I hear how a Raphael or a Veronese is glorified with the veiled intention of denigrating what came after them, . . . I ask myself whether an achievement which must be rated *at least* equal to theirs . . . is not infinitely *more meritorious,* because it triumphed in a hostile atmosphere and place."[204]—Baudelaire was fond of contextualizing his theses crassly—placing them in baroque lighting, as it were. It was part of his theoretical *raison d'état* to obscure the connections among them—wherever connections existed. Such obscure passages [*Schattenpartien*] can almost always be illuminated by his letters. Without having to resort to such a procedure, one can see a clear link between the above passage from 1859 and another passage that was written ten years earlier and is particularly strange. The following chain of reflections will reconstruct this link.

The resistance that modernity offers to the natural productive élan of an individual is out of all proportion to his strength. It is understandable if a person becomes exhausted and takes refuge in death. Modernity must stand under the sign of suicide, an act which seals a heroic will that makes no concessions to a mentality inimical toward this will. Such a suicide is not resignation but heroic passion. It is *the* achievement of modernity in the realm of the passions.[205] In this form, as the *passion particulière de la vie moderne,* suicide appears in the classic passage devoted to the theory of the modern. The voluntary suicide of heroes in the ancient world is an exception. "Apart from Heracles on Mount Oeta, Cato of Utica, and Cleopatra, . . . where does one find suicides in ancient accounts?"[206] Not that Baudelaire could find them in modern accounts; the reference to Rousseau and Balzac which follows this sentence is a meager one. But modernity does keep the raw material for such presentations in readiness, and it awaits its master. This raw material has deposited itself in those very strata that have turned out to be the foundation of modernity. The first notes on the theory of the modern were made in 1845. Around that time, the idea of suicide became familiar to the working masses. "People are scrambling for copies of a lithograph depicting an English worker who is taking his life because he despairs of earning a livelihood. One worker even goes to Eugène Sue's apartment and hangs himself there. In his hand is a slip of paper with this note: 'I thought dying would be easier for me if I died under the roof of a man who stands up for us and loves us.'"[207] In 1841 Adolphe Boyer, a printer, published a small book entitled *De l'état des ouvriers et de son amélioration par l'organisation du travail.* Taking a moderate approach, it sought to recruit for the workers' associations the old corporations of itinerant journeymen which stuck to guild practices. His work was unsuccessful. The author took his own life and in an open letter invited his companions in misfortune to follow suit. Someone like Baudelaire could very well have viewed suicide as the only heroic act still available to the *multitudes maladives* of the cities in reactionary times. Perhaps he saw Rethel's *Dance of Death,* which he greatly admired, as the work of a subtle artist who stood before an easel sketching on a canvas the ways in which suicides died.[208] As to the colors of Rethel's images, fashion offered its palette.

With the July Monarchy, blacks and grays began to predominate in men's clothes. Baudelaire concerned himself with this innovation in "Salon de 1845," his first work. In the conclusion to that piece, he wrote: "More than anyone else, *the* painter, the true painter, will be the man who extracts from present-day life its epic aspects and teaches us in lines and colors to understand how great and poetic we are in our patent-leather shoes and our neckties.—May the real pioneers next year give us the exquisite pleasure of being allowed to celebrate the advent of the *new.*"[209] One year later, he wrote: "Regarding the attire, the covering of the modern hero, . . . does it not have a beauty and a charm of its own? . . . Is this not an attire that is needed by our age, which is suffering, and dressed up to its thin black narrow shoulders in the symbol of constant mourning? The black suit and the frock coat not only have their political beauty as an expression of general equality, but also their poetic beauty as an expression of the public mentality: an immense cortège of undertakers—political undertakers, amorous undertakers, bourgeois undertakers. We are all attendants at some kind of funeral.—The unvarying livery of hopelessness testifies to equality. . . . And don't the folds in the material—those folds that make grimaces and drape themselves around mortified flesh like snakes—have their own secret charm?"[210] These mental images are part of the profound fascination which the *femme passante* dressed in mourning—the passer-by in his sonnet—exerted upon the poet. The text of 1846 concludes as follows: "For the heroes of the *Iliad* cannot hold a candle to you, O Vautrin, O Rastignac, O Birotteau; or to you, O Fontanarès, who did not dare to confess publicly the sorrows you were feeling under the macabre frock coat which seems tightened as if by a cramp, the frock coat which all of us wear; or to you, O Honoré de Balzac, the most heroic, the most singular, the most romantic, and the most poetic of all the characters you have drawn from your fertile bosom."[211]

Fifteen years later, the southern-German Democrat Friedrich Theodor Vischer wrote a critique of men's fashion in which he arrived at insights similar to Baudelaire's.[212] But his work has a different emphasis. What provides a hue for the dusky prospectus of the modern in Baudelaire is a shiny argument of political struggle in Vischer. Contemplating the reaction that had held sway since 1850, Vischer writes: "To show one's true colors is regarded as ridiculous; to be trim is thought to be childish. Then how could clothes keep from becoming colorless, slack, and tight at the same time?"[213] The extremes meet where the matter is expressed metaphorically; Vischer's political critique overlaps with an early image of Baudelaire's. In his sonnet "The Albatross"—inspired by the overseas trip which, it was hoped, would reform the young poet—Baudelaire recognizes himself in these birds, describing their awkwardness on the deck where the crew has put them:

> A peine les ont-ils déposés sur les planches,
> Que ces rois de l'azur, maladroits et honteux,

Laissent piteusement leurs grandes ailes blanches
Comme des avirons trainer à côté d'eux.

Ce voyageur ailé, comme il est gauche et veule![214]

[Hardly have they been set down on the planks of the deck—
   deposed,
These monarchs of the blue—than, awkward and ashamed,
They let their great white wings drag piteously
At their sides, like oars.
This winged voyager—how clumsy and enfeebled he is!]

Vischer writes as follows about the type of man's jacket whose wide sleeves cover the wrists: "Those are not arms any more but the rudiments of wings—stumps of penguin wings and fins of fishes. And the movements of the shapeless appendages when a man walks look like foolish, silly gesticulating, shoving, rowing."[215] The same view of the matter, and the same image.

Baudelaire more clearly defines the face of the modern, without denying the mark of Cain on its brow: "The majority of the writers who have concerned themselves with really modern subjects have contented themselves with the certified, official subjects, with our victories and our political heroism. They do this reluctantly, and only because the government orders them and pays them for it. Yet there are subjects from private life which are heroic in quite another way. The spectacle of elegant life and of the thousands of marginal existences eked out in the basements of a big city by criminals and kept women: *La Gazette des Tribunaux* and *Le Moniteur* demonstrate that we need only open our eyes to recognize our heroism."[216] The image of the hero here includes the apache. He represents the characteristics which Bounoure sees in Baudelaire's solitude—"a *noli me tangere,* an encapsulation of the individual in his difference."[217] The apache abjures virtue and laws; he terminates the *contrat social* forever. Thus, he sees himself as a world away from the bourgeois and fails to recognize in him the features of the philistine accomplice which Hugo was soon to describe with such powerful effect in *Les*

Châtiments. Baudelaire's illusions, to be sure, were destined to have far greater staying power. They engendered the poetry of apachedom and contributed to a genre which has lasted more than eighty years. Baudelaire was the first to tap this vein. Poe's hero is not the criminal but the detective. Balzac, for his part, knows only the great outsiders of society. Vautrin experiences a rise and a fall; he has a career, just as all of Balzac's heroes do. A criminal career is a career like any other. Ferragus, too, has big ideas and makes long-range plans; he is a Carbonari type.[218] Before Baudelaire, the apache, who lived out his life within the precincts of society and of the big city, had had no place in literature. The most striking depiction of this subject in *Les Fleurs du mal*, "Le Vin de l'assassin," inaugurated a Parisian genre. The café known as Le Chat Noir became its "artistic headquarters." "Passant, sois moderne!" was the inscription it bore during its early, heroic period.[219]

The poets find the refuse of society on their streets and derive their heroic subject from this very refuse. This means that a common type is, as it were, superimposed upon their illustrious type. This new type is permeated by the features of the ragpicker, who made frequent appearances in Baudelaire's work. One year before Baudelaire wrote "Le Vin des chiffonniers," he published a prose description of the figure: "Here we have a man whose job it is to gather the day's refuse in the capital. Everything that the big city has thrown away, everything it has lost, everything it has scorned, everything it has crushed underfoot he catalogues and collects. He collates the annals of intemperance, the capharnaum of waste. He sorts things out and selects judiciously; he collects, like a miser guarding a treasure, refuse which will assume the shape of useful or gratifying objects between the jaws of the goddess of Industry."[220] This description is one extended metaphor for the poetic method, as Baudelaire practiced it. Ragpicker and poet: both are concerned with refuse, and both go about their solitary business while other citizens are sleeping; they even move in the same way. Nadar speaks of Baudelaire's "pas saccadé."[221] This is the gait of the poet who roams the city in search of rhyme-booty; it is also the gait of the ragpicker, who is obliged to come to a halt every few moments to gather up the refuse he encounters. There is much evidence indicating that Baudelaire secretly wished to develop this analogy. It contains a prophecy in any case. Sixty years later a brother of the poet—a kinsman who has deteriorated into a ragpicker—appears in Apollinaire. His name is Croniamantal, the *poète assassiné*, the first victim of the pogrom that is aimed at annihilating the entire race of lyric poets from the world.[222]

The poetry of apachedom appears in an uncertain light. Do the dregs of society supply the heroes of the big city? Or is the hero the poet who fashions his work from such material?[223]—The theory of the modern admits both. But in a late poem, "Les Plaintes d'un Icare," the aging Baudelaire indicates that he no longer relates to the kind of people among whom he sought heroes in his youth.

> Les amants des prostituées
> Sont heureux, dispos et repus;
> Quant à moi, mes bras sont rompus
> Pour avoir étreint des nuées.[224]

> [Lovers of whores
> Are happy—fit and satisfied;
> As for me, my arms are broken
> from having clasped the clouds.]

The poet, who, as the poem's title indicates, is a stand-in for the hero of ancient times, has had to give way to the modern hero whose deeds are reported by *La Gazette des Tribunaux*.[225] In truth, this abstinence is already inherent in the concept of the modern hero. He is destined for doom, and no tragic poet need come forward to explain the conditions for this downfall. But once modernity has received its due, its time will have run out. Then it will be put to the test. After its end, it will be seen whether it itself will ever be able to become antiquity.

Baudelaire always remained aware of this question. He took the ancient claim to immortality as his claim to being read as an ancient writer someday. "That all modernity is really worthy of becoming antiquity someday"[226]—to him, this defined the artistic mission generally. In Baudelaire, Gustave Kahn very aptly noticed a "refus de l'occasion, tendu par la nature du prétexte lyrique."[227] What made him indifferent toward opportunities and occasions was his awareness of that mission. In the period in which he lived, nothing came closer to the "task" of the ancient hero—to the "labors" of a Hercules—than the task imposed upon him as his very own: to give shape to modernity.

Among all the relations that have involved modernity, its relation to classical antiquity stands out. Baudelaire thought this was clearly apparent in the works of Victor Hugo: "Fate led him . . . to remodel the classical ode and classical tragedy . . . into the poems and dramas he has given us."[228] "Modernity" designates an epoch; it also denotes the energies which are at work in this epoch to bring it close [*anverwandeln*] to antiquity. Baudelaire conceded such energies to Hugo reluctantly and in only a few cases. Wagner, on the other hand, seemed to him an unbounded, unadulterated effusion of this energy. "If in his choice of subjects and his dramatic method Wagner approaches classical antiquity, his passionate power of expression makes him the most important representative of modernity at the present time."[229] This sentence contains Baudelaire's theory of modern art in a nutshell. In his view, antiquity can serve as a model only where construction is concerned; the substance and the inspiration of a work are the concern of modernity. "Woe to him who studies aspects of antiquity other than pure art, logic, or general method! He who becomes excessively absorbed in antiquity . . . forfeits the privileges opportunity offers him."[230] And in the final passage of his essay on Guys, he says: "Everywhere he sought the transitory, fleeting beauty of our present life—the character of what the reader has permitted us to call *modernity*."[231] In summary form, his doctrine reads: "A constant, immutable element . . . and a relative, limited element cooperate to produce beauty. . . . The latter element is supplied by the period, by fashion, by morality, and by the passions. Without this second element, . . . the first would be unassimilable."[232] One cannot say that this is a profound analysis.

In Baudelaire's view of modernity, the theory of modern art is the weakest point. His general view brings out the modern themes; his theory of art should probably have concerned itself with classical art, but Baudelaire never attempted anything of the kind. His theory did not come to grips with the renunciation which, in his work, appears as a loss of nature and naïveté. Its dependence on Poe—right down to its formulation—is one mark of its limitations. Its polemical orientation is another; it stands out against the gray background of historicism, against the academic Alexandrism which was favored by Villemain and Cousin.[233] None of their aesthetic reflections showed modernity in its interpenetration with classical antiquity—something that occurs in certain poems of *Les Fleurs du mal.*

Among these, "Le Cygne" is paramount. It is no accident that this poem is allegorical. The ever-changing city grows rigid. It becomes as brittle as glass—and as transparent, insofar as its meaning is concerned. "La forme d'une ville / Change plus vite, hélas! que le coeur d'un mortel."[234] The condition of Paris is fragile; it is surrounded by symbols of fragility—living creatures (the black woman and the swan) and historical figures (Andromache, "widow of Hector and wife of Helenus"). What they share are mourning for what was and lack of hope for what is to come. In the final analysis, this decrepitude constitutes the closest link between modernity and antiquity. Wherever Paris appears in *Les Fleurs du mal,* it gives evidence of this decrepitude. "Le Crépuscule du matin" consists of the sobs of an awakening person as these are reproduced through the material of a city. "Le Soleil" shows the city threadbare, like a bit of worn fabric in the sunlight. The old man who resignedly reaches for his tools day after day because even in his old age he has not been freed from want is an allegory of the city; and among its inhabitants, old women—"Les Petites Vieilles"—are the only spiritualized ones. That these poems have traveled through the decades unchallenged is the result of a certain reservation which protects them. It is a reservation about the big city, and it distinguishes these poems from almost all later big-city poetry. A stanza by Verhaeren suffices for us to understand what is involved here.

> Et qu'importent les maux et les heures démentes
> Et les cuves de vice où la cité fermente
> Si quelque jour, du fond des brouillards et des voiles
> Surgit un nouveau Christ, en lumière sculpté
> Qui soulève vers lui l'humanité
> Et la baptise au feu de nouvelles étoiles.[235]

> [And of what consequence are the evils and the lunatic hours
> And the vats of vice in which the city ferments,
> If someday a new Christ, sculpted of light,
> Arises from the fog and the veils,
> Lifts humanity toward himself,
> And baptizes it by the fire of new stars?]

Baudelaire knows no such perspectives. His idea of the decrepitude of the big city is the basis for the permanence of the poems he has written about Paris.

The poem "Le Cygne," too, is dedicated to Hugo, one of the few men whose work, it seemed to Baudelaire, produced a new antiquity. To the extent that one can speak of a source of inspiration in Hugo's case, it was fundamentally different from Baudelaire's. Hugo did not have the capacity to become rigid which—if a biological term may be used—manifests itself a hundredfold in Baudelaire's writings as a kind of mimesis of death. On the other hand, one could speak of Hugo's chthonian bent. Although it is not specifically mentioned, it is brought out in the following remarks by Charles Péguy, which reveal where the difference between Hugo's and Baudelaire's conceptions of classical antiquity lies. "One thing is certain: when Hugo saw a beggar by the road, he saw him the way he is, really saw him the way he really is, . . . saw him, the ancient beggar, the ancient suppliant, on the ancient road. When he saw the marble inlay of one of our fireplaces or the cemented bricks on one of our modern fireplaces, he saw them as what they are—namely, the stones from the hearth, the stones from the ancient hearth. When he saw the door of a house and the threshold, which is usually a squared stone, he recognized in this squared stone the antique line, the line of the sacred threshold that it is."[236] There is no better commentary on the following passage of *Les Misérables:* "The taverns of the Faubourg Saint-Antoine resembled the taverns of the Aventine, which are built over the sibyl's cave and are connected with sacred inspiration; the tables of these taverns were almost tripods, and Ennius speaks of the sibylline wine that was drunk there."[237] The same way of viewing things engendered the work in which the first image of a "Parisian antiquity" appears: Hugo's poetic cycle "A l'Arc de Triomphe." The glorification of this architectural monument proceeds from the vision of a Paris Campagna, an "immense campagne" in which only three monuments of the vanished city have survived: the Sainte-Chapelle, the Vendôme column, and the Arc de Triomphe. The great significance of this cycle in Hugo's work derives from its role in the genesis of a picture of Paris in the nineteenth century which is modeled upon classical antiquity. Baudelaire undoubtedly knew this cycle, which was written in 1837.

Seven years earlier, in his letters from Paris and France in the year 1830, the historian Friedrich von Raumer had written: "Yesterday I surveyed the enormous city from the Notre Dame tower. Who built the first house? When will the last one collapse and the ground of Paris look like the ground of Thebes and Babylon?"[238] Hugo has described this soil as it will be one day, when "this bank where the water surges against echoing bridge-arches will have been restored to the murmuring, bending reeds":[239] "Mais non, tout sera mort. Plus rien dans cette plaine / Qu'un peuple évanoui dont elle est encore pleine."[240] ["But no, everything will be dead. Nothing more on this plain / Than a vanished people, with which it is still pregnant."] One hundred years after Raumer, Léon Daudet took a look at Paris from the church of Sacré-Coeur, another elevated place in the city. In his eyes the history of "modernity" up to that time was mirrored in a frightening contraction:

From above, one looks down on this agglomeration of palaces, monuments, houses, and barracks, and one gets the feeling that they are destined for catastrophe, or several catastrophes—natural or social. . . . I have spent hours on Fourvières with a view of Lyons, on Notre-Dame de la Garde with a view of Marseilles, on Sacré-Coeur with a view of Paris. . . . What becomes most apparent from these heights is a threat. The agglomerations of human beings are threatening. . . . Aman needs work—that is correct. But he has other needs, too. . . . Among his other needs is suicide, something that is inherent in him and in the society which forms him, and it is stronger than his drive for self-preservation. Thus, when one stands on Sacré-Coeur, Fourvières, and Notre-Dame de la Garde and looks down, one is surprised that Paris, Lyons, and Marseilles are still there.[241]

This is the face that the *passion moderne* which Baudelaire recognized in suicide has received in this century.

The city of Paris entered the twentieth century in the form which Haussmann gave it. He revolutionized the physiognomy of the city with the humblest means imaginable: spades, pickaxes, crowbars, and the like. What destruction was caused by even these crude tools! And as the big cities grew, the means of razing them developed in tandem. What visions of the future this evokes!—Haussmann's activity was at its height and entire neighborhoods were being torn down when Maxime Du Camp found himself on the Pont Neuf one afternoon in 1862.[242] He was near an optician's shop, waiting for his eyeglasses.

The author, who was at the threshold of old age, experienced one of those moments when a man who thinks about his past life finds his own melancholy reflected in everything. The slight deterioration of his eyesight which had been demonstrated on his visit to the optician reminded him of the law of the inevitable infirmity of all human things. . . . It suddenly occurred to this man—who had traveled widely in the Orient, who was acquainted with the desert sands made of the dust of the dead—that this city, too, the city bustling all around him, would have to die someday, the way so many capitals had died. It occurred to him how extraordinarily interesting an accurate description of Athens at the time of Pericles, Carthage at the time of Barca, Alexandria at the time of the Ptolemies, and Rome at the time of the Caesars would be to us today. . . . In a flash of inspiration, the kind that occasionally furnishes one with an extraordinary subject, he resolved to write the kind of book about Paris that the historians of antiquity had failed to write about their cities. . . . In his mind's eye, he could see the work of his mature old age.[243]

In Hugo's sequence "A l'Arc de Triomphe" and in Du Camp's great portrait of his city from the administrative point of view, one discerns the same inspiration that became decisive for Baudelaire's idea of modernity.

Haussmann set to work in 1859. His project had long been regarded as necessary, and the way for it had been prepared by legislation. "After 1848," wrote Du Camp in the above-mentioned book, "Paris was on the verge of becoming uninhabitable. The constant expansion of the railway network . . . brought increases in traffic and in the city's population. The people were choking in the narrow, dirty, convoluted old streets, where they remained packed in because there was no alternative."[244] At the beginning of the 1850s, the population of Paris began to get used to the idea that a great face-cleaning of the city was inevitable. In its incubation period, this cleanup could presumably have had at least as great an effect on a fertile imagination as the work of urban renewal itself. "Les poètes sont plus inspirés par les images que par la présence même des objets," said Joubert.[245] The same is true of artists. When one knows that something will soon be removed from one's gaze, that thing becomes an image. Presumably this is what happened to the streets of Paris at that time. In any case, the work that undoubtedly had the closest subterranean connection to the great transformation of Paris was finished a few years before this urban renewal began. The work was Meryon's sequence of engraved views of Paris.[246] No one was more impressed with them than Baudelaire. To him, the archaeological view of future catastrophe, the basis of Hugo's dreams, was not the really moving one. He envisioned antiquity as springing suddenly from an intact modernity, like an Athena from the head of an unharmed Zeus. Meryon brought out the ancient face of the city without abandoning a single cobblestone. It was this view of the matter that Baudelaire had unceasingly pursued in the idea of *la modernité*. He was a passionate admirer of Meryon.

The two men had an elective affinity to each other. They were born in the same year, and their deaths occurred only months apart. Both died lonely and deeply disturbed—Meryon as a deranged patient at Charenton, Baudelaire speechless in a private clinic. Both were late in achieving fame.[247] Baudelaire was virtually the only person who championed Meryon in the latter's lifetime. Few of his prose works are as fine as his short piece on Meryon. In its treatment of Meryon it pays homage to modernity, but it also pays homage to aspects of antiquity in modernity. For in Meryon, too, there is an interpenetration of classical antiquity and modernity, and in him, too, the form of this superimposition—allegory—appears unmistakably. The captions under his etchings are significant. If the texts are touched by madness, their obscurity only underlines their "meaning." As an interpretation, Meryon's lines under his view of the Pont Neuf are, despite their sophistry, closely related to the "Squelette laboureur":

> Ci-gît du vieux Pont-Neuf
> L'exacte ressemblance
> Tout radoubé de neuf
> Par récente ordonnance.
> O savants médecins,
> Habiles chirurgiens,

De nous pourquoi ne faire
Comme du pont de pierre.[248]

[Here lies the old Pont Neuf's
Exact likeness,
All newly refurbished
In accord with a recent ordinance.
O learned physicians
And skillful surgeons, why not do with us
As was done with this stone bridge.]

Geffroy sees the uniqueness of these pictures in the fact "that, although they are made directly from life, they give an impression of expired life, something that is dead or on the verge of dying."[249] He thus shows that he understands the essence of Meryon's work, as well as its relationship to Baudelaire, and he is particularly aware of the faithfulness with which Meryon reproduces Paris—a city that was soon to be pocked with mounds of rubble. Baudelaire's Meryon essay contains a subtle reference to the significance of this Parisian antiquity. "Seldom has the natural solemnity of a great city been depicted with more poetic power: the majesty of the piles of stone; those spires pointing their fingers at the sky; the obelisks of industry vomiting their legions of smoke against the heavens;[250] the enormous scaffolds encircling monuments under repair, pressing the paradoxical beauty of their spider-web tracery against the monuments' solid bodies; the steamy sky, pregnant with rage and heavy with rancor; and the wide vistas whose poetry resides in the dramas that one imparts to them in one's imagination—none of the complex elements that compose the painful and glorious décor of civilization has been forgotten."[251] Among the plans whose failure one can mourn like a loss is that of the publisher Delâtre, who wanted to issue Meryon's series with texts by Baudelaire. That these texts were never written was the fault of the artist: he was unable to conceive of Baudelaire's task as anything other than an inventory of the houses and streets he had depicted. If Baudelaire had undertaken that project, Proust's remark about "the role of ancient cities in the work of Baudelaire and the scarlet color they occasionally give it"[252] would make more sense than it does today. Among these cities, Rome was paramount for him. In a letter to Leconte de Lisle, he confesses his "natural predilection" for that city.[253] This attraction was probably inspired by Piranesi's *Vedute,* in which the unrestored ruins and the new city still appear as an integrated whole.[254]

The thirty-ninth poem of *Les Fleurs du mal*—a sonnet—begins as follows:

> Je te donne ces vers afin que si mon nom
> Aborde heureusement aux époques lointaines,
> Et fait rêver un soir les cervelles humaines,
> Vaisseau favorisé par un grand aquilon,
>
> Ta mémoire, pareille aux fables incertaines,
> Fatigue le lecteur ainsi qu'un tympanon.[255]
>
> [I give you these verses so that, if my name
> Should arrive safely on the shores of a far-distant future
> And set men's minds to dreaming after dark—
> Vessel favored by a good north wind—
> Then the memory of you, like some old tale that won't come
>   clear,
> Will nag at the reader's spirits as might the song of a dul-
>   cimer.]

Baudelaire wanted to be read like a classical poet. With astonishing speed his claim was made good, for the distant future, that of the "époques lointaines" mentioned in the sonnet, has arrived—mere decades after his death, though he may have envisioned as many centuries elapsing. To be sure, Paris is still standing and the great tendencies of social development are still the same. But the more constant they have remained, the more everything that stood under the sign of the "truly new" has been rendered obsolete by the experience of them. Modernity has changed most of all, and the antiquity it was supposed to contain really presents a picture of the obsolete. "Herculaneum is found again under the ashes—yet a few years are enough to bury the mores of a society more effectively than all the dust of the volcanoes."[256]

Baudelaire's antiquity is Roman antiquity. In only one place does Greek antiquity extend into his world: Greece supplies him with the image of the heroine which seemed to him worthy and capable of being carried over into modern times. In one of the greatest and most famous poems of *Les Fleurs du mal,* the women bear Greek names, Delphine and Hippolyte. The poem is devoted to lesbian love. The lesbian is the heroine of *la modernité.* In her, one of Baudelaire's erotic ideals—the woman who signifies hardness and virility—has combined with a historical ideal, that of greatness in the ancient world. This makes the position of the lesbian in *Les Fleurs du mal* unmistakable. It explains why Baudelaire long considered using the title "Les Lesbiennes." Incidentally, he was by no means the first to bring the lesbian into art. Balzac had already done this in his *Fille aux yeux d'or,* and so had Gautier in *Mademoiselle de Maupin* and Delatouche in *Fragoletta.* Baudelaire also encountered her in the work of Delacroix; in a critique of Delacroix's paintings, he speaks, somewhat elliptically, of "the modern woman in her heroic manifestation, in the sense of infernal or divine."[257]

The motif is found in Saint-Simonianism, which in its cultic imaginings often used the idea of the androgyne. One of these is the temple that was to be a showpiece of Duveyrier's "New City."[258] A disciple of the school wrote about it as follows: "The temple must represent an androgyne, a man and a woman. . . . The same division must be planned for the entire city—indeed, for the entire kingdom and the whole earth. There will be a hemisphere of man and a hemisphere of woman."[259] So far as its anthropological content is concerned, the Saint-Simonian utopia is more comprehensible in the ideas of Claire Démar than in this structure, which was never built. Over the grandiloquent fantasies of Enfantin, Claire Démar has been forgotten.[260] Yet the manifesto that she left behind is closer to the essence of Saint-Simonian theory—the hypostatization of industry as the force that moves the world—than is Enfantin's mother-myth. Her text is likewise concerned with the mother, but in a sense substantially different from those who set out from France to seek "the Mother" in the Orient. In the widely ramified literature of those days which deals with the future of women, Démar's manifesto is unique in its power and passion. It appeared under the title *Ma loi d'avenir*. In the concluding section, she writes: "No more motherhood! No law of the blood. I say: no more motherhood. Once a woman has been freed from men who pay her the price of her body, . . . she will owe her existence . . . only to her own creativity. To this end, she must devote herself to a task and fulfill a function. . . . So you will have to resolve to take a newborn child from the breast of its natural mother and place it in the hands of a social mother, a nurse employed by the state. In this way, the child will be brought up more effectively. . . . Only then and not earlier will men, women, and children be freed from the law of blood, the law of mankind's self-exploitation."[261]

Here the image of the heroic woman—an image that Baudelaire absorbed—is seen in its original version. Its lesbian variant was not the work of writers but a product of the Saint-Simonian circle. Whatever documentation is involved here surely was not in the best of hands with the chroniclers of this school. Yet we do have the following peculiar confession by a woman who was an adherent of Saint-Simon's doctrine: "I began to love my fellow woman as much as I loved my fellow man. . . . I conceded the physical strength of men, as well as the kind of intelligence that is peculiar to them, but I placed alongside men's qualities, as their equal, the physical beauty of women and the intellectual gifts peculiar to them."[262] A surprising critical reflection by Baudelaire sounds like an echo of this confession. It deals with Flaubert's first heroine. "In her optimal vigor and her most ambitious goals, as well as in her deepest dreams, Madame Bovary . . . has remained a man. Like Pallas Athena, who sprang from the head of Zeus, this strange androgyne has been given all the seductive power of a masculine spirit in an enchanting woman's body."[263] And about the author himself, he writes: "All *intellectual* women will be grateful to him for having raised the 'little woman' to such a high level . . . and for endowing her with the dual nature that makes up a perfect human being: a nature that is as capable of calculation as of dreaming."[264] With the kind of *coup de main* that was typical of him, Baudelaire raises Flaubert's petty-bourgeois wife to the status of a heroine.

There are a number of important and even obvious facts about Baudelaire's work that have gone unnoticed. Among them is the antithetical relation between the two lesbian poems that appear one after the other in the sequence titled "Les Epaves." "Lesbos" is a hymn to lesbian love; "Femmes damnées: Delphine et Hippolyte," on the other hand, is a condemnation of this passion, whatever the nature of the compassion that infuses the reproach.

> Que nous veulent les lois du juste et de l'injuste?
> Vierges au coeur sublime, honneur de l'Archipel,
> Votre religion comme une autre est auguste,
> Et l'amour se rira de l'Enfer et du Ciel![265]

> [What do laws of right and wrong have to do with us?
> You virgins sublime of heart, who do honor to the
>   Archipelago,
> Your religion is venerable as any other,
> And love makes sport of Hell as much as Heaven!]

These lines are taken from the first poem. In the second poem Baudelaire says: "—Descendez, descendez, lamentables victimes, / Descendez le chemin de l'enfer éternel!"[266] ["—Descend, descend, lamentable victims, / Follow the pathway to everlasting hell!"] This striking dichotomy may be explained as follows. Just as Baudelaire did not view the lesbian as either a social or a physical problem, he had, as it were, no attitude toward her in real life. He found room for her within the image of modernity, but did not recognize her in reality. This is why he could say casually: "We have known the female philanthropist who was a writer, . . . the republican poetess, the poetess of the future, be she a Fourierist or a Saint-Simonian.[267] But we have never been able to accustom our eyes . . . to all this solemn and repulsive behavior, . . . these sacrilegious imitations of the masculine spirit."[268] It would be wrong to assume that Baudelaire ever thought of championing lesbians publicly in his writings. This is proved by the proposals he made to his attorney for the latter's plea in the *Fleurs du mal* trial. To him, social ostracism was inseparable from the heroic nature of lesbian passion. "Descendez, descendez, lamentables victimes" were the last words that Baudelaire addressed to lesbians. He abandoned them to their doom, and they could not be saved, because Baudelaire's conception of them comprises elements that are inextricably tangled.

During the nineteenth century, women were for the first time used in large numbers in the production process outside the home. This was done for the most part in a primitive way, by employing them in factories. As a result, masculine traits were bound to appear in these women eventually. These were caused, in particular, by the distorting influence of factory work. Higher forms of production, as well as the political struggle per se, fostered masculine characteristics of a more refined nature. The Vésuviennes movement can perhaps be understood in such a way. It supplied the February Revolution with a corps composed of women. "We call ourselves Vésuviennes," it says in the statutes, "to indicate that a revolutionary volcano is at work in every woman who belongs to our group."[269] Such a change in the feminine habitus brought out tendencies capable of firing Baudelaire's imagination. It would not be surprising if his profound antipathy to pregnancy was a factor here.[270] The masculinization of woman was in keeping with this, so Baudelaire approved of the process. At the same time, however, he sought to free it from economic bondage. Thus, he reached the point where he gave a purely sexual emphasis to this development. What he could not forgive George Sand was, perhaps, that she had desecrated the image of the lesbian through her affair with Musset.[271]

The deterioration of the "realistic" element in Baudelaire's attitude toward lesbians is characteristic of him in other things as well. It struck attentive observers as strange. In 1895, Jules Lemaître wrote:

> One confronts a work full of artifice and intentional contradictions. . . . Even as he gives the rawest descriptions of the bleakest details of reality, he indulges in a spiritualism which greatly distracts us from the immediate impression that things make upon us. . . . Baudelaire regards a woman as a slave or animal, but he renders her the same homage as he does the Holy Virgin. . . . He curses "progress," he loathes the century's industrial activity, yet he enjoys the special flavor that this industrial activity has imparted to contemporary life. . . . What is uniquely Baudelairean, I believe, is the readiness always to unite two opposite modes of reaction . . . One could call these a past mode and a present mode. A masterpiece of the will, . . . the latest innovation in the sphere of emotional life.[272]

To present this attitude as a great achievement of the will accorded with Baudelaire's spirit. But the other side of the coin is a lack of conviction, insight, and steadiness. In all his endeavors, Baudelaire was subject to abrupt, shock-like changes; his vision of another way of living life to extremes was thus all the more alluring. This way becomes apparent in the incantations which emanate from many of his perfect verses; in some of them, it even gives its name.

> Vois sur ces canaux
> Dormir ces vaisseaux
> Dont l'humeur est vagabonde;
> C'est pour assouvir
> Ton moindre désir
> Qu'ils viennent du bout du monde.[273]

[See, on the canals,
Those sleeping ships—
They have a vagabond spirit.

It is to satisfy
Your least desire
That they come from the ends of the earth.]

This famous stanza has a rocking rhythm; its movement seizes the ships which lie moored in the canals. To be rocked between extremes: this is the privilege of ships, and this is what Baudelaire longed for. The ships emerge at the site of the profound, secret, and paradoxical image of his dreams: the vision of being supported and sheltered by greatness. "These beautiful big ships that lie on the still water imperceptibly rocking, these strong ships that look so idle and so nostalgic—are they not asking us in a mute language: When do we set sail for happiness?"[274] The ships combine airy casualness with readiness for the utmost exertion. This gives them a secret significance. There is a special constellation in which greatness and indolence meet in human beings, too. This constellation governed Baudelaire's life. He deciphered it and called it "modernity." When he loses himself in the spectacle of the ships lying at anchor, he does so in order to derive a parable from them. The hero is as strong, as ingenious, as harmonious, and as well-built as those boats. But the high seas beckon to him in vain, for his life is under the sway of an ill star. Modernity turns out to be his doom. There are no provisions for him in it; it has no use for his type. It moors him fast in the secure harbor forever and abandons him to everlasting idleness. Here, in his last incarnation, the hero appears as a dandy. If you encounter one of these figures, who thanks to their strength and composure are perfect in their every gesture, you say to yourself: "Here is perhaps a rich man—but more certainly a Hercules with no labors to accomplish."[275] The dandy seems to be supported by his greatness. Hence it is understandable that at certain times Baudelaire thought his flânerie was endowed with the same dignity as the exertion of his poetic powers.

To Baudelaire, the dandy appeared to be a descendant of great ancestors. Dandyism, he thought, was "the last gleam of the heroic in times of decadence."[276] It pleased him to discover in Chateaubriand a reference to American Indian dandies—evidence of a past flowering of those tribes.[277] Indeed, the features that combine in the dandy bear a very definite historical stamp. The dandy is a creation of the English, who were leaders in world trade. The trade network that spans the globe was in the hands of the London stock exchange; its meshes were subject to extraordinarily varied, numerous, and unforeseeable tremors. A merchant had to react to these, but he could not publicly display his reactions. The dandies took over the management of the conflicts thus created. They developed the ingenious training necessary to overcome these conflicts. They combined extremely quick reactions with a relaxed, even slack demeanor and facial expression. The tic, which for a time was regarded as fashionable, is, as it were, a clumsy, inferior manifestation of the problem. The following statement is very revealing: "The face of an elegant man must always have something convulsive and distorted about it. Such a grimace can, if one wishes, be ascribed to a natural satanism."[278] This is how the figure of the London dandy appeared in the mind of a Paris boulevardier, and this was its physiognomic reflection in Baudelaire. His love for dandyism was unsuccessful. He did not have the gift of pleasing, which is such an important element in the dandy's art of not pleasing. There were traits inherent in his character that were bound to strike people as strange; turning these traits into mannerisms, he became profoundly lonely, particularly since his inaccessibility increased as he became more isolated.

Unlike Gautier, Baudelaire found nothing to like about the age he lived in, and unlike Leconte de Lisle he was unable to deceive himself about it. He did not have the humanitarian idealism of a Lamartine or a Hugo, and it was not given to him, as it was to Verlaine, to take refuge in religious devotion. Because he did not have any convictions, he assumed ever new forms himself. Flâneur, apache, dandy, and ragpicker were so many roles to him. For the modern hero is no hero; he is a portrayer of heroes. Heroic modernity turns out to be a Trauerspiel in which the hero's part is available.[279] Baudelaire indicated this, half-hidden in a *remarque,* in his poem "Les Sept Vieillards."

Un matin, cependant que dans la triste rue
Les maisons, dont la brume allongeait la hauteur,
Simulaient les deux quais d'une rivière accrue,
Et que, décor semblable à l'âme de l'acteur,
Un brouillard sale et jaune inondait tout l'espace,
Je suivais, roidissant mes nerfs comme un héros
Et discutant avec mon âme déjà lasse,
Le faubourg secoué pas les lourds tombereaux.[280]

[One morning, when in the dreary street
The houses, made taller by the mist,
Simulated the two quays of a river in flood,
And when—scenery resembling the actor's soul—

A dirty yellow fog filled all the space,
I took my way—steeling my nerves like a hero
And pursuing a dialogue with my already weary soul—
Through the outlying neighborhoods shaken by the passage
    of heavy carts.]

The scenery, the actor, and the hero meet in these stanzas in an un-mistakable way. Baudelaire's contemporaries did not need the reference. When Courbet was painting Baudelaire, he complained that his subject looked different every day. And Champfleury said that Baudelaire had the ability to change his facial expression like a fugitive from a chain gang.[281] Vallès, in a malicious obituary that displays a fair amount of acuity, called Baudelaire a *cabotin*.[282]

Behind the masks which he used to their fullest extent, the poet in Baudelaire preserved his incognito. He was as circumspect in his work as he was capable of seeming provocative in his personal associations. The incognito was the law of his poetry. His prosody is like the map of a big city in which one can move about inconspicuously, shielded by blocks of houses, gateways, courtyards. On this map, words are given clearly designated positions, just as conspirators are given designated positions before the outbreak of a revolt. Baudelaire conspires with language itself. He calculates its effects step by step.

That he always avoided revealing himself to the reader has been emphasized by the most competent observers. Gide noticed a very calculated disharmony between the image and the object.[283] Rivière has emphasized how Baudelaire proceeds from the remote word—how he teaches it to tread softly as he cautiously brings it closer to the object.[284] Lemaître speaks of forms that are designed to check an eruption of passion.[285] And Laforgue focuses on Baudelaire's similes, which, as it were, belie the poet's lyrical façade and get into the text as disturbing intruders. Laforgue quotes "La nuit s'épaississait ainsi qu'une cloison,"[286] and adds: "A wealth of other examples could be found."[287]

The segregation of words into those that seemed suitable for elevated speech and those that were to be excluded from it influenced poetic production generally, and from the beginning applied to tragedy no less than to lyric poetry. In the first decades of the nineteenth century, this convention was in undisputed force. When Lebrun's *Cid* was performed, the word *chambre* evoked mutterings of disapproval.[288] *Othello,* in Alfred de Vigny's translation, failed because of the word *mouchoir*—a term that seemed intolerable in a tragedy. Victor Hugo had begun smoothing out, in literature, the difference between words of colloquial language and those of elevated speech. Sainte-Beuve had proceeded in a similar fashion. In his life of Joseph Delorme, he explained: "I have tried to be original in my own way, in a modest, homely way. I called the things of intimate life by their names; but when I did so, a hut was closer to me than a boudoir."[289] Baudelaire transcended both Victor Hugo's linguistic Jacobinism and Sainte-Beuve's bucolic liberties. His images are original because the objects they bring into relation are so humble. He is on the lookout for banal incidents in order to liken them to poetic events. He speaks of "les vagues terreurs de ces affreuses nuits / Qui compriment le coeur comme un papier qu'on froisse."[290] This linguistic gesture, characteristic of the artist in Baudelaire, becomes truly significant only in the allegorist. It gives his type of allegory the disconcerting quality that distinguishes it from the ordinary kind. Lemercier had been the last to populate the Parnassus of the Empire with such ordinary allegories, thus marking the nadir of neoclassical literature.[291] Baudelaire was unconcerned about that. He took up myriad allegories and altered their character fundamentally by virtue of the linguistic context in which he placed them. *Les Fleurs du mal* is the first book of poetry to use not only words of ordinary provenance but words of urban origin as well. Yet Baudelaire by no means avoids locutions which, free from any poetic patina, strike one with the brilliance of their coinage. He uses *quinquet, wagon, omnibus,* and does not shrink from *bilan, réverbère, voirie.* This is the nature of the lyric vocabulary, in which allegory may appear suddenly and without prior preparation. If Baudelaire's linguistic spirit can be perceived anywhere, it is in such abrupt contrasts. Claudel gave it its definitive formulation when he said that Baudelaire combined the style of Racine with the style of a journalist of the Second Empire.[292] Not a word of his vocabulary is intended for allegory from the outset. A word receives this charge in a particular case, depending on what is involved, on which topic is in line to be reconnoitered, besieged, and occupied. For the *coup de main* which Baudelaire calls writing poetry, he takes allegories into his confidence. They alone have been let in on the secret. Wherever one comes across *la Mort* or *le Souvenir, le Repentir* or *le Mal,* one finds a locus of poetic strategy. The lightning-like flashing up of these charges—recognizable by their capitalization—in a text which does not disdain the most banal word betrays Baudelaire's hand. His technique is the technique of the putsch.

A few years after Baudelaire's death, Blanqui crowned his career as a conspirator with a memorable feat. It was after the murder of Victor Noir.[293] Blanqui wished to take an inventory of his troops. He knew only his lieutenants personally, and it is not certain how many of his other men knew him. He communicated with Granger, his adjutant, who made arrangements for a review of the Blanquists.[294] Geffroy has described it as follows:

> Blanqui left his house armed, said goodbye to his sisters, and took up his post on the Champs-Elysées. According to his agreement with Granger, the troops serving under the myste-

rious General Blanqui were to pass in review. He knew his subcommanders, and now he was supposed to see, following each of them, their people march past him in regular formation. It all took place as arranged. Blanqui held his review without anyone's having an inkling of the strange spectacle. The old man stood leaning against a tree among a crowd of people, who were watching just as he was, and paid close attention to his friends; they marched past in columns, approaching silently amid a murmuring that was continually interrupted by shouts.[295]

Baudelaire's poetry has preserved in words the strength that made such a thing possible.

On some occasions, Baudelaire tried to discern the image of the modern hero in the conspirator as well. "No more tragedies!" he wrote in *Le Salut public* during the February days. "No more histories of ancient Rome! Aren't we today greater than Brutus?"[296] "Greater than Brutus" was, to be sure, less than great. For when Napoleon III came to power, Baudelaire did not recognize the Caesar in him. In this, Blanqui was more perceptive than he was. But the differences between them are superficial compared to their profound similarities: their obstinacy and their impatience, the power of their indignation and their hatred, as well as the impotence which was their common lot. In a famous line, Baudelaire lightheartedly bids farewell to "a world in which action is not the sister of dreams."[297] His dream was not as hopeless as it seemed to him. Blanqui's action was the sister of Baudelaire's dream. The two are conjoined. They are the joined hands on the stone under which Napoleon III buried the hopes of the June fighters.

Addenda

Sundering truth from falsehood is the goal of the materialist method, not its point of departure.[298] In other words, its point of departure is the object riddled with error, with *doxa*.[299] The distinctions that form the basis of the materialist method, which is discriminative from the outset, are distinctions within this extremely heterogeneous object; it would be impossible to present this object as too heterogeneous or too uncritical. If the materialist method claimed to approach the matter [*die Sache*] "in truth," it would do nothing but greatly reduce its chances of success. These chances, however, are considerably augmented if the materialist method increasingly abandons such a claim, thus preparing for the insight that "the matter in itself" is not "in truth."

Of course, one is tempted to pursue "the matter in itself." In the case of Baudelaire, it offers itself in profusion. The sources flow as abundantly as one could wish, and where they converge to form the stream of tradition, they flow along between well-laid-out slopes as far as the eye can reach. Historical materialism is not led astray by this spectacle. It does not seek the image of the clouds in this stream, but neither does it turn away from the stream to drink "from the source" and pursue "the matter itself" behind men's backs. Whose mills does this stream drive? Who is utilizing its power? Who dammed it? These are the questions that historical materialism asks, changing our impressions of the landscape by naming the forces that have been operative in it.

This seems like a complex process, and it is. Isn't there a more direct, more decisive one? Why not simply confront the poet Baudelaire with present-day society and determine what he has to say to this society's progressive cadres by referring to his works—without, to be sure, failing to consider whether he has anything to say to them at all? What contravenes this is precisely that when we read Baudelaire, we are given a course of historical lessons by bourgeois society. These lessons can never be ignored. A critical reading of Baudelaire and a critical revision of these lessons are one and the same thing. For it is an illusion of vulgar Marxism that one can determine the social function of a material or intellectual product without reference to the circumstances and the bearers of its tradition. "The concept of culture—as the embodiment of creations considered independent, if not of the production process in which they originate, then of a production process in which they continue to survive—has a fetishistic quality."[300] The tradition of Baudelaire's works is a very brief one, but it already bears historical scars which cannot but be of interest to critical observers.

Taste

Taste develops when commodity production clearly surpasses any other kind of production. The manufacture of products as commodities for a market ensures that the conditions of their production—not only societal conditions, in the form of exploitation, but technological ones as well—will gradually vanish from the perceived world of the people. The consumer, who is more or less expert when he gives an order to an artisan (in individual cases, he is advised by the master craftsman himself), is not usually knowledgeable when he acts as a buyer. Added to this is the fact that mass production, which aims at turning out inexpensive commodities, must strive to disguise bad quality. In most cases, mass production actually benefits when the buyer has little expertise. The more industry progresses, the more perfect are the imitations it offers on the market. A profane glimmer [*Schein*] makes the commodity phosphorescent; this has nothing in common with the semblance that produces its "theological niceties."[301] Yet it is of some importance to society. On July 17, 1824, in a speech about trademarks, Chaptal said: "Don't tell me that in the final analysis a shopper will know about the different qualities of a material. No, gentlemen, a consumer is no judge of them; he will go only by the appearance of the commodity. But are looking and touching enough to determine the permanence of colors, the fineness of a material, or the quality and nature of its finish?"[302]

As the expertness of a customer declines, the importance of his taste increases proportionately—both for him and for the manufacturer. For the consumer, it serves as a more or less elaborate masking of his lack of expertness. For the manufacturer, it serves as a fresh stimulus to consumption, which in some cases is satisfied at the expense of other consumer needs that would be more costly for the manufacturer to meet.

It is precisely this development which literature reflects in *l'art pour l'art.*[303] This doctrine and its corresponding practice for the first time give taste a dominant position in poetry. (To be sure, taste does not seem to be the object there; it is not mentioned anywhere. But this is no more significant than the fact that taste was often discussed in the aesthetic debates of the eighteenth century. Actually, these debates centered on content.) In *l'art pour l'art,* the poet for the first time faces language the way the buyer faces the commodity on the open market. To an extreme extent, he has ceased to be familiar with the process of its production. The poets of *l'art pour l'art* are the last poets who can be said to have come "from the people." They have nothing to say with such urgency that it could determine the *coining* of their words. Rather, they are forced to choose their words. The "chosen word" soon became the motto of Jugendstil literature.[304] The poet of *l'art pour l'art* wanted to bring *himself* to language above all else—with all the idiosyncrasies, nuances, and imponderabilities of his nature. These elements are precipitated in taste. The poet's taste guides him in his choice of words. But the choice is made only among words which have not already been stamped by the *matter* itself—that is, which have not been included in its process of production.

Actually, the theory of *l'art pour l'art* assumed decisive importance around 1852, at a time when the bourgeoisie sought to wrest its "cause" from the hands of the writers and the poets. In *The Eighteenth Brumaire,* Marx recollects this moment, when "the extra-parliamentary masses of the bourgeoisie, . . . through the brutal abuse of their own press," called upon Napoleon III "to destroy their speaking and writing segment, their politicians and literati, so that they might confidently pursue their private affairs under the protection of a strong and untrammeled government." At the end of this development, we find Mallarmé and the theory of *la poésie pure.* Here the poet has become so far removed from the cause of his own class that the problem of a literature without an object becomes the center of discussion. This discussion is clearly evident in Mallarmé's poems, which revolve around *blanc, absence, silence, vide.* This, to be sure—particularly in Mallarmé—is the face of a coin whose obverse is by no means insignificant. It shows that the poet no longer supports any of the causes pursued by the class to which he belongs. To found a production process on such a basic renunciation of all the manifest experiences of this class engenders specific and considerable difficulties—difficulties that make this poetry highly esoteric. Baudelaire's works are not esoteric. The social experiences which are precipitated in his work are, to be sure, nowhere derived from the production process—least of all in its most advanced form, the industrial process; without exception, they all originated in long, roundabout ways. But these roundabout ways are quite apparent in his works. The most important are the experiences of the neurasthenic, of the big-city dweller, and of the retail customer.

Written in the summer and fall of 1938; unpublished in Benjamin's lifetime. *Gesammelte Schriften*, I, 511–604, 1160–61, 1167–69. Translated by Harry Zohn.

Central Park

[1]

Laforgue's hypothesis concerning Baudelaire's conduct in the bordello puts his entire psychoanalytic interpretation of Baudelaire into proper perspective.[1] This view agrees point by point with the conventional approach of "literary history."

The special beauty of so many of the openings of Baudelaire's poems lies in this: a rising up from the abyss.

In translating "Spleen et idéal" as "Trübsinn und Vergeistigung," George hit upon the true meaning of the ideal in Baudelaire.[2]

If it can be said that for Baudelaire modern life is the reservoir of dialectical images, this implies that he stood in the same relation to modern life as the seventeenth century did to antiquity.

If we call to mind just how much Baudelaire as a poet had to respect his own precepts, his own insights, and his own taboos, and how strictly circumscribed, on the other hand, the tasks of his poetic labor were, then we may come to see in him a heroic trait.

[2]

Spleen as a bulwark against pessimism. Baudelaire is no pessimist. This is because, with Baudelaire, a taboo is placed on the future. That is what distinguishes his heroism most clearly from Nietzsche's.[3] His writings contain no reflections on the future of bourgeois society—an astonishing fact, in view of the nature of his *Journaux intimes*. From this alone, we can see how little he relied on striking effects for the longevity of his work, and to what extent the structure of *Les Fleurs du mal* is monadological.

The structure of *Les Fleurs du mal* is not based on any ingenious arrangement of the individual poems, still less on some secret key. It results from the relentless exclusion of any lyric theme that does not bear the stamp of Baudelaire's own profoundly sorrowful experience. And precisely because Baudelaire was aware that his form of suffering—spleen, the *taedium vitae*—is a very ancient one, he was able to make the signature of his own experience stand out in bold relief against it. One suspects that few things could have given him a greater sense of his own originality than a reading of the Roman satirists.

[3]

The "enshrinement," or apologia, is meant to cover up the revolutionary moments in the course of history. At bottom, it seeks to establish continuity. It sets store only by those elements of a work which have already emerged and played a part in its reception. It ignores the peaks and crags, which offer footing to those who want to move beyond this view.

The cosmic shudder in Victor Hugo never has the quality of the naked terror that seized Baudelaire in his spleen.[4] This descended on the poet from a cosmic space that was made for the *intérieur* in which he felt at home. He felt perfectly at home in this spirit world. It is the complement of the coziness of his domestic existence, which was itself not without its terrors.

"Dans le coeur immortel qui toujours veut fleurir": use this to elucidate the meaning of the flowers of evil and of infertility. *Vendanges* in Baudelaire—his most melancholy word ("Semper eadem"; "L'Imprévu").[5]

The contradiction between the theory of natural correspondences[6] and the repudiation of nature. How is this to be resolved?

Sudden attacks, mystery-mongering, surprising decisions belong to the *raison d'état* of the Second Empire and were characteristic of Napoleon III.[7] They are the crucial gestures [*Gestus*] informing Baudelaire's theoretical pronouncements.

[4]

The decisively new ferment that enters the *taedium vitae* and turns it into spleen is self-estrangement. In Baudelaire's melancholy [*Trauer*], all that is left of the infinite regress of reflection—which in Romanticism playfully expanded the space of life into ever-wider circles and reduced it within ever narrower frames—is the "somber and lucid tête-à-tête" of the subject with itself. The specific "seriousness" of Baudelaire's work is located here. It prevented the poet from truly assimilating the Catholic worldview, which could be reconciled with allegory only under the aegis of play. Here, unlike the situation in the Baroque, the semblance implicit in allegory is no longer acknowledged.[8]

Baudelaire was not based in any style, and he had no school. This greatly impeded his reception.

•

The introduction of allegory is a far more significant response to the crisis in art than the doctrine of art for art's sake, which sought to combat the crisis around 1852. This crisis in art had its roots in both the technological situation and the political situation.

[5]

There are two legends of Baudelaire. One—which he disseminated himself—presents him as the inhuman bogeyman of the solid citizen. The other—which arose with his death and is the basis of his fame—presents him as a martyr. This false theological nimbus should be dispelled right down the line. Monnier has a formula for this nimbus.[9]

It can be said that happiness penetrated him like a shudder; the same cannot be said of unhappiness. In the state of nature, misfortune cannot pass into us.

Spleen is the feeling that corresponds to catastrophe in permanence.

The course of history, seen in terms of the concept of catastrophe, can actually claim no more attention from thinkers than a child's kaleidoscope, which with every turn of the hand dissolves the established order into a new array. There is profound truth in this image. The concepts of the ruling class have always been the mirrors that enabled an image of "order" to prevail.—The kaleidoscope must be smashed.

The grave as the secret chamber in which Eros and Sexus settle their ancient quarrel.

The stars in Baudelaire represent a picture puzzle of the commodity. They are the ever-same in great masses.

•

The devaluation of the world of things in allegory is surpassed within the world of things itself by the commodity.

[6]

Jugendstil is to be presented as art's second attempt to come to terms with technology.[10] The first attempt was realism. For realism, the problem was more or less present in the consciousness of the artists, who were uneasy about the new processes of technological reproduction. (Loci! Perhaps in the papers for the "Reproducibility" essay.) In Jugendstil, the problem as such was already prey to repression. Jugendstil no longer saw itself threatened by the competing technology; hence, the critique of technology concealed within it was all the more total and aggressive. Its real purpose was to arrest technological development. Its recourse to technological motifs arises from the effort . . .[11]

In Rollinat, what was allegory in Baudelaire has lapsed into genre.[12]

The motif of the *perte d'auréole*[13] is to be developed as the decisive contrast to Jugendstil.

Essence as a motif of Jugendstil.

To write history means giving calendar dates their physiognomy.

Prostitution of space in hashish, where it serves all that has been (spleen).

From the perspective of spleen, the buried man is the "transcendental subject"[14] of historical consciousness.

Jugendstil was especially fond of the aureole. Never was the sun more pleased with itself than in its radiant halo; never was the human eye more lustrous than in Fidus.[15]

[7]

The motif of androgyny, the lesbian, the unfruitful woman, should be treated in connection with the destructive power of the allegorical intention.—The rejection of the "natural" must be dealt with earlier—in connection with the city as the poet's subject.

Meryon: the sea of buildings, the ruins, the clouds; the majesty and decrepitude of Paris.[16]

The interplay between antiquity and modernity must be transferred from the pragmatic context—in which it first appears in Baudelaire—to the context of allegory.

Spleen interposes centuries between the present moment and the one just lived. It is spleen that tirelessly generates "antiquity."

"Modernity" in Baudelaire is not based solely or primarily on sensibility. It gives expression to extreme spontaneity. Modernity in Baudelaire is a conquest; it has an armature. Apparently Jules Laforgue, speaking of Baudelaire's "Americanism," is the only one who has noticed this.[17]

[8]

Baudelaire did not have the humanitarian idealism of a Victor Hugo or a Lamartine.[18] The emotional buoyancy of a Musset was not at his disposal.[19] He did not, like Gautier, take pleasure in his times, nor could he deceive himself about them like Leconte de Lisle.[20] It was not given to him to find a refuge in devotions, like Verlaine, nor to heighten the youthful vigor of his lyric élan through the betrayal of his adulthood, like Rimbaud.[21] As rich as Baudelaire is in knowledge of his art, he is relatively lacking in stratagems to face the times. How far did even the "modernity" he was so proud of discovering really engage with those times? Those who wielded power in the Second Empire were not modeled on the bourgeois types created by Balzac. Modernity finally became a role which perhaps only Baudelaire himself could fill. A tragic role, in which the dilettante—who, for want of other parts, had to perform it—often cut a comical figure, like the heroes Daumier caricatured with Baudelaire's approbation.[22] All this Baudelaire no doubt recognized. The eccentricities in which he took such pleasure were his way of acknowledging it. Assuredly, therefore, he was not a savior, a martyr, or even a hero. But he had about him something of the mime who apes the "poet" before an audience and a society which no longer need a real poet, and which grant him only the latitude of mimicry.

[9]

Neurosis creates the mass-produced article in the psychic economy. There it takes the form of the obsessional idea, which, manufactured in countless copies, appears in the household of the neurotic mind as the ever selfsame. Conversely, in Blanqui the idea of eternal return itself takes the form of an obsessional idea.[23]

The idea of eternal recurrence transforms the historical event itself into a mass-produced article. But this conception also displays, in another respect—on its obverse side, one could say—a trace of the economic circumstances to which it owes its sudden topicality. This was manifest at the moment the security of the conditions of life was considerably diminished through an accelerated succession of crises. The idea of eternal recurrence derived its luster from the fact that it was no longer possible, in all circumstances, to expect a recurrence of conditions across any interval of time shorter than that provided by eternity. The recurrence of quotidian constellations became gradually less frequent and there could arise, in consequence, the obscure presentiment that henceforth one must rest content with cosmic constellations. Habit, in short, made ready to surrender some of its prerogatives. Nietzsche says, "I love short-lived habits";[24] and before this, Baudelaire was throughout his life incapable of developing regular habits.

[10]

On the melancholic's Via Dolorosa, allegories are the stations. The role of the skeleton in Baudelaire's erotology? "L'élégance sans nom de l'humaine armature."[25]

It is impotence that makes for the Via Dolorosa of male sexuality. The historical index of this impotence. From this impotence springs [Baudelaire's] attachment to the seraphic image of woman, as well as his fetishism. Witness the clarity and precision of the phenomenon of woman in Baudelaire. Keller's "sin of the poet"—namely, "inventing sweet images of women, / such as bitter earth never harbors"—is certainly not his.[26] Keller's women have the sweetness of chimeras because they are informed by his own impotence. Baudelaire, in his female figures, is more precise and, in a word, more French, because with him the fetishistic and the seraphic elements almost never coincide, as they do in Keller.

Social reasons for impotence: the imagination of the bourgeois class ceases to be occupied with the future of the productive forces it has unleashed. (Comparison between classical utopias and those of the mid-nineteenth century.) In order to concern itself further with this future, the bourgeois class in fact would first have had to renounce the idea of private income. In my study on Fuchs, I showed how the specific midcentury "coziness" goes hand in hand with this demonstrable flagging of the social imagination. Compared to the images of the future engendered by the social imagination, the wish to have children is, perhaps, a weaker stimulant to potency. At any rate, Baudelaire's doctrine of children as the beings closest to original sin is somewhat revealing here.

[11]

Baudelaire's strategy in the literary market: through his deep experience of the nature of the commodity, he was enabled, or compelled, to recognize the market as an objective court of appeals (see his *Conseils aux jeunes littérateurs*). Through his negotiations with editors, he was continuously in contact with the market. His techniques: defamation (Musset), and counterfeit (Hugo). Baudelaire was perhaps the first to conceive of a market- oriented originality, which for that very reason was more original in its day than any other *(créer un poncif)*.[27] This *création* entailed a certain intolerance. Baudelaire wanted to make room for his poems, and to this end he had to push aside others. He managed to devalue certain poetic liberties of the Romantics through his classical deployment of the alexandrine, and to devalue classicist poetics through the characteristic ruptures and defects he introduced into classical verse. In short, his poems contained special provisions for the elimination of competitors.

[12]

The figure of Baudelaire plays a decisive part in his fame. For the petty-bourgeois mass of readers, his story was an *image d'Epinal*,[28] an illustrated "life history of a libertine." This image has contributed greatly to Baudelaire's reputation, little though its purveyors may have numbered among his friends. Over this image another was laid, one that has had a much less widespread but—for that very reason— perhaps more lasting effect: it shows Baudelaire as the exemplar of an aesthetic Passion, such as Kierkegaard conceived of around the same time (in *Either-Or*).[29] No study of Baudelaire can fully explore the vitality of its subject without dealing with the image of his life. This image was actually determined by the fact that he was the first to realize, and in the most productive way, that the bourgeoisie was about to annul its contract with the poet. Which social contract would replace it? That question could not be addressed to any class; only the market and its crises could provide an answer. What concerned Baudelaire was not manifest and short-term demand but latent and long-term demand. *Les Fleurs du mal* demonstrates that he correctly assessed this demand. But the medium of the market through which it revealed itself to him dictated a mode of production and of living which differed sharply from those known to earlier poets. Baudelaire was obliged to lay claim to the dignity of the poet in a society that had no more dignity of any kind to confer. Hence the *bouffonerie* of his public appearances.

[13]

In Baudelaire, the poet for the first time stakes a claim to exhibition value. Baudelaire was his own impresario. The *perte d'auréole* concerned the poet first of all. Hence his mythomania.

The elaborate theorems with which the principle of "art for art's sake" was enunciated—not only by its original proponents but above all by literary history (not to mention its present devotees)—ultimately came down to a specific thesis: that sensibility is the true subject of poetry. Sensibility, by its nature, is involved in suffering. If it experiences its highest concretization, its richest determination, in the sphere of the erotic, then it must find its absolute consummation, which coincides with its transfiguration, in the Passion. The poetics of *l'art pour l'art* issued directly in the poetic Passion of *Les Fleurs du mal.*

Flowers adorn the individual stations of this Calvary. They are flowers of evil.

That which the allegorical intention has fixed upon is sundered from the customary contexts of life: it is at once shattered and preserved. Allegory holds fast to the ruins. It offers the image of petrified unrest.[30] Baudelaire's destructive impulse is nowhere concerned with the abolition of what falls prey to it.

The description of confusion is not the same as a confused description.[31]

Victor Hugo's "Attendre c'est la vie": the wisdom of exile.

The new *desolation* of Paris (see the passage on *croque-morts*) is an essential moment in the image of modernity (see Veuillot; D2,2).[32]

[14]

The figure of the lesbian is, in the precise sense, one of Baudelaire's heroic exemplars. He himself says as much in the language of his satanism. It is no less comprehensible in the unmetaphysical, critical language in which he declares his adherence to "modernity" in its political sense. The nineteenth century began openly and without reserve to include woman in the process of commodity production. All the theoreticians were united in their opinion that her specific femininity was thereby endangered; masculine traits must necessarily manifest themselves in women after a while. Baudelaire affirms these traits; at the same time, however, he seeks to free them from the domination of the economy. Hence the purely sexual accent which he comes to give this developmental tendency in women. The paradigm of the lesbian woman represents the protest of "modernity" against technological development. (One would have to determine how his aversion to George Sand[33] had its roots in this context.)

Woman in Baudelaire: the most precious booty in the "triumph of allegory"—the life which signifies death. This quality is most inalienably the whore's. It is the only thing about her that cannot be bought, and for Baudelaire it is the only thing that matters.

[15]

To interrupt the course of the world—that was Baudelaire's deepest intention. The intention of Joshua. Not so much the prophetic one, for he gave no thought to any sort of reform. From this intention sprang his violence, his impatience, and his anger; from it, too, sprang the ever-renewed attempts to stab the world in the heart or sing it to sleep. In this intention he provides death with an accompaniment: his encouragement of its work.

One must assume that the subjects at the center of Baudelaire's poetry could not be arrived at by a planned, purposeful effort; thus, he does not aim at these radically new subjects—the big city, the masses—as such. The melody he seeks is not in them. It is in satanism, spleen, and deviant eroticism. The true subjects of *Les Fleurs du mal* are found in inconspicuous places. To pursue the image: they are in the previously untouched strings of the instrument whose sound had never been heard before and on which Baudelaire's works were improvised.

[16]

The labyrinth is the right path for the person who always arrives early enough at his destination. This destination is the marketplace.

Games of chance, flânerie, collecting—activities pitted against spleen.

Baudelaire shows how the bourgeoisie in its decline can no longer assimilate asocial elements. When was the Garde Nationale dissolved?[34]

•

With the new manufacturing processes that lead to imitations, semblance is consolidated in commodities.

For people as they are now, there is only one radical novelty—and always the same one: death.

Petrified unrest is also the formula for Baudelaire's life history, which knows no development.

[17]

One of the arcana which prostitution came to possess with the advent of the big city is the phenomenon of the masses.[35] Prostitution opens the possibility of a mythical communion with the mass. The masses came into being at the same time as mass production. Prostitution seems to offer the possibility of enduring a life in which the most immediate objects of our use have turned more and more into mass commodities. In big-city prostitution, the woman herself becomes a mass-produced article. It is this wholly new characteristic of urban life which gives Baudelaire's reception of the dogma of original sin its true significance. The oldest concept seemed to him just proven enough to master a thoroughly new and disconcerting phenomenon.

The labyrinth is the habitat of the dawdler. The path followed by someone reluctant to reach his goal easily becomes labyrinthine. A drive, in the stages leading to its satisfaction, acts likewise. But so, too, does a humanity (a class) which does not want to know where its destiny is taking it.

If it is imagination that presents correspondences to the memory, it is thinking that consecrates allegories to it. Memory brings about the convergence of imagination and thought.

[18]

The magnetic attraction which a few basic situations continually exerted on the poet is one of the symptoms of his melancholy. Baudelaire's imagination is occupied by stereotyped images. He seems to have been subject to a very general compulsion to return at least once to each of his motifs. This is doubtless comparable to the compulsion which repeatedly draws the felon back to the scene of his crime. Baudelaire's allegories are sites where he atoned for his destructive drive. This may explain the unique correspondence between so many of his prose pieces and particular poems from *Les Fleurs du mal*.

To attempt (like Lemaître) to judge Baudelaire's intellectual powers on the basis of his philosophical digressions would be a grave error.[36] Baudelaire was a bad philosopher, a good theoretician; but only as a brooder was he incomparable. He has the characteristics of the brooder: the stereotypical quality of his motifs, his imperturbability in warding off disturbance, his perpetual readiness each time to put the image at the beck and call of thought. The brooder, as a historically distinct type of thinker, is at home among allegories.

For Baudelaire, prostitution is the yeast that causes the great urban masses to rise in his imagination.

[19]

Majesty of the allegorical intention: to destroy the organic and the living—to eradicate semblance [*Schein*]. One must note the highly revealing passage where Baudelaire writes about his fascination with painted stage backdrops.[37] The renunciation of the magic of distance is a decisive moment in Baudelaire's lyric poetry. It has found its sovereign formulation in the first stanza of "Le Voyage."

•

Regarding the eradication of semblance: "L'Amour du mensonge."[38]

"Une Martyre" and "La Mort des amants"—Makart interior and Jugendstil.[39]

The wrenching of things from their familiar contexts—the normal state for goods on display—is a procedure highly characteristic of Baudelaire. It is linked to the destruction of organic contexts in the allegorical intention. See the nature motifs in "Une Martyre," third and fifth stanzas, and in the first stanza of "Madrigal triste."[40]

Derivation of the aura as the projection of a human social experience onto nature: the gaze is returned.

The dissolution of semblance [*die Scheinlosigkeit*] and the decay of the aura are identical phenomena. Baudelaire places the artistic device of allegory in their service.

It belongs to the Via Dolorosa of male sexuality that Baudelaire regarded pregnancy as a kind of unfair competition.

The stars, which Baudelaire banished from his world, are for Blanqui precisely the theater of eternal recurrence.

[20]

More and more relentlessly, the objective environment of human beings is coming to wear the expression of the commodity. At the same time, advertising seeks to disguise the commodity character of things. What resists the mendacious transfiguration of the commodity world is its distortion into allegory. The commodity wants to look itself in the face. It celebrates its incarnation in the whore.

The refunctioning [*Umfunktionierung*] of allegory in the commodity economy must be described. Baudelaire's enterprise was to make manifest the peculiar aura of commodities. He sought to humanize the commodity heroically. This endeavor has its counterpart in the concurrent bourgeois attempt to humanize the commodity sentimentally: to give it, like the human being, a home. The means used were the étuis, covers, and cases in which the domestic utensils of the time were sheathed.

The Baudelairean allegory—unlike the Baroque allegory—bears traces of the rage needed to break into this world, to lay waste its harmonious structures.

In Baudelaire, the heroic is the sublime manifestation—while spleen is the abject manifestation—of the demonic. Yet these categories of his aesthetic must be deciphered. They cannot be taken at face value.—Connection of the heroic to Latin antiquity.

[21]

Shock as a poetic principle in Baudelaire: the urban scene traced out by the *fantasque escrime*[41] of "Tableaux parisiens" is no longer a homeland. It is a spectacle, a foreign place.

How well can the image of the big city turn out when the inventory of its physical dangers is as incomplete as it is in Baudelaire?

Emigration as a key to the big city.

Baudelaire never wrote a poem on prostitution from the standpoint of the prostitute (compare [Brecht's] *Lesebuch für Städtebewohner* 5).[42]

The solitude of Baudelaire and the solitude of Blanqui.

Baudelaire's physiognomy as that of the mime.

•

Depict Baudelaire's misery against the background of his "aesthetic Passion."

Baudelaire's violent temper goes hand in hand with his destructive animus. We get nearer the matter when we recognize that here, too, in these bursts of anger, there is *un étrange sectionnement du temps.*[43]

The basic motif of Jugendstil is the transfiguration of infertility. The body is portrayed, preferably, in its prepubescent forms. This idea is to be linked to the regressive interpretation of technology.

Lesbian love carries spiritualization forth into the very womb of the woman. There it raises its lily-banner of "pure" love, which knows no pregnancy and no family.

The title *Les Limbes* should perhaps be dealt with in the first part, so that each part contains a commentary on a title; *Les Lesbiennes,* in the second part; and *Les Fleurs du mal,* in the third.[44]

[22]

Baudelaire's reputation—unlike the more recent fame of Rimbaud, for example—has not yet waned. The uncommon difficulty one encounters when approaching the core of Baudelaire's poetry can be summed up by the formula: in this poetry, nothing yet is outdated.

The signature of heroism in Baudelaire: to live in the heart of unreality (semblance). In keeping with this is the fact that Baudelaire knew nothing of nostalgia. Kierkegaard!

Baudelaire's poetry reveals the new in the ever-selfsame, and the ever-selfsame in the new.

•

Show with maximum force how the idea of eternal recurrence emerged at about the same time in the worlds of Baudelaire, Blanqui, and Nietzsche. In Baudelaire, the accent is on the new, which is wrested with heroic effort from the "ever-selfsame"; in Nietzsche, it is on the "ever-selfsame" which the human being faces with heroic composure. Blanqui is far closer to Nietzsche than to Baudelaire; but in his work, resignation predominates. In Nietzsche, this experience is projected onto a cosmological plane, in his thesis that nothing new will occur.

[23]

Baudelaire would never have written poems if he'd had nothing more than the usual motives poets have for writing poetry.

This study will need to furnish the historical projection of the experiences underlying *Les Fleurs du mal.*

Some very precise observations by Adrienne Monnier: his specifically French quality—*la rogne.*[45] She sees him as a man in revolt, comparing him to Fargue: "maniacal, rebelling against his own impotence, and aware of doing so."[46] She also mentions Céline. *Gauloiserie* is the French quality in Baudelaire.[47]

Another observation by Adrienne Monnier: Baudelaire's readers are men. His work does not appeal to women. For men, he represents the image and transcendence of the *côté ordurier* of their instinctual life.[48] Indeed, the Passion of Baudelaire takes on this aspect for many readers, as a redemption of certain sides of their instinctual life.

For the dialectician, what matters is having the wind of world history in one's sails. For him, thinking means setting the sails. What is important is *how* they are set. Words are for him merely the sails. The way they are set turns them into concepts.

[24]

The uninterrupted resonance which *Les Fleurs du mal* has found up through the present day is closely linked to a certain aspect of the big city, which here entered poetry for the first time. It is the aspect least of all expected. What makes itself felt through the evocation of Paris in Baudelaire's verse is the infirmity and decrepitude of this great city. This is perhaps nowhere more perfectly conveyed than in "Le Crépuscule du matin"; but the aspect itself is common to almost all the poems in "Tableaux parisiens." It is expressed in the transparency of the city, as conjured up by "Le Soleil," no less than in the effect of contrast in "Rêve parisien."

The crucial basis of Baudelaire's production is the tension between an extremely heightened sensitivity and an extremely intense contemplation. This tension is reflected theoretically in the doctrine of *correspondances* and in the principle of allegory. Baudelaire never made the slightest attempt to establish any sort of relations between these two forms of speculation, both of the greatest concern to him. His poetry springs from the interaction of the two tendencies, which are rooted in his temperament. What first aroused interest in his work (Pechméja),[49] and lived on in *poésie pure,* was the sensitive side of his genius.

[25]

Silence as aura. Maeterlinck pushes the unfolding of the auratic to the point of absurdity.[50]

Brecht remarked that, in speakers of Romance languages, a refinement of the sensorium does not diminish the power of apprehension. In those who speak German, on the other hand, the refinement and development of the capacity for enjoyment is always purchased with a decline in the power of apprehension. The capacity for pleasure loses in concentration what it gains in sensibility. This observation apropos of the *odeur de futailles* in "Le Vin des chiffonniers."[51]

Still more important is the following observation: the eminent sensual refinement of a Baudelaire has nothing at all to do with any sort of coziness. This fundamental incompatibility of sensual pleasure with what is called *Gemütlichkeit* is the criterion for a true culture of the senses. Baudelaire's snobbism is the eccentric formula for this steadfast repudiation of complacency, and his "satanism" is nothing other than the constant readiness to subvert this habit of mind wherever and whenever it should appear.

[26]

Les Fleurs du mal does not contain even the rudiments of a visual description of Paris. That is enough to distinguish it emphatically from later "city poetry." Baudelaire mingles his voice with the roar of the city as one might mingle one's voice with the breakers on the shore. His speech is clear to the extent that it is perceptible. But something merging with it muffles its sound. And it remains mingled with this roar, which carries it onward while endowing it with a dark meaning.

For Baudelaire, the *fait divers* is the yeast that causes the great urban masses to rise in his imagination.

What proved so fascinating to Baudelaire in Latin literature, particularly that of the late period, may have been, in part, the way in which late Latin literature used the names of gods—a usage that was less abstract than allegorical. In this he may have recognized a procedure with affinities to his own.

Baudelaire's opposition to nature involves first and foremost a deep-seated protest against the "organic." Compared to the inorganic, organic nature has only the most limited instrumental quality. It is less available for use. Compare Courbet's testimony that Baudelaire's appearance was different every day.[52]

[27]

The heroic bearing of Baudelaire is intimately related to that of Nietzsche. Although Baudelaire adheres to Catholicism, his experience of the universe is in exact accord with the experience comprehended by Nietzsche in the phrase "God is dead."

The sources nourishing Baudelaire's heroic bearing spring from the deepest foundations of the social order that was being established in the mid-nineteenth century. They consist solely of the experiences which apprised Baudelaire of the radical changes taking place in the conditions of artistic production. These changes consisted in the fact that the commodity form was being far more directly and forcefully expressed in the work of art—and the form of the masses expressed in its public—than ever before. These changes, in conjunction with others in the realm of art, contributed more than anything else to the decline of lyric poetry. It is the unique distinction of *Les Fleurs du mal* that Baudelaire responded to these altered conditions with a book of poems. This is also the most extraordinary example of heroic conduct to be found in the course of his existence.

"L'appareil sanglant de la Destruction":[53] the household effects scattered, in the innermost chamber of Baudelaire's poetry, at the feet of the whore who has inherited all the powers of Baroque allegory.

[28]

The brooder whose startled gaze falls on the fragment in his hand becomes an allegorist.

•

A question to be reserved until the end: How is it possible that a stance seemingly so "untimely" as allegory should have taken such a prominent place in the poetic work of the century?

Allegory should be shown as the antidote to myth. Myth was the comfortable route from which Baudelaire abstained. A poem like "La Vie antérieure," whose very title invites every sort of compromise, shows how far removed Baudelaire was from myth.

End with the Blanqui quotation, "Hommes du dix-neuvième siècle . . ."[54]

To the image of "rescue" belongs the firm, seemingly brutal grasp.

The dialectical image is that form of the historical object which satisfies Goethe's requirements for a synthetic object.[55]

[29]

As someone dependent on handouts, Baudelaire put this society continuously to the test. His artificially maintained dependence on his mother had not only a psychological cause (underscored by psychoanalysts) but a social one.

Important to the idea of eternal recurrence is the fact that the bourgeoisie no longer dared count on the future development of the system of production which they had set in motion. Zarathustra's idea of eternal recurrence, and the embroidered pillowcase-motto "Just fifteen little minutes," are complementary.

Fashion is the eternal recurrence of the new.—Yet can motifs of redemption be found specifically in fashion?

•

The interior, in Baudelaire's poems, is often inspired by the dark side of the bourgeois interior. Its opposite is the transfigured interior of Jugendstil. Proust, in his observations, touched only on the former.[56]

Baudelaire's aversion to travel makes the preponderance of exotic images in many of his poems all the more remarkable. In this predominance his melancholy finds expression. It also attests to the strength of the claim which the auratic element made on his sensibility. "Le Voyage" is an abjuration of travel.

The correspondence between antiquity and modernity is the sole constructive concept of history in Baudelaire. It excluded, more than contained, a dialectical conception.

[30]

An observation by Leiris: the word *familier* in Baudelaire is full of mystery and disquiet, standing for something it had never stood for before.[57]

One of the hidden anagrams of Paris in "Spleen (I)" is the word *mortalité*.[58]

The first line of "La Servante au grand coeur": the words "dont vous étiez *jalouse*"[59] do not carry the stress one would expect. The voice draws back, as it were, from *jaloux*. And this ebbing of the voice is something highly characteristic of Baudelaire.

A remark by Leiris: the noise of Paris is not communicated through the numerous literal references—such as *lourds tombereaux*[60]—but penetrates the rhythm of Baudelaire's verse.

•

The line "Où tout, même l'horreur, tourne aux enchantements" could hardly be better exemplified than by Poe's description of the crowd.[61]

Leiris remarks that *Les Fleurs du mal* is the most irreducible book of poetry. This could be understood to mean that the experience underlying it has scarcely at all been converted into something else.

[31]

Male impotence: the key figure of solitude. Under its aegis the stagnation of productive forces is enacted—an abyss divides the human being from others.

Fog as the consolation of solitude.

The "vie antérieure"[62] opens a temporal abyss within things; solitude opens a spatial abyss before the human being.

The tempo of the flâneur should be compared with that of the crowd, as described by Poe. It is a protest against the tempo of the crowd. Compare the fashion for tortoises in 1839 (D2a,1).[63]

Boredom in the production process arises as the process accelerates (through machinery). The flâneur protests against the production process with his ostentatious nonchalance.

One encounters an abundance of stereotypes in Baudelaire, as in the Baroque poets.

A series of types, from the national guardsman Mayeux through Vireloque and Baudelaire's ragpicker to Gavroche and the *lumpen-proletarian* Ratapoil.[64]

•

Look for an invective against Cupid. In connection with the allegorist's invectives against mythology, which so precisely match those of early medieval clerics. In the passage in question, Cupid might have the epithet *joufflu*.[65] Baudelaire's aversion to this figure has the same roots as his hatred for Béranger.[66]

Baudelaire's candidacy for the Académie was a sociological experiment.

The doctrine of eternal recurrence as a dream of the immense discoveries imminent in the field of reproduction technology.

[32]

If, as generally agreed, the human longing for a purer, more innocent, more spiritual existence than the one given to us necessarily seeks some pledge of that existence in nature, this is usually found in some entity from the plant or animal kingdom. Not so in Baudelaire. His dream of such an existence disdains community with any terrestrial nature and holds only to clouds. This is explicit in the first prose poem in *Le Spleen de Paris*. Many of his poems contain cloud motifs. What is most appalling is the defilement of the clouds ("La Béatrice").

Les Fleurs du mal bears a hidden resemblance to Dante in the emphatic way it traces the itinerary of a creative life. There is no other book of poems in which the poet presents himself with so little vanity and so much force. According to Baudelaire's experience, autumn is the true ground of creative genius. The great poet is, as it were, a creature of autumn. "L'Ennemi," "Le Soleil."

"De l'essence du rire"[67] contains nothing other than the theory of satanic laughter. In this essay, Baudelaire goes so far as to view even smiling from the standpoint of such laughter. Contemporaries often testified to something frightful in his own manner of laughing.

The dialectic of commodity production: the product's novelty (as a stimulant to demand) takes on a significance hitherto unknown; in mass production the ever-selfsame manifests itself overtly for the first time.

[32a]

The souvenir [*Andenken*] is a secularized relic.

The souvenir is the complement to "isolated experience."[68] In it is precipitated the increasing self-estrangement of human beings, whose past is inventoried as dead effects. In the nineteenth century, allegory withdrew from the world around us to settle in the inner world. The relic comes from the cadaver; the souvenir comes from the defunct experience [*Erfahrung*] which thinks of itself, euphemistically, as living [*Erlebnis*].

Les Fleurs du mal is the last book of poems to have had an impact throughout Europe. Before that, perhaps Ossian? *Das Buch der Lieder?*[69]

Allegorical emblems return as commodities.

Allegory is the armature of modernity.

There is, in Baudelaire, a reluctance to awaken echoes—whether in the soul or in space. His poetry is occasionally coarse, but is never sonorous. His mode of expression deviates as little from his experience as the gestures of a consummate prelate deviate from his person.

[33]

Jugendstil appears as the productive misunderstanding by which the "new" became the "modern." Naturally, this misunderstanding originates in Baudelaire.

Modernity stands opposed to antiquity; the new, to what is always the same. (Modernity: the masses. Antiquity: the city of Paris.)

The streets of Paris, in Meryon's rendering: chasms—and high above them float the clouds.

The dialectical image is an image that flashes up. The image of what has been—in this case, the image of Baudelaire—must be caught in this way, flashing up in the now of its recognizability.[70] The redemption enacted in this way, and solely in this way, is won only against the perception of what is being irredeemably lost. The metaphorical passage from the introduction to Jochmann should be introduced here.[71]

[34]

The concept of exclusive copyright was not nearly so widely accepted in Baudelaire's day as it is today. Baudelaire often republished his poems two or three times without having anyone object. He ran into difficulties with this only toward the end of his life, with the *Petits poèmes en prose.*

Inspiration for Hugo: words present themselves to him, like images, as a surging mass. Inspiration for Baudelaire: words appear in their place as if by magic—the result of a highly studied procedure. In this procedure, the image plays a decisive role.

•

Something that must be clarified: the importance of heroic melancholy for intoxication [*Rausch*] and for the inspiration of images.

When yawning, the human being himself opens like an abyss. He makes himself resemble the time stagnating around him.

What good is talk of progress to a world sinking into rigor mortis? Baudelaire found the experience of such a world set down with incomparable power in the work of Poe, who thus became irreplaceable for him. Poe described the world in which Baudelaire's whole poetic enterprise had its prerogative. Compare the Medusa's head in Nietzsche.

[35]

Eternal recurrence is an attempt to combine the two antinomic principles of happiness: that of eternity and that of the "yet again."—The idea of eternal recurrence conjures the speculative idea (or phantasmagoria) of happiness from the misery of the times. Nietzsche's heroism has its counterpoint in the heroism of Baudelaire, who conjures the phantasmagoria of modernity from the misery of philistinism.

The concept of progress must be grounded in the idea of catastrophe. That things are "status quo" *is* the catastrophe. It is not an ever-present possibility but what in each case is given. Strindberg's idea: hell is not something that awaits us, but *this life here and now.*

Redemption depends on the tiny fissure in the continuous catastrophe.

The reactionary attempt to turn technologically determined forms—that is, dependent variables—into constants can be found not only in Jugendstil but in Futurism.

•

The development which led Maeterlinck, in the course of a long life, to an attitude of extreme reaction is a logical one.

Explore the question of how far the extremes to be encompassed within redemption are those of "too early" and "too late."

That Baudelaire was hostile to progress was the indispensable condition for his ability to master Paris in his verse. Compared to his poetry of the big city, later work of this type is marked by weakness, not least where it sees the city as the throne of progress. But: Walt Whitman??

[36]

It was the weighty social grounds for male impotence which in fact turned the Golgotha-way trod by Baudelaire into one socially ordained. Only this explains why, to sustain him on his travels, he received a precious old coin from the treasury amassed by European society. On its face it showed the figure of Death; on its reverse, Melancholia sunk in brooding meditation. This coin was allegory.

Baudelaire's Passion as an *image d'Epinal* in the style of the usual Baudelaire literature.

"Rêve parisien" as a fantasy about productive forces that have been shut down.

Machinery in Baudelaire becomes a figure for destructive powers. The human skeleton is not the least part of such machinery.

The residential character of the rooms in early factories, despite all their impractical barbarity, has this one peculiarity: the factory owner can be imagined in them as a kind of incidental figure in a painting, sunk in contemplation of his machines and dreaming not only of his own future greatness but of theirs. Fifty years after Baudelaire's death, this dream was over.

Baroque allegory sees the corpse only from the outside. Baudelaire sees it also from within.

That the stars are absent from Baudelaire's poetry is the most conclusive sign of its tendency to eradicate semblance [*Tendenz seiner Lyrik zur Scheinlosigkeit*].

[37]

That Baudelaire was attracted to late Latin culture may have been linked to the strength of his allegorical intention.

Considering the importance of forbidden forms of sexuality in Baudelaire's life and work, it is remarkable that the bordello plays not the slightest part in either his private documents or his work. There is no counterpart, within this sphere, to a poem such as "Le Jeu." (But see "Les Deux Bonnes Soeurs.")[72]

The introduction of allegory must be deduced from the situation in which art is conditioned by technological development; and the melancholic temper of this poetry can be portrayed only in terms of allegory.

In the flâneur, one might say, is reborn the sort of idler that Socrates picked out from the Athenian marketplace to be his interlocutor. Only, there is no longer a Socrates, so there is no one to address the idler. And the slave labor that guaranteed him his leisure has likewise ceased to exist.

The key to Baudelaire's relationship with Gautier should be sought in the younger man's more or less clear awareness that even in art his destructive impulse encounters no inviolable limit. For the allegorical intention, this limit was certainly not absolute. Baudelaire's reactions to the neo-pagan school reveal this situation clearly. He could hardly have written his essay on Dupont, had not his own critique of the concept of art been at least as radical as Dupont's.[73] Baudelaire tried successfully to conceal these tendencies with his invocation of Gautier.

[38]

The peculiarities both of Hugo's faith in progress and of his pantheism were surely not unrelated to the messages received in spiritualist séances. This dubious circumstance, however, pales before that of the constant communication between his poetry and the world of poltergeists. In fact, the special quality of his poetry lay far less in its real or apparent adoption of motifs of spiritualist revelation than in the fact that his poetry was exhibited, so to speak, before the spirit world. This spectacle is difficult to reconcile with the attitude of other poets.

In Hugo, it is through the crowd that nature exercises its elemental rights over the city. (J32,1.)

On the concept of the *multitude* and the relationship between "the crowd" and "the masses."

Baudelaire's original interest in allegory is not linguistic but optical. "Les images, ma grande, ma primitive passion."[74]

Question: When does the commodity begin to emerge in the image of the city? Here it would be very important to have statistics on the intrusion of display windows into building façades.

[39]

Mystification, in Baudelaire, is a form of apotropaic magic, similar to the lie among prostitutes.

Many of his poems have their incomparable moment at the beginning—where they are, so to speak, new. This has often been pointed out.

The mass-produced article was Baudelaire's model. His "Americanism" has its firmest foundation here. He wanted to create a *poncif*. Lemaître assured him that he had succeeded.

The commodity has taken the place of the allegorical mode of apprehension.

In the form which prostitution has taken in big cities, the woman appears not only as a commodity but, in the most graphic sense, as a mass-produced article. This can be seen in the way the individual expression is artificially concealed by a professional one, as happens with the use of cosmetics. That this aspect of the whore was sexually crucial for Baudelaire is indicated not least by the fact that the background for his numerous evocations of the whore is never the bordello, but often the street.

[40]

In Baudelaire, it is very important that the "new" in no way contributes to progress. At any rate, serious attempts to come to terms with the idea of progress are hardly ever found in his work. His hatred was directed above all at "faith in progress," as at a heresy, a false teaching, not a commonplace error. Blanqui, on the other hand, displays no antipathy to the belief in progress; he quietly heaps scorn on the idea. One should not necessarily conclude from this that he was untrue to his political credo. The activities of a professional conspirator like Blanqui certainly do not presuppose any belief in progress—they merely presuppose a determination to do away with present injustice. This firm resolve to snatch humanity at the last moment from the catastrophe looming at every turn is characteristic of Blanqui—more so than of any other revolutionary politician of the time. He always refused to develop plans for what comes "later." One can easily see how Baudelaire's conduct in 1848 accords with all this.

[41]

Confronted with the scant success of his work, Baudelaire threw himself into the bargain. He flung himself after his work, and thus, to the end, confirmed in his own person what he had said: that prostitution was an unavoidable necessity for the poet.

One of the decisive questions for an understanding of Baudelaire's poetry is how the face of prostitution was changed by the rise of the great cities. For this much is certain: Baudelaire gives expression to the change—it is one of the great themes of his poetry. With the emergence of big cities, prostitution comes to possess new arcana. Among the earliest of these is the labyrinthine character of the city itself. The labyrinth, whose image has become part of the flâneur's flesh and blood, seems to have been given, as it were, a colored border by prostitution. The first arcanum known to prostitution is thus the mythical aspect of the city as labyrinth. This includes, as one would expect, an image of the Minotaur at its center. That he brings death to the individual is not the essential fact. What is crucial is the image of the deadly power he embodies. And this, too, for inhabitants of the great cities, is something new.

[42]

Les Fleurs du mal as an arsenal: Baudelaire wrote certain of his poems in order to destroy others written before his own. Valéry's well-known remarks could be developed further in this direction.[75]

To elaborate on Valéry's comments: It is highly significant that Baudelaire encountered competitive relations in the production of poetry. Of course, personal rivalries between poets are as old as the hills. But here the rivalry is transposed into competition on the open market. The goal was victory in that arena, not the patronage of a prince. In this context, it was a real discovery for Baudelaire that he was not competing against *individuals*. The disorganization of poetic schools, of "styles," is the complement of the open market, which reveals itself to the poet as his audience. In Baudelaire, the public as such comes into view for the first time—this was the reason he did not fall victim to the "semblance" of poetic schools. And conversely, because the "school" was for him a mere epiphenomenon, he experienced the public as a more authentic reality.

[43]

Difference between allegory and parable.

Baudelaire and Juvenal. The decisive difference is that when Baudelaire describes degeneracy and vice, he always includes himself. The gestus of the satirist is foreign to him. Admittedly, this applies only to Les Fleurs du mal, which differs entirely in this regard from the prose pieces.

Fundamental observations on the relation between the theoretical writings of poets and their poetry. In the latter, they disclose a region of their inner life which is not generally available to their reflection.

This should be demonstrated in Baudelaire—with reference to others such as Kafka and Hamsun.[76]

The lastingness of a literary work's effect is inversely proportional to the obviousness of its material content. (Its truth content? See the study on *Elective Affinities*.)[77]

Les Fleurs du mal undoubtedly gained importance from the fact that Baudelaire left no novel.

[44]

Melanchthon's phrase "Melencolia illa heroica" provides the most perfect definition of Baudelaire's genius.[78] But melancholy in the nineteenth century was different from what it had been in the seventeenth. The key figure in early allegory is the corpse. In late allegory, it is the "souvenir" [*Andenken*]. The "souvenir" is the schema of the commodity's transformation into an object for the collector. The *correspondances* are, objectively, the endlessly varied resonances between one souvenir and the others. "J'ai plus de souvenirs que si j'avais mille ans."[79]

The heroic tenor of Baudelairean inspiration lies in the fact that in his work memory gives way to the souvenir. In his work, there is a striking lack of "childhood memories."

Baudelaire's eccentric individuality was a mask behind which he tried to conceal—out of shame, one might say—the supra-individual necessity of his way of life and, to a certain extent, his fate.

From the age of seventeen, Baudelaire led the life of a *littérateur*. One cannot say that he ever thought of himself as an "intellectual" [*Geistiger*], or devoted himself to "the life of the mind" [*das Geistige*]. The registered trademark for artistic production had not yet been devised.

[45]

On the truncated endings of materialist studies (in contrast to the close of the book on the Baroque.)[80]

The allegorical viewpoint, which generated literary style in the seventeenth century, had lost this role by the nineteenth. As an allegorist, Baudelaire was isolated, and his isolation was in a sense that of a straggler. (In his theories, this belatedness is sometimes provocatively emphasized.) If the stylistic impetus of allegory in the nineteenth century was slight, so too was its tendency to encourage routine, which left such diverse traces in the seventeenth century. To some extent, this routine mitigated the destructive tendency of allegory—its stress on the artwork's fragmentary nature.

Written ca. April 1938–February 1939; unpublished in Benjamin's lifetime. *Gesammelte Schiften,* I, 655–690. Translated by Edmund Jephcott and Howard Eiland.

On Some Motifs in Baudelaire

I

Baudelaire envisaged readers to whom the reading of lyric poetry would present difficulties. The introductory poem of *Les Fleurs du mal* is addressed to these readers. Willpower and the ability to concentrate are not their strong points. What they prefer is sensual pleasure; they are familiar with the "spleen" which kills interest and receptiveness. It is strange to come across a lyric poet who addresses himself to such readers—the least rewarding type of audience. There is of course a ready explanation for this. Baudelaire wanted to be understood; he dedicates his book to those who are like him. The poem addressed to the reader ends with the salutation: "Hypocrite lecteur,—mon semblable,—mon frère!"[1] It might be more fruitful to put it another way and say: Baudelaire wrote a book which from the very beginning had little prospect of becoming an immediate popular success. The kind of reader he envisaged is described in the introductory poem, and this turned out to have been a far-sighted judgment. He would eventually find the reader his work was intended for. This situation—the fact, in other words, that the conditions for the reception of lyric poetry have become increasingly unfavorable—is borne out by three particular factors, among others. First of all, the lyric poet has ceased to represent the poet per se. He is no longer a "minstrel," as Lamartine still was; he has become the representative of a genre.[2] (Verlaine is a concrete example of this specialization; Rimbaud must already be regarded as an esoteric figure, a poet who, ex officio, kept a distance between his public and his work.)[3] Second, there has been no success on a mass scale in lyric poetry since Baudelaire. (The lyric poetry of Victor Hugo was still capable of evoking powerful reverberations when it first appeared. In Germany, Heine's *Buch der Lieder* marks a watershed.)[4] The third factor follows from this—namely, the greater coolness of the public, even toward the lyric poetry that has been handed down as part of its own cultural heritage. The period in question dates back roughly to the mid-nineteenth century. Throughout this span, the fame of *Les Fleurs du mal* has steadily increased. This book, which the author expected would be read by the least indulgent of readers and which was at first read by only a few indulgent ones, has, over the decades, acquired the stature of a classic and become one of the most widely printed ones as well.

If conditions for a positive reception of lyric poetry have become less favorable, it is reasonable to assume that only in rare instances does lyric poetry accord with the experience of its readers. This may be due to a change in the structure of their experience. Even though one may approve of this development, one may find it difficult to specify the nature of the change. Turning to philosophy for an answer, one encounters a strange situation. Since the end of the nineteenth century, philosophy has made a series of attempts to grasp "true" experience, as opposed to the kind that manifests itself in the standardized, denatured life of the civilized masses. These efforts are usually classified under the rubric of "vitalism." Their point of departure, understandably enough, has not been the individual's life in society. Instead they have invoked poetry, or preferably nature—most recently, the age of myths. Dilthey's book *Das Erlebnis und die Dichtung* represents one of the earliest of these efforts, which culminate with Klages and Jung, who made common cause with fascism.[5] Towering above this literature is Bergson's early monumental work, *Matière et mémoire*.[6] To a greater extent than the other writings in this field, it preserves links with empirical research. It is oriented toward biology. As the title suggests, it regards the structure of memory [*Gedächtnis*] as decisive for the philosophical structure of experience [*Erfahrung*].[7] Experience is indeed a matter of tradition, in collective existence as well as private life. It is the product less of facts firmly anchored in memory [*Erinnerung*] than of accumulated and frequently unconscious data that flow together in memory [*Gedächtnis*]. Of course, the historical determination of memory is not at all Bergson's intention. On the contrary, he rejects any historical determination of memory. He thus manages to stay clear of that experience from which his own philosophy evolved, or, rather, in reaction to which it arose. It was the alienating, blinding experience of the age of large-scale industrialism. In shutting out this experience, the eye perceives a complementary experience—in the form of its spontaneous afterimage, as it were. Bergson's philosophy represents an attempt to specify this afterimage and fix it as a permanent record. His philosophy thus indirectly furnishes a clue to the experience which presented itself undistorted to Baudelaire's eyes, in the figure of his reader.

II

The reader of *Matière et mémoire*, with its particular definition of the nature of experience in *durée*,[8] is bound to conclude that only a poet can be the adequate subject of such an experience. And it was indeed a poet who put Bergson's theory of experience to the test. Proust's work *A la Recherche du temps perdu* may be regarded as an attempt to produce experience, as Bergson imagines it, in a synthetic way under today's social conditions, for there is less and less hope that it will come into being in a natural way. Proust, incidentally, does not evade the question in his work. He even introduces a new factor, one that involves an immanent critique of Bergson. Bergson emphasized the antagonism between the *vita activa* and the specific *vita contemplativa* which arises from memory. But he leads us to believe that turning to the contemplative realization of the stream of life is a matter of free choice. From the start, Proust indicates his divergent view in his choice of terms. In his work the *mémoire pure* of Bergson's theory becomes a *mémoire involontaire*. Proust immediately confronts this involuntary memory with a voluntary memory, one that is in the service of the intellect. The first pages of his great novel are devoted to making this relationship clear. In the reflection which introduces the term, Proust tells us that for many years he had a very indistinct memory of the town of Combray, where he had spent part of his childhood. One afternoon, the taste of a kind of pastry called a *madeleine* (which he later mentions often) transported him back to the past, whereas before then he had been limited to the promptings of a memory which obeyed the call of conscious attention. This he calls *mémoire volontaire*. Its signal characteristic is that the information it gives about the past retains no trace of that past. "It is the same with our own past. In vain we try to conjure it up again; the efforts of our intellect are futile." In sum, Proust says that the past is situated "somewhere beyond the reach of the intellect and its field of operations, in some material object . . . , though we have no idea which one it is. And whether we come upon this object before we die, or whether we never encounter it, depends entirely on chance."[9]

According to Proust, it is a matter of chance whether an individual forms an image of himself, whether he can take hold of his experience. But there is nothing inevitable about the dependence on chance in this matter. A person's inner concerns are not by nature of an inescapably private character. They attain this character only after the likelihood decreases that one's external concerns will be assimilated to one's experience. Newspapers constitute one of many indications of such a decrease. If it were the intention of the press to have the reader assimilate the information it supplies as part of his own experience, it would not achieve its purpose. But its intention is just the opposite, and it is achieved: to isolate events from the realm in which they could affect the experience of the reader. The principles of journalistic information (newness, brevity, clarity, and, above all, lack of connection between the individual news items) contribute as much to this as the layout of the pages and the style of writing. (Karl Kraus never tired of demonstrating the extent to which the linguistic habitus of newspapers paralyzes the imagination of their readers.)[10] Another reason for the isolation of information from experience is that the former does not enter "tradition." Newspapers appear in large editions. Few readers can boast of having any information that another reader may need from them.—Historically, the various modes of communication have competed with one another. The replacement of the older relation by information, and of information by sensation, reflects the increasing atrophy of experience. In turn, there is a contrast between all these forms and the story, which is one of the oldest forms of communication. A story does not aim to convey an event per se, which is the purpose of information; rather, it embeds the event in the life of the storyteller in order to pass it on as experience to those listening. It thus bears the trace of the storyteller, much the way an earthen vessel bears the trace of the potter's hand.

Proust's eight-volume novel gives some idea of the effort it took to restore the figure of the storyteller to the current generation. Proust undertook this task with magnificent consistency. From the outset, this involved him in a fundamental problem: reporting on his own childhood. In saying that it was a matter of chance whether the problem could be solved at all, he took the measure of its difficulty. In connection with these reflections, he coined the phrase *mémoire involontaire*. This concept bears the traces of the situation that engendered it; it is part of the inventory of the individual who is isolated in various ways. Where there is experience [*Erfahrung*] in the strict sense of the word, certain contents of the individual past combine in the memory [*Gedächtnis*] with material from the collective past.[11] Rituals, with their ceremonies and their festivals (probably nowhere recalled in Proust's work), kept producing the amalgamation of these two elements of memory over and over again. They triggered recollection[12] at certain times and remained available to memory throughout people's lives. In this way, voluntary and involuntary recollection cease to be mutually exclusive.

III

In seeking a more substantial definition of what appears in Proust's *mémoire de l'intelligence* as a by-product of Bergson's theory, we would do well to go back to Freud. In 1921 Freud published his essay *Beyond the Pleasure Principle,* which hypothesizes a correlation between memory (in the sense of *mémoire involontaire*) and consciousness.[13] The following remarks, though based on that essay, are not intended to confirm it; we shall have to content ourselves with testing the fruitfulness of Freud's hypothesis in situations far removed from the ones he had in mind when he wrote. Such situations are more likely to have been familiar to Freud's pupils. Some of Reik's writings on his own theory of memory are in line with Proust's distinction between involuntary and voluntary recollection.[14] "The function of memory [*Gedächtnis*]," Reik writes, "is to protect our impressions; reminiscence [*Erinnerung*] aims at their dissolution. Memory is essentially conservative; reminiscence, destructive."[15] Freud's fundamental thought, on which these remarks are based, is the assumption that "emerging consciousness takes the place of a memory trace."[16] Therefore, "it would be the special characteristic of consciousness that, unlike what happens in all other systems of the psyche, the excitatory process does not leave behind a permanent change in its elements, but expires, as it were, in the phenomenon of becoming conscious." The basic formula of this hypothesis is that "becoming conscious and leaving behind a memory trace are incompatible processes within one and the same system." Rather, vestiges of memory are "often most powerful and most enduring when the incident which left them behind was one that never entered consciousness." Put in Proustian terms, this means that only what has not been experienced explicitly and consciously, what has not happened to the subject as an isolated experience [*Erlebnis*], can become a component of *mémoire involontaire*. According to Freud, the attribution of "permanent traces as the basis of memory" to processes of stimulation is reserved for "other systems," which must be thought of as different from consciousness. In Freud's view, consciousness as such receives no memory traces whatever, but has another important function: protection against stimuli. "For a living organism, protection against stimuli is almost more important than the reception of stimuli. The protective shield is equipped with its own store of energy and must above all strive to preserve the special forms of conversion of energy operating in it against the effects of the excessive energies at work in the external world—effects that tend toward an equalization of potential and hence toward destruction." The threat posed by these energies is the threat of shocks. The more readily consciousness registers these shocks, the less likely they are to have a traumatic effect. Psychoanalytic theory strives to understand the nature of these traumatic shocks "in terms of how they break through the shield that protects against stimuli." According to this theory, fright gains "significance" in proportion to the "absence of any preparedness for anxiety."

Freud's investigation was occasioned by the sort of dream that may afflict accident survivors—those who develop neuroses which cause them to relive the catastrophe in which they were involved. Dreams of this kind, according to Freud, "endeavor to master the stimulus retroactively, by developing the anxiety whose omission was the cause of the traumatic neurosis." Valéry seems to have had something similar in mind. The coincidence is worth noting, for Valéry was among those interested in the special functioning of psychic mechanisms under present-day conditions.[17] (Moreover, Valéry was able to reconcile this interest with his poetic production, which remained exclusively lyric. He thus emerges as the only author who goes back directly to Baudelaire.) "The impressions and sense perceptions of humans," Valéry writes, "actually belong in the category of surprises; they are evidence of an insufficiency in humans. . . .

Recollection is . . . an elemental phenomenon which aims at giving us the time for organizing 'the reception of stimuli' which we initially lacked."[18] The reception of shocks is facilitated by training in coping with stimuli; if need be, dreams as well as recollection may be enlisted. As a rule, however—so Freud assumes—this training devolves upon the wakeful consciousness, located in a part of the cortex which is "so frayed by the effect of the stimulus" that it offers the most favorable situation for the reception of stimuli. That the shock is thus cushioned, parried by consciousness, would lend the incident that occasions it the character of an isolated experience [*Erlebnis*], in the strict sense. If it were incorporated directly in the register of conscious memory, it would sterilize this incident for poetic experience [*Erfahrung*].

One wonders how lyric poetry can be grounded in experience [*einer Erfahrung*] for which exposure to shock [*Chockerlebnis*] has become the norm. One would expect such poetry to have a large measure of consciousness; it would suggest that a plan was at work in its composition. This is indeed true of Baudelaire's poetry; it establishes a connection between him and Poe, among his predecessors, and with Valéry, among his successors. Proust's and Valéry's reflections on Baudelaire complement each other providentially. Proust wrote an essay on Baudelaire which is actually surpassed in significance by certain reflections in his novels. In his "Situation de Baudelaire," Valéry supplies the classic introduction to *Les Fleurs du mal.* "Baudelaire's problem," he writes, "must have posed itself in these terms: 'How to be a great poet, but neither a Lamartine nor a Hugo nor a Musset.'[19] I do not say that this ambition was consciously formulated, but it must have been latent in Baudelaire's mind; it even constituted the essential Baudelaire. It was his *raison d'état*."[20] There is something odd about referring to "reason of state" in the case of a poet. There is something remarkable about it: the emancipation from isolated experiences [*Erlebnisse*]. Baudelaire's poetic production is assigned a mission. Blank spaces hovered before him, and into these he inserted his poems. His work cannot be categorized merely as historical, like anyone else's, but it intended to be so and understood itself as such.

IV

The greater the shock factor in particular impressions, the more vigilant consciousness has to be in screening stimuli; the more efficiently it does so, the less these impressions enter long experience [*Erfahrung*] and the more they correspond to the concept of isolated experience [*Erlebnis*]. Perhaps the special achievement of shock defense is the way it assigns an incident a precise point in time in consciousness, at the cost of the integrity of the incident's contents. This would be a peak achievement of the intellect; it would turn the incident into an isolated experience. Without reflection, there would be nothing but the sudden start, occasionally pleasant but usually distasteful, which, according to Freud, confirms the failure of the shock defense. Baudelaire has portrayed this process in a harsh image. He speaks of a duel in which the artist, just before being beaten, screams in fright. This duel is the creative process itself. Thus, Baudelaire placed shock experience [*Chockerfahrung*] at the very center of his art. This self-portrait, which is corroborated by evidence from several contemporaries, is of great significance. Since Baudelaire was himself vulnerable to being frightened, it was not unusual for him to evoke fright. Vallès tells us about his eccentric grimaces; on the basis of a portrait by Nargeot, Pontmartin establishes Baudelaire's alarming appearance; Claudel stresses the cutting quality he could give to his utterances; Gautier speaks of the italicizing Baudelaire indulged in when reciting poetry; Nadar describes his jerky gait.[21]

Psychiatry is familiar with traumatophile types. Baudelaire made it his business to parry the shocks, no matter what their source, with his spiritual and physical self. This shock defense is rendered in the image of combat. Baudelaire describes his friend Constantin Guys,[22] whom he visits when Paris is asleep: "How he stands there, bent over his table, scrutinizing the sheet of paper just as intently as he does the objects around him by day; how he *stabs away* with his pencil, his pen, his brush; how he spurts water from his glass to the ceiling and tries his pen on his shirt; how he pursues his work swiftly and intensely, as though he were afraid his images might escape him. Thus, he is combative even when alone, parrying his own blows." In the opening stanza of "Le Soleil," Baudelaire portrays himself engaged in just such fantastic combat; this is probably the only passage in *Les Fleurs du mal* that shows the poet at work.

Le long du vieux faubourg, où pendent aux masures
Les persiennes, abri des secrètes luxures,
Quand le soleil cruel frappe à traits redoublés
Sur la ville et les champs, sur les toits et les blés,
Je vais m'exercer seul à ma fantasque escrime,
Flairant dans tous les coins les hasards de la rime,
Trébuchant sur les mots comme sur les pavés,
Heurtant parfois des vers depuis longtemps rêvés.

[Through decrepit neighborhoods on the outskirts of town,
    where
Slatted shutters hang at the windows of hovels that shelter
    secret lusts;
At a time when the cruel sun beats down with redoubled
    force
On city and countryside, on rooftops and cornfields,
I go out alone to practice my fantastical fencing,
Scenting chances for rhyme on every street corner,
Stumbling over words as though they were cobblestones,
Sometimes knocking up against verses dreamed long ago.]

Shock is among those experiences that have assumed decisive importance for Baudelaire's personality. Gide has dealt with the intermittences between image and idea, word and thing, which are the real site of Baudelaire's poetic excitation.[23] Rivière has pointed to the subterranean shocks by which Baudelaire's poetry is shaken; it is as though they caused words to collapse.[24] Rivière has indicated such collapsing words.

> Et qui sait si les fleurs nouvelles que je rêve
> Trouveront dans ce sol lavé comme une grève
> Le mystique aliment qui *ferait* leur vigueur.

> [And who knows whether my dreams' new flowers
> Will find within this soil, washed like a shore,
> The mystic nourishment that *would make* them strong?]

Or: "Cybèle, qui les aime, *augmente ses verdures*" ["Cybele, who loves them, *augments her verdure*"]. Another example is this famous first line: "La servante au grand coeur dont vous étiez *jalouse*" ["That good-hearted servant of whom you were *jealous*"].

To give these covert laws their due outside his verses as well was Baudelaire's intention in *Spleen de Paris*, his collection of prose poems. In the book's dedication to the editor-in-chief of *La Presse*, Arsène Houssaye,[25] Baudelaire wrote: "Who among us has not dreamed, in his ambitious moments, of the miracle of a poetic prose, musical, yet without rhythm and without rhyme, supple and resistant enough to adapt to the lyrical stirrings of the soul, the undulations of reverie, and the sudden leaps of consciousness. This obsessive ideal is born, above all, from the experience of giant cities, from the intersecting of their myriad relations."

This passage suggests two insights. For one thing, it tells us about the close connection in Baudelaire between the figure of shock and contact with the urban masses. For another, it tells us what is really meant by these masses. They do not stand for classes or any sort of collective; rather, they are nothing but the amorphous crowd of passers-by, the people in the street.[26] This crowd, whose existence Baudelaire is always aware of, does not serve as the model for any of his works; but it is imprinted on his creativity as a hidden figure, just as it constitutes the figure concealed in the excerpt quoted above. We can discern the image of the fencer in it: the blows he deals are designed to open a path for him through the crowd. To be sure, the neighborhoods through which the poet of "Le Soleil" makes his way are deserted. But the hidden constellation—in which the profound beauty of that stanza becomes thoroughly transparent—is no doubt a phantom crowd: the words, the fragments, the beginnings of lines, from which the poet, in the deserted streets, wrests poetic booty.

V

The crowd: no subject was more worthy of attention from nineteenth-century writers. It was getting ready to take shape as a public consisting of broad strata that had acquired facility in reading. It gave out commissions; it wished to find itself portrayed in the contemporary novel, as wealthy patrons did in the paintings of the Middle Ages. The most successful author of the century met this demand out of inner necessity. To him, "the crowd" meant—almost in the ancient sense—the crowd of clients, the public. Victor Hugo was the first to address the crowd in his titles: *Les Misérables, Les Travailleurs de la mer.* In France, Hugo was the only writer able to compete with the serial novel. As is generally known, Eugène Sue was the master of this genre, which came to be the source of revelation for the man in the street. In 1850 an overwhelming majority elected him to the Chamber of Deputies as a representative from the city of Paris. It is no accident that the young Marx chose Sue's *Mystères de Paris* for an attack.[27] At an early date, he realized it was his task to forge the amorphous masses—then being wooed by an aesthetically appealing socialism—into the iron of the proletariat. Engels' description of these masses in his early writings may be regarded as a prelude, however modest, to one of Marx's themes. In his book *The Condition of the Working Class in England,* Engels writes:

> A town such as London, where a man may wander for hours together without reaching the beginning of the end, without meeting the slightest hint which could lead to the inference

that there is open country within reach, is a strange thing. This colossal centralization, this heaping together of two and a half million human beings at one point, has multiplied the power of these two and a half million people a hundredfold. . . . But the sacrifices which all this has cost become apparent later. After roaming the streets of the capital for a day or two, making headway with difficulty through the human turmoil and the endless lines of vehicles, after visiting the slums of the metropolis, one realizes for the first time that these Londoners have been forced to sacrifice the best qualities of their human nature in order to bring to pass all the marvels of civilization which crowd their city; that a hundred powers which slumbered within them have remained inactive, have been suppressed. . . . The very turmoil of the streets has something repulsive about it, something against which human nature rebels. The hundreds of thousands of people of all classes and ranks crowding past one another—are they not all human beings with the same qualities and powers, and with the same interest in being happy? . . . And still they crowd by one another as though they had nothing in common, nothing to do with one another, and their only agreement is a tacit one: that each should keep to his own side of the pavement, so as not to delay the opposing streams of the crowd, while it occurs to no man to honor another with so much as a glance. The brutal indifference, the unfeeling isolation of each person in his private interest becomes the more repellent and offensive, the more these individuals are crowded together within a limited space.[28]

This description differs markedly from those found in minor French masters, such as Gozlan, Delvau, or Lurine.[29] It lacks the skill and nonchalance which the flâneur displays as he moves among the crowds in the streets and which the journalist eagerly learns from him. Engels is dismayed by the crowd. He responds with a moral reaction, and an aesthetic one as well; the speed with which people rush past one another unsettles him. The charm of his description lies in the blend of unshakable critical integrity with old-fashioned views. The writer came from a Germany that was still provincial; he may never have been tempted to lose himself in a stream of people. When Hegel went to Paris for the first time, not long before his death, he wrote to his wife: "When I walk through the streets, people look just as they do in Berlin. They wear the same clothes, and their faces are about the same—they have the same aspect, but in a populous mass."[30] To move in this mass of people was natural for a Parisian. No matter how great the distance an individual wanted to keep from it, he still was colored by it and, unlike Engels, was unable to view it from without. As for Baudelaire, the masses were anything but external to him; indeed, it is easy to trace in his works his defensive reaction to their attraction and allure.

The masses had become so much a part of Baudelaire that it is rare to find a description of them in his works. His most important subjects are hardly ever encountered in descriptive form. As Desjardins so aptly put it, he was "more concerned with implanting the image in the memory than with adorning and elaborating it."[31] It is futile to search in Les Fleurs du mal or in Spleen de Paris for any counterpart to the portrayals of the city that Victor Hugo composed with such mastery. Baudelaire describes neither the Parisians nor their city. Avoiding such descriptions enables him to invoke the former in the figure of the latter. His crowds are always the crowds of a big city; his Paris is invariably overpopulated. It is this that makes him so superior to Barbier, whose descriptive method divorced the masses from the city.[32] In Tableaux parisiens, the secret presence of a crowd is demonstrable almost everywhere. When Baudelaire takes the dawn as his theme, the deserted streets emit something of that "silence of a throng" which Hugo senses in nocturnal Paris. As Baudelaire looks at the illustrations in the books on anatomy being sold on the dusty banks of the Seine, a crowd of departed souls takes the place of the singular skeletons on those pages. In the figures of the danse macabre, he sees a compact mass on the move. The heroism of the wizened old women whom the cycle "Les Petites Vieilles" follows on their rounds consists in their standing apart from the urban crowd, unable to keep up with it, no longer mentally participating in the present. The masses were an agitated veil, and Baudelaire views Paris through this veil. The presence of the masses informs one of the most famous poems in *Les Fleurs du mal.*

In the sonnet "A une passante," the crowd is nowhere named in either word or phrase. Yet all the action hinges on it, just as the progress of a sailboat depends on the wind.

> La rue assourdissante autour de moi hurlait.
> Longue, mince, en grand deuil, douleur majestueuse,
> Une femme passa, d'une main fastueuse
> Soulevant, balançant le feston et l'ourlet;
>
> Agile et noble, avec sa jambe de statue.
> Moi, je buvais, crispé comme un extravagant,
> Dans son oeil, ciel livide où germe l'ouragan,
> La douceur qui fascine et le plaisir qui tue.
>
> Un éclair . . . puis la nuit!—Fugitive beauté
> Dont le regard m'a fait soudainement renaître,
> Ne te verrai-je plus que dans l'éternité?
>
> Ailleurs, bien loin d'ici! Trop tard! *Jamais* peut-être!
> Car j'ignore où tu fuis, tu ne sais où je vais,
> O toi que j'eusse aimée, ô toi qui le savais!
>
> [The deafening street was screaming all around me.
> Tall, slender, in deep mourning—majestic grief—
> A woman made her way past, with fastidious hand
> Raising and swaying her skirt-border and hem;
>
> Agile and noble, with her statue's limbs.
> And me—I drank, contorted like a wild eccentric,
> From her eyes, that livid sky which gives birth to hurricanes,
> Gentleness that fascinates, pleasure that kills.

A lightning-flash . . . then night!—O fleeting beauty
Whose glance suddenly gave me new life,
Shall I see you again only in eternity?

Far, far from here! Too late! Or maybe *never*?
For I know not where you flee, you know not where I go,
O you whom I would have loved, O you who knew it too!]

In a widow's veil, mysteriously and mutely borne along by the
crowd, an unknown woman crosses the poet's field of vision. What
this sonnet conveys is simply this: far from experiencing the crowd as
an opposing, antagonistic element, the city dweller discovers in the
crowd what fascinates him. The delight of the urban poet is love—
not at first sight, but at last sight. It is an eternal farewell, which coincides in the poem with the moment of enchantment. Thus, the sonnet deploys the figure of shock, indeed of catastrophe. But the nature
of the poet's emotions has been affected as well. What makes his
body contract in a tremor—"crispé comme un extravagant," Baudelaire says—is not the rapture of a man whose every fiber is suffused
with eros; rather, it is like the sexual shock that can beset a lonely
man. The fact that "these verses could have been written only in a
big city," as Thibaudet put it, is not very meaningful.[33] They reveal
the stigmata which life in a metropolis inflicts upon love. Proust read
the sonnet in this light, and that is why he gave to his own echo of
the woman in mourning (which appeared to him one day in the
form of Albertine) the evocative epithet "La Parisienne." "When Albertine came into my room again, she wore a black satin dress. It
made her look pale. She resembled the kind of fiery yet pale Parisian
woman who is not used to fresh air and has been affected by living among the masses, possibly in an atmosphere of vice—the kind
you can recognize by her gaze, which seems unsteady if there is no
rouge on her cheeks."[34] This is the gaze—evident even as late as
Proust—of the object of a love which only a city dweller experiences,
which Baudelaire captured for poetry, and which one might not in-

frequently characterize as being spared, rather than denied, fulfillment.[35]

VI

A story by Poe which Baudelaire translated can be seen as the classic example among the older versions of the motif of the crowd. It is marked by certain peculiarities which, upon closer inspection, reveal aspects of social forces of such power and hidden depth that we may include them among the only ones that are capable of exerting both a subtle and a profound effect on artistic production. The story is entitled "The Man of the Crowd." It is set in London, and its narrator is a man who, after a long illness, ventures out again for the first time into the hustle and bustle of the city. On a late afternoon in autumn, he takes a seat by the window in a big London coffeehouse. He gazes around at the other customers and pores over advertisements in the paper, but he is mainly interested in the throng of people he sees through the window, surging past in the street.

> The latter is one of the principal thoroughfares of the city, and had been very much crowded during the whole day. But, as the darkness came on, the throng momently increased; and by the time the lamps were well lighted, two dense and continuous tides of population were rushing past the door. At this particular period of the evening I had never before been in a similar situation, and the tumultuous sea of human heads filled me, therefore, with a delicious novelty of emotion. I gave up, at length, all care of things within the hotel, and became absorbed in contemplation of the scene without.

Important as it is, let us disregard the narrative to which this is the prelude and examine the setting.

The appearance of the London crowd as Poe describes it is as gloomy and fitful as the light of the gas lamps overhead. This applies not only to the riffraff that is "brought forth from its den" as night falls. The employees of higher rank, "the upper clerks of staunch firms," Poe describes as follows: "They had all slightly bald heads, from which the right ears, long used to pen-holding, had an odd habit of standing off on end. I observed that they always removed or settled their hats with both hands, and wore watches, with short gold chains of a substantial and ancient pattern." Even more striking is his description of the crowd's movements.

> By far the greater number of those who went by had a satisfied business-like demeanour, and seemed to be thinking only of making their way through the press. Their brows were knit, and their eyes rolled quickly; when pushed against by fellow-wayfarers they evinced no symptom of impatience, but adjusted their clothes and hurried on. Others, still a numerous class, were restless in their movements, had flushed faces, and talked and gesticulated to themselves, as if feeling in solitude on account of the very denseness of the company around. When impeded in their progress, these people suddenly ceased muttering, but redoubled their gesticulations, and awaited, with an absent and overdone smile upon the lips, the course of the persons impeding them. If jostled, they bowed profusely to the jostlers, and appeared overwhelmed with confusion.[36]

One might think he was speaking of half-drunken wretches. Actually, they were "noblemen, merchants, attorneys, tradesmen, stock-jobbers."[37]

Poe's image cannot be called realistic. It shows a purposely distorting imagination at work, one that takes the text far from what is commonly advocated as the model of socialist realism. Barbier, perhaps one of the best examples of this type of realism, described things in a less eccentric way. Moreover, he chose a more transparent subject: the oppressed masses. Poe is not concerned with these; he deals with "people," pure and simple. For him, as for Engels, there was something menacing in the spectacle they presented. It is precisely this image of big-city crowds that became decisive for Baudelaire. If he succumbed to the force that attracted him to them and that made him, as a flâneur, one of them, he was nevertheless unable to rid himself of a sense of their essentially inhuman character. He becomes their accomplice even as he dissociates himself from them. He becomes deeply involved with them, only to relegate them to oblivion with a single glance of contempt. There is something compelling about this ambivalence, wherever he cautiously admits it. Perhaps the charm of his "Crépuscule du soir," so difficult to account for, is bound up with this.

VII

Baudelaire was moved to equate the man of the crowd, whom Poe's narrator follows throughout the length and breadth of nocturnal London, with the flâneur. It is hard to accept this view. The man of the crowd is no flâneur. In him, composure has given way to manic behavior. He exemplifies, rather, what had to become of the flâneur after the latter was deprived of the milieu to which he belonged. If London ever provided it for him, it was certainly not the setting described by Poe. In comparison, Baudelaire's Paris preserved some features that dated back to the old days. Ferries were still crossing the Seine at points that would later be spanned by bridges. In the year of Baudelaire's death, it was still possible for some entrepreneur to cater to the comfort of the well-to-do with a fleet of five hundred sedan chairs circulating about the city. Arcades where the flâneur would not be exposed to the sight of carriages, which did not recognize pedestrians as rivals, were enjoying undiminished popularity.[38] There was the pedestrian who would let himself be jostled by the crowd, but there was also the flâneur, who demanded elbow room and was unwilling to forgo the life of a gentleman of leisure. Let the many attend to their daily affairs; the man of leisure can indulge in the perambulations of the flâneur only if as such he is already out of place. He is as much out of place in an atmosphere of complete leisure as in the feverish turmoil of the city. London has its man of the crowd. His counterpart, as it were, is Nante, the boy who loiters on the street corner, a popular figure in Berlin before the March Revolution of 1848. The Parisian flâneur might be said to stand midway between them.[39]

How the man of leisure views the crowd is revealed in a short piece by E. T. A. Hoffmann, his last story, entitled "The Cousin's Corner Window."[40] It antedates Poe's story by fifteen years and is probably one of the earliest attempts to capture the street scene of a large city. The differences between the two pieces are worth noting. Poe's narrator watches the street from the window of a public coffee-house, whereas the cousin is sitting at home. Poe's observer succumbs to the fascination of the scene, which finally lures him out into the whirl of the crowd. The cousin in Hoffmann's tale, looking out from his corner window, has lost the use of his legs; he would not be able to go with the crowd even if he were in the midst of it. His attitude toward the crowd is, rather, one of superiority, inspired as it is by his observation post at the window of an apartment building. From this vantage point he scrutinizes the throng; it is market day, and all the passers-by feel in their element. His opera glasses enable him to pick out individual genre scenes. Employing the glasses is thoroughly in keeping with the inner disposition of their user. He confesses he would like to initiate his visitor in the "principles of the art of seeing."[41] This consists of an ability to enjoy *tableaux vivants*— a favorite pursuit of the Biedermeier period. Edifying sayings provide the interpretation.[42] One can then view Hoffmann's narrative as describing an attempt which at that time was being made. But it is obvious that the conditions under which it was made in Berlin prevented it from being a complete success. If Hoffmann had ever set foot in Paris or London, or if he had been intent on depicting the masses as such, he would not have focused on a marketplace; he would not have portrayed the scene as being dominated by women. He would perhaps have seized on the motifs that Poe derives from the swarming crowds under the gas lamps. Actually, there would have been no need for these motifs in order to bring out the uncanny or sinister elements that other students of the physiognomy of the big city have felt. A thoughtful observation by Heine is relevant here. "He was having a bad time with his eyes in the spring," wrote a correspondent in an 1838 letter to Varnhagen.[43] "On our last meeting, I accompanied him part of the way along the boulevard. The splendor and vitality of that unique thoroughfare moved me to boundless admiration, while, against this, Heine now laid weighty emphasis on the horrors attending this center of the world."[44]

VIII

Fear, revulsion, and horror were the emotions which the big-city crowd aroused in those who first observed it. For Poe, it has something barbaric about it; discipline barely manages to tame it. Later, James Ensor never tired of confronting its discipline with its wildness; he liked to depict military groups amid carnival mobs, and show them getting along in model fashion—that is, according to the model of totalitarian states, in which the police make common cause with looters.[45] Valéry, who had a fine eye for the cluster of symptoms called "civilization," has highlighted one of the pertinent facts. "The inhabitant of the great urban centers," he writes, "reverts to a state of savagery—that is, of isolation. The feeling of being dependent on others, which used to be kept alive by need, is gradually blunted in the smooth functioning of the social mechanism. Any improvement of this mechanism eliminates certain modes of behavior and emotions."[46] Comfort isolates; on the other hand, it brings those enjoying it closer to mechanization. In the mid-nineteenth century, the invention of the match brought forth a number of innovations which have one thing in common: a single abrupt movement of the hand triggers a process of many steps. This development is taking place in many areas. A case in point is the telephone, where the lifting of a receiver has taken the place of the steady movement that used to be required to crank the older models. With regard to countless movements of switching, inserting, pressing, and the like, the "snapping" by the photographer had the greatest consequences. Henceforth a touch of the finger sufficed to fix an event for an unlimited period of time. The camera gave the moment a posthumous shock, as it were. Haptic experiences of this kind were joined by optic ones, such as are supplied by the advertising pages of a newspaper or the traffic of a big city. Moving through this traffic involves the individual in a series of shocks and collisions. At dangerous intersections, nervous impulses flow through him in rapid succession, like the energy from a battery. Baudelaire speaks of a man who plunges into the crowd as into a reservoir of electric energy. Circumscribing the experience of the shock, he calls this man "a kaleidoscope endowed with consciousness."[47] Whereas Poe's passers-by cast glances in all directions, seemingly without cause, today's pedestrians are obliged to look about them so that they can be aware of traffic signals. Thus, technology has subjected the human sensorium to a complex kind of training. There came a day when a new and urgent need for stimuli was met by film. In a film, perception conditioned by shock [*chockförmige Wahrnehmung*] was established as a formal principle. What determines the rhythm of production on a conveyor belt is the same thing that underlies the rhythm of reception in the film.

Marx had good reason to stress the great fluidity of the connection between segments in manual labor. This connection appears to the factory worker on an assembly line in an independent, objectified form. The article being assembled comes within the worker's range of action independently of his volition, and moves away from him just as arbitrarily. "It is a common characteristic of all capitalist production. . . ," wrote Marx, "that the worker does not make use of the working conditions. The working conditions make use of the worker; but it takes machinery to give this reversal a technologically concrete form."[48] In working with machines, workers learn to coordinate "their own movements with the uniformly constant movements of an automaton." These words shed a peculiar light on the absurd kind of uniformity that Poe wants to impose on the crowd—uniformities of attire and behavior, but also a uniformity of facial expression. Those smiles provide food for thought. They are probably the familiar kind, as expressed these days in the phrase "keep smiling";[49] in Poe's story, they function as a mimetic shock absorber.—"All machine work," says Marx in the same passage cited above, "requires prior training of the workers." This training must be differentiated from practice. Practice, which was the sole determinant in handcrafting, still had a function in manufacturing. With practice as the basis, "each particular area of production finds its appropriate technical form in *experience* and *slowly* perfects it." To be sure, each area quickly crystallizes this form "as soon as a certain degree of maturity has been attained." On the other hand, this same system of manufacture produces "in every handicraft it appropriates a class of so-called unskilled laborers which the handicraft system strictly excluded. In developing a greatly simplified specialty to the point of virtuosity, at the cost of overall production capacity, it starts turning the lack of any development into a specialty. In addition to rankings, we get the simple division of workers into the skilled and the unskilled." The unskilled worker is the one most deeply degraded by machine training. His work has been sealed off from experience; practice counts for nothing in the factory.[50] What the amusement park achieves with its dodgem cars and other similar amusements is nothing but a taste of the training that the unskilled laborer undergoes in the factory—a sample which at times was for him the entire menu; for the art of the eccentric, an art in which an ordinary man could acquire training in places like an amusement park, flourished concomitantly with unemployment. Poe's text helps us understand the true connection between wildness and discipline. His pedestrians act as if they had adapted themselves to machines and could express themselves only automatically. Their behavior is a reaction to shocks. "If jostled, they bowed profusely to the jostlers."

IX

The shock experience [*Chockerlebnis*] which the passer-by has in the crowd corresponds to the isolated "experiences" of the worker at his machine. This does not entitle us to assume that Poe knew anything about industrial work processes. Baudelaire, at any rate, did not have the faintest notion of them. He was, however, captivated by a process in which the reflexive mechanism that the machine triggers in the workman can be studied closely, as in a mirror, in the idler. To say that this process is represented in games of chance may appear paradoxical. Where could one find a starker contrast than the one between work and gambling? Alain puts this convincingly when he writes: "It is inherent in the concept of gambling . . . that no game is dependent on the preceding one. Gambling cares nothing for any secured position. . . . It takes no account of winnings gained earlier, and in this it differs from work. Gambling gives short shrift to the weighty past on which work bases itself."[51] The work that Alain has in mind here is the highly specialized kind (which, like intellectual effort, probably retains certain features of handicraft); it is not that of most factory workers, and least of all unskilled work. The latter, to be sure, lacks any touch of adventure, of the mirage that lures the gambler. But it certainly does not lack futility, emptiness, an inability to complete something—qualities inherent in the activity of a wage slave in a factory. Even the worker's gesture produced by the automated work process appears in gambling, for there can be no game without the quick movement of the hand by which the stake is put down or a card is picked up. The jolt in the movement of a machine is like the so-called *coup* in a game of chance. The hand movement of the worker at the machine has no connection with the preceding gesture for the very reason that it repeats that gesture exactly. Since each operation at the machine is just as screened off from the preceding operation as a *coup* in a game of chance is from the one that preceded it, the drudgery of the laborer is, in its own way, a counterpart to the drudgery of the gambler. Both types of work are equally devoid of substance.

There is a lithograph by Senefelder which depicts a gambling club.[52] Not one of the individuals in the scene is pursuing the game in ordinary fashion. Each man is dominated by an emotion: one shows unrestrained joy; another, distrust of his partner; a third, dull despair; a fourth evinces belligerence; another is getting ready to take leave of the world. All these modes of conduct share a concealed characteristic: the figures presented show us how the mechanism to which gamblers entrust themselves seizes them body and soul, so that even in their private sphere, and no matter how agitated they may be, they are capable only of reflex actions. They behave like the pedestrians in Poe's story. They live their lives as automatons and resemble Bergson's fictitious characters who have completely liquidated their memories.

Baudelaire does not seem to have been a devotee of gambling, though he had words of sympathetic understanding, even homage, for those addicted to it. The motif he treats in his night piece "Le Jeu" [The Game] is integral to his view of modernity, and writing this poem formed part of his mission. In Baudelaire, the image of the gambler becomes the characteristically modern counterpart to the archaic image of the fencer; both are heroic figures to him. Ludwig Börne was looking at things through Baudelaire's eyes when he wrote: "If all the energy and passion . . . that are expended every year at Europe's gambling tables . . . were stored up, an entire Roman people and Roman history could be created from them. But this is precisely the point. Because every man is born a Roman, bourgeois society seeks to de- Romanize him, and this is why there are games of chance, as well as parlor games, novels, Italian operas, and fashionable newspapers."[53] Gambling did not become a common diversion among the bourgeoisie until the nineteenth century; in the eighteenth, only the aristocracy gambled. Games of chance, which were disseminated by Napoleon's armies, henceforth became a pastime "both among the fashionable set and among the thousands of people living unsettled lives in big-city basements"—became part of the spectacle in which Baudelaire claimed he saw the heroic, "as it typifies our age."

If we look at gambling from the psychological as well as the technical point of view, Baudelaire's conception of it appears even more significant. It is obvious that the gambler is out to win. Yet his desire to win and make money cannot really be termed a "wish" in the strict sense of the word. He may be inwardly motivated by greed or by some sinister design. At any rate, his frame of mind is such that he cannot make much use of experience.[54] A wish, however, appertains to the order of experience. "What one wishes for in one's youth, one has in abundance in old age," said Goethe.[55] The earlier in life one makes a wish, the greater one's chances that it will be fulfilled. The further a wish reaches out in time, the greater the hopes for its fulfillment. But it is experience [*Erfahrung*] that accompanies one to the far reaches of time, that fills and articulates time. Thus, a wish fulfilled is the crowning of experience. In folk symbolism, distance in space can take the place of distance in time; that is why the shooting star, which plunges into infinite space, has become the symbol of a fulfilled wish. The ivory ball that rolls into the *next* compartment, the *next* card that lies on top, are the very antithesis of a falling star. The instant in which a shooting star flashes before human eyes consists of the sort of time that Joubert has described with his customary assurance. "Time," he says, "is found even in eternity; but it is not earthly, worldly time. . . . It does not destroy; it merely completes."[56] It is the antithesis of time in hell, which is the province of those who are not allowed to complete anything they have started. The disrepute of games of chance is actually based on the fact that the player himself has a hand in it. (Someone who compulsively buys lottery tickets will not be shunned in the same way as someone who "gambles" in the stricter sense.)

This process of continually starting all over again is the regulative idea of gambling, as it is of work for wages. Thus, it is highly significant that in Baudelaire the second-hand of the clock—"la Seconde"—appears as the gambler's partner: "*Souviens-toi* que le Temps est un joueur avide / Qui gagne sans tricher, à tout coup! c'est la loi!"[57] ["*Keep in mind* that Time is a rabid gambler Who wins without cheating—every time! It's the law!"]. Elsewhere Satan himself takes the place of this second. In the poem "Le Jeu," compulsive gamblers are relegated to the silent corner of a cave that is doubtless part of Satan's realm:

> Voilà le noir tableau qu'en un rêve nocturne
> Je vis se dérouler sous mon oeil clairvoyant.
> Moi-même, dans un coin de l'antre taciturne,

Je me vis accoudé, froid, muet, enviant,
Enviant de ces gens la passion tenace.

[Here you see the hellish picture that one night in a dream
I saw unfolding before my clairvoyant eyes.
My own self was in a corner of the silent cave;
I saw myself, hunched, cold, wordless, envious,
Envying those people for their tenacious passion.]

The poet does not participate in the game. He stays in his corner, no happier than those who are playing. He too has been cheated out of his experience—a modern man. The only difference is that he rejects the narcotics the gamblers use to dull the consciousness that has forced them to march to the beat of the second-hand.[58]

Et mon coeur s'effraya d'envier maint pauvre homme
Courant avec ferveur à l'abîme béant,
Et qui, soûl de son sang, préférerait en somme
La douleur à la mort et l'enfer au néant!

[And my heart took fright at the idea of envying many a
    poor man
Who ran avidly to the gaping abyss,
And who, drunk with the pulsing of his blood, preferred
Suffering to death, and hell to nothingness!]

In this last stanza, Baudelaire presents impatience as the substrate of the passion for gambling. He found it in himself in its purest form. His violent temper had the expressiveness of Giotto's *Iracondia* at Padua.[59]

X

According to Bergson, it is the actualization of *durée* that rids man's soul of the obsession with time. Proust shared this belief, and from it he developed the lifelong exercises in which he strove to bring to light past things saturated with all the reminiscences that had penetrated his pores during the sojourn of those things in his unconscious. Proust was an incomparable reader of *Les Fleurs du mal,* for he sensed that it contained kindred elements. Familiarity with Baudelaire must include Proust's experience with his work. Proust writes: "Time is peculiarly dissociated in Baudelaire; only a very few days can appear, and they are significant ones. Thus, it is understandable why turns of phrase like 'if one evening' occur frequently in his works."[60] These significant days are days of the completing time, to paraphrase Joubert. They are days of recollection [*Eingedenken*], not marked by any immediate experience [*Erlebnis*]. They are not connected with other days, but stand out from time. As for their substance, Baudelaire has defined it in the notion of *correspondances*—a concept that in Baudelaire is concomitant but not explicitly linked with the notion of "modern beauty."[61]

Disregarding the scholarly literature on *correspondances* (the common property of mystics; Baudelaire encountered them in Fourier's writings), Proust no longer fusses about the artistic variations on this phenomenon that result from synaesthesia.[62] The important thing is that *correspondances* encompass a concept of experience which includes ritual elements. Only by appropriating these elements was Baudelaire able to fathom the full meaning of the breakdown which he, as a modern man, was witnessing. Only in this way was he able to recognize it as a challenge meant for him alone, a challenge that he incorporated in *Les Fleurs du mal.* If there really is a secret architecture in the book—and many speculations have been devoted to this question—the cycle of poems that opens the volume is probably oriented toward something irretrievably lost. This cycle includes two sonnets dealing with the same motif. The first, entitled "Correspondances," begins with these lines:

> La Nature est un temple où de vivants piliers
> Laissent parfois sortir de confuses paroles;

L'homme y passe à travers des forêts de symboles
Qui l'observent avec des regards familiers.

Comme de longs échos qui de loin se confondent
Dans une ténébreuse et profonde unité,
Vaste comme la nuit et comme la clarté,
Les parfums, les couleurs et les sons se répondent.

[Nature is a temple whose living pillars
Sometimes give forth a babel of words;
Man wends his way through forests of symbols
Which look at him with their familiar glances.

Like resounding echoes that blend from afar
In a somber, profound unity,
Vast as the night or as the brightness of day,
Scents, colors, and sounds respond to one another.]

What Baudelaire meant by *correspondances* can be described as an experience which seeks to establish itself in crisis-proof form. This is possible only within the realm of ritual. If it transcends this realm, it presents itself as the beautiful. In the beautiful, ritual value appears as the value of art.[63] *Correspondances* are the data of recollection— not historical data, but data of prehistory. What makes festive days great and significant is the encounter with an earlier life. Baudelaire recorded this in a sonnet entitled "La Vie antérieure." The images of caves and vegetation, of clouds and waves which are evoked at the beginning of this second sonnet rise from the warm vapor of tears—tears of homesickness. "The wanderer looks into the tear-veiled distance, and hysterical tears well up in his eyes," writes Baudelaire in his review of the poems of Marceline Desbordes-Valmore.[64] There are no simultaneous correspondences, such as were cultivated later by the Symbolists. What is past murmurs in the correspondences, and the canonical experience of them has its place in a previous life:

Les houles, en roulant les images des cieux,
Mêlaient d'une façon solennelle et mystique
Les tout-puissants accords de leur riche musique
Aux couleurs du couchant reflété par mes yeux.

C'est là que j'ai vécu.

[The breakers, tumbling the images of the heavens,
Blended, in a solemn and mystical way,
The all-powerful chords of their rich music
With the colors of the sunset reflected in my eyes.
There is where I lived.]

The fact that Proust's restorative will remains within the limits of earthly existence, whereas Baudelaire's transcends it, may be regarded as symptomatic of the vastly more elemental and powerful counterforces that announced themselves to Baudelaire. And it is likely he never achieved greater perfection than when he seems resigned to being overcome by them. "Recueillement" [Contemplation] traces the allegories of the old years set off against the deep sky: ". . . Vois se pencher les défuntes Années / Sur les balcons du ciel, en robes surannées." [". . . See the dead departed Years leaning over / Heaven's balconies, in old-fashioned dresses."] In these lines, Baudelaire resigns himself to paying homage to bygone times that escaped him in the guise of the outdated. When Proust in the last volume of his novel harks back to the sensation that suffused him at the taste of a madeleine, he imagines the years which appear on the balcony as being loving sisters of the years of Combray. "In Baudelaire . . . these reminiscences are even more numerous. It is obvious they do not occur by chance, and this, to my mind, is what gives them crucial importance. No one else pursues the interconnected *correspondances* with such leisurely care, fastidiously yet nonchalantly—in a woman's scent, for instance, in the fragrance of her hair or her breasts— *correspondances* which then inspire him with lines like 'the azure of the vast, vaulted sky' or 'a harbor full of flames and masts.'"[65] This passage is a confessional motto for Proust's work. It bears a relation to Baudelaire's work, which has assembled the days of recollection into a spiritual year.

But *Les Fleurs du mal* would not be what it is if all it contained were this success. It is unique because, from the inefficacy of the same consolation, the breakdown of the same fervor, the failure of the same work, it was able to wrest poems that are in no way inferior to those in which the *correspondances* celebrate their triumphs. "Spleen et idéal" is the first of the cycles in *Les Fleurs du mal*. The *idéal* supplies the power of recollection; *spleen* rallies the multitude of the seconds against it. It is their commander, just as the devil is the lord of the flies. One of the "Spleen" poems, "Le Goût du néant" [The Taste of Nothingness], says: "Le Printemps adorable a perdu son odeur!" ["Spring, the beloved, has lost its scent!"] Here Baudelaire expresses something extreme with extreme discretion; this makes the line unmistakably his. The word *perdu* acknowledges that the experience he once shared is now collapsed into itself. The scent is the inaccessible refuge of *mémoire involontaire*. It is unlikely to associate itself with a visual image; out of all possible sensual impressions, it will ally itself only with the same scent. If the recognition of a scent can provide greater consolation than any other memory, this may be because it deeply anesthetizes the sense of time. A scent may drown entire years in the remembered odor it evokes. This imparts a sense of boundless desolation to Baudelaire's verse. For someone who is past experiencing, there is no consolation. Yet it is this very inability to experience that explains the true nature of rage. An angry man "won't listen." His prototype, Timon, rages against people indiscriminately; he is no longer capable of telling his proven friend from his mortal enemy. Barbey d'Aurevilly very perceptively recognized this habit of mind in Baudelaire, calling him "a Timon with the genius of Archilochus."[66] The rage explodes in time to the ticking of the seconds that enslaves the melancholy man. "Et le Temps m'engloutit minute par minute, / Comme la neige immense un corps pris de roideur." ["And, minute by minute, Time engulfs me, / The way an immense snowfall engulfs a body grown stiff."] These lines immediately follow the ones quoted above. In spleen, time is reified: the minutes cover a man like snowflakes. This time is historyless, like that of the *mémoire involontaire*. But in spleen the perception of time is supernaturally keen. Every second finds consciousness ready to intercept its shock.[67]

Although chronological reckoning subordinates duration to regularity, it cannot prevent heterogeneous, conspicuous fragments from remaining within it. Combining recognition of a quality with measurement of quantity is the accomplishment of calendars, where spaces for recollection are left blank, as it were, in the form of holidays. The man who loses his capacity for experiencing feels as though he has been dropped from the calendar. The big-city dweller knows this feeling on Sundays; Baudelaire expresses it *avant la lettre* in one of his "Spleen" poems.

> Des cloches tout à coup sautent avec furie
> Et lancent vers le ciel un affreux hurlement,
> Ainsi que des esprits errants et sans patrie
> Qui se mettent à geindre opiniâtrement.

> [Suddenly bells are tossing with fury,
> Hurling a hideous howling to the sky
> Like wandering homeless spirits
> Who break into stubborn wailing.]

The bells, which once played a part in holidays, have been dropped from the calendar like the human beings. They are like the poor souls that wander restlessly but have no history. If Baudelaire in "Spleen" and "Vie antérieure" holds in his hands the scattered fragments of genuine historical experience, Bergson in his conception of *durée* has become far more estranged from history. "Bergson the metaphysician suppresses death."[68] The fact that death has been eliminated from Bergson's *durée* isolates it effectively from a historical (as well as prehistorical) order. Bergson's concept of *action* is in keeping with this. The "sound common sense" which distinguishes the "practical man" is its godfather.[69] The *durée* from which death has been eliminated has the bad infinity of an ornament. Tradition is excluded from it.[70] It is the quintessence of an isolated experience [*Erlebnis*] that struts about in the borrowed garb of long experience [*Erfahrung*]. Spleen, on the other hand, exposes the isolated experience in all its nakedness. To his horror, the melancholy man sees the earth revert to a mere state of nature. No breath of prehistory surrounds it—no aura. This is how the earth emerges in the lines of "Le Goût du néant" which follow the ones quoted above. "Je contemple d'en haut le globe en sa rondeur, / Et je n'y cherche plus l'abri d'une cahute." ["I contemplate, from on high, the globe in its roundness, / And no longer look there for the shelter of a hut."]

XI

If we think of the associations which, at home in the *mémoire involontaire,* seek to cluster around an object of perception, and if we call those associations the aura of that object, then the aura attaching to the object of a perception corresponds precisely to the experience [*Erfahrung*] which, in the case of an object of use, inscribes itself as long practice. The techniques inspired by the camera and subsequent analogous types of apparatus extend the range of the *mémoire volontaire;* these techniques make it possible at any time to retain an event—as image and sound—through the apparatus. They thus represent important achievements of a society in which long practice is in decline.—To Baudelaire, there was something profoundly unnerving and terrifying about daguerreotypy; he speaks of the fascination it exerted as "cruel and surprising."[71] Thus, he must have sensed—though he certainly did not understand them completely—the connections of which we have spoken. His perpetual willingness to grant the modern its place and, especially in art, to assign it a specific function also determined his attitude toward photography. Whenever he felt photography as a threat, he tried to put this down to "badly applied advances" in the field; yet he admitted that the latter had been promoted by "the stupidity of the masses." "The masses demanded an ideal that would conform to their aspirations and the nature of their temperament. . . . Their prayers were granted by a vengeful god, and Daguerre became his prophet."[72] Still, Baudelaire tried to take a more conciliatory view. Photography should be free to stake a claim on ephemeral things—those that have a right to "a place in the archives of our memory"—so long as it stops short of the "realm of the intangible and the imaginative": that is, the realm of art, in which only those things "granted the imprint of man's soul" are allotted a place. This judgment is not exactly Solomonic. The perpetual readiness of voluntary, discursive memory, encouraged by the technology of reproduction, reduces the imagination's scope for play [*Spielraum*]. "Imagination" can perhaps be defined as an ability to give expression to desires of a special kind—desires that have "something beautiful" as their intended fulfillment. Valéry has set out the conditions for this fulfillment: "We recognize a work of art by the fact that no idea it inspires in us, no mode of behavior it suggests we adopt, could ever exhaust it or dispose of it. We may inhale the smell of a sweet-smelling flower as long as we like; we cannot rid ourselves of the fragrance that has aroused our senses, and no recollection, no thought, no mode of behavior can obliterate its effect or release us from the hold it has on us. Anyone who undertakes to create a work of art aims at the same effect."[73] According to this view, the painting we look at reflects back at us that of which our eyes will never have their fill. What it contains that fulfills the original desire would be the very same stuff on which the desire continuously feeds. The distinction between photography and painting is therefore clear. It is also clear why there can be no comprehensive principle of "form-endowing" [*Gestaltung*] which is applicable to both: to the gaze that will never get its fill of a painting, photography is rather like food for the hungry or drink for the thirsty.

The crisis of artistic reproduction that emerges in this way can be seen as an integral part of a crisis in perception itself.—What makes our delight in the beautiful unquenchable is the image of the primeval world, which for Baudelaire is veiled by tears of nostalgia. "Ah— in times gone by, you were my sister or my wife!"[74]—this declaration of love is the tribute which the beautiful as such is entitled to claim. Insofar as art aims at the beautiful and, on however modest a scale, "reproduces" it, it retrieves it (as Faust does Helen) out of the depths of time.[75] This does not happen in the case of technological reproduction. (The beautiful has no place in it.) Proust, complaining of the barrenness and lack of depth in the images of Venice that his *mémoire volontaire* presented to him, notes that the very word "Venice" made those images seem to him as vapid as an exhibition of photographs. If the distinctive feature of the images arising from *mémoire involontaire* is seen in their aura, then photography is decisively implicated in the phenomenon of a "decline of the aura." What was inevitably felt to be inhuman—one might even say deadly—in daguerreotypy was the (prolonged) looking into the camera, since the camera records our likeness without returning our gaze. Inherent in the gaze, however, is the expectation that it will be returned by that on which it is bestowed. Where this expectation is met (which, in the case of thought processes, can apply equally to an intentional gaze of awareness and to a glance pure and simple), there is an experience [*Erfahrung*] of the aura in all its fullness. "Perceptibility," as Novalis puts it, "is an attentiveness."[76] The perceptibility he has in mind is none other than that of the aura. Experience of the aura thus arises from the fact that a response characteristic of human relationships is transposed to the relationship between humans and inanimate or natural objects. The person we look at, or who feels he is being looked at, looks at us in turn. To experience the aura of an object we look at means to invest it with the ability to look back at us.[77] This ability corresponds to the data of *mémoire involontaire*. (These data, incidentally, are unique: they are lost to the memory that seeks to retain them. Thus, they lend support to a concept of the aura that involves the "unique apparition of a distance."[78] This formulation has the advantage of clarifying the ritual character of the phenomenon. The essentially distant is the unapproachable; and unapproachability is a primary quality of the ritual image.) That Proust was quite familiar with the problem of the aura needs no emphasis. It is nonetheless notable that he sometimes alludes to it in concepts that comprehend its theory: "People who are fond of secrets occasionally flatter themselves that objects retain something of the gaze that has rested on them." (The objects, it seems, have the ability to return the gaze.) "They believe that monuments and pictures appear only through a delicate veil which centuries of love and reverence on the part of so many admirers have woven about them. This chimera," Proust concludes evasively, "would become truth if they related it to the only reality that is valid for the individual—namely, the world of his emotions."[79] Akin to this, but reaching further because of its objective orientation, is Valéry's characterization of perception in dreams as an auratic perception: "To say 'Here I see such-and-such an object' does not establish an equation between me and the object. . . . In dreams, however, there *is* an equation. The things I look at see me just as much as I see them."[80] Of a piece with perception in dreams is the nature of temples, which Baudelaire was describing when he wrote: "L'homme y passe à travers des forêts de symboles / Qui l'observent avec des regards familiers."[81] ["Man wends his way through forests of symbols / Which look at him with their familiar glances."]

The greater Baudelaire's insight into this phenomenon, the more unmistakably was his lyric poetry marked by the disintegration of the aura. This occurred in the form of a sign, which we encounter in nearly all those passages of *Les Fleurs du mal* where the gaze of the human eye is invoked. (That Baudelaire was not following some preconceived scheme goes without saying.) What happens here is that the expectation aroused by the gaze of the human eye is not fulfilled. Baudelaire describes eyes that could be said to have lost the ability to look. Yet this gives them a charm which to a large, perhaps overwhelming extent serves as a means of defraying the cost of his instinctual desires. It was under the spell of these eyes that *sexus* in Baudelaire detaches itself from *eros*. If in "Selige Sehnsucht"[82] the lines "Keine Ferne macht dich schwierig, / Kommst geflogen und gebannt" ["No distance weighs you down; / You come flying and entranced"] must be regarded as the classic description of love that is sated with the experience of the aura, then lyric poetry could hardly effect a more decisive repudiation of those lines than the following ones from Baudelaire:

> Je t'adore à l'égal de la voûte nocturne,
> O vase de tristesse, o grande taciturne,
> Et t'aime d'autant plus, belle, que tu me fuis,
> Et que tu me parais, ornement de mes nuits,
> Plus ironiquement accumuler les lieues
> Qui séparent mes bras des immensités bleues.[83]

> [I adore you as much as the vault of night,
> O vessel of sorrow, O deeply silent one,
> And I love you even more, my lovely, because you flee me
> And because you seem, ornament of my nights,
> More ironically, to multiply the miles
> That separate my arms from blue immensities.]

Glances may be all the more compelling, the more complete the viewer's absence that is overcome in them. In eyes that look at us with mirrorlike blankness, the remoteness remains complete. It is precisely for this reason that such eyes know nothing of distance. Baudelaire incorporated the glassiness of their stare in a cunning rhyme: "Plonge tes yeux dans les yeux fixes / Des Satyresses ou des Nixes."[84] ["Let your eyes plunge into the fixed stare / Of Satyresses or Water Sprites."] Female satyrs and water sprites are no longer members of the family of man. Theirs is a world apart. Significantly, Baudelaire's poem incorporates the look of the eye encumbered by distance as *un regard familier*. The poet who never founded a family imbues the word *familier* with a tone of mingled promise and renunciation. He has yielded to the spell of eyes-without-a-gaze, and submits to their sway without illusions.

> Tes yeux, illuminés ainsi que des boutiques
> Et des ifs flamboyants dans les fêtes publiques,
> Usent insolemment d'un pouvoir emprunté.[85]

[Your eyes, lit up like shopwindows
Or like yew-trees illuminated for public celebrations,
Insolently wield borrowed power.]

"Dullness," says Baudelaire in one of his earliest publications, "is frequently one of beauty's adornments. This is the reason eyes may be sad and translucent like blackish swamps, or their gaze may have the oily inertness of tropical seas."[86] When such eyes come alive, it is with the self-protective wariness of a carnivore hunting for prey. (Thus, the eye of a prostitute scrutinizing passers-by is at the same time on the lookout for police. The physiognomic type bred by this kind of life, Baudelaire noted, is delineated in Constantin Guys' numerous drawings of prostitutes. "Her eyes, like those of a wild animal, are fixed on the distant horizon; they have the restlessness of a wild animal . . . , but sometimes also the animal's sudden tense vigilance.")[87] That the eye of the city dweller is overburdened with protective functions is obvious. Georg Simmel refers to some of its less obvious tasks. "Someone who sees without hearing is much more uneasy than someone who hears without seeing. In this, there is something characteristic of the sociology of the big city. Interpersonal relationships in big cities are distinguished by a marked preponderance of visual activity over aural activity. The main reason for this is the public means of transportation. Before the development of buses, railroads, and trams in the nineteenth century, people had never been in situations where they had to look at one another for long minutes or even hours without speaking to one another."[88]

In the protective eye, there is no daydreaming surrender to distance and to faraway things. The protective eye may bring with it something like pleasure in the degradation of such distance. This is probably the sense in which the following curious sentences should be read. In his "Salon of 1859" Baudelaire lets the landscapes pass in review, concluding with this admission: "I long for the return of the dioramas, whose brutal and enormous magic has the power to impose on me a useful illusion. I would rather go to the theater and feast my eyes on the scenery, in which I find my dearest dreams treated with consummate skill and tragic concision. These things, because they are false, are infinitely closer to the truth, whereas the majority of our landscape painters are liars, precisely because they fail to lie."[89] One is inclined to attach less importance to the "useful illusion" than to the "*tragic* concision." Baudelaire insists on the magic of distance; he goes so far as to judge landscapes by the standard of paintings sold in booths at fairs. Does he mean the magic of distance to be broken through, as necessarily happens when the viewer steps too close to the depicted scene? This motif enters into a great passage from *Les Fleurs du mal:* "Le Plaisir vaporeux fuira vers l'horizon / Ainsi qu'une sylphide au fond de la coulisse."[90] ["Nebulous Pleasure horizonward will flee / Like a sylph darting into the wings."]

XII

Les Fleurs du mal was the last lyric work that had a broad European reception; no later writings penetrated beyond a more or less limited linguistic area. Added to this is the fact that Baudelaire expended his productive capacity almost entirely on this one volume. And finally, it cannot be denied that some of his motifs—those which the present study has discussed—render the possibility of lyric poetry problematic. These three facts define Baudelaire historically. They show that he held steadfastly to his cause and focused single-mindedly on his mission. He went so far as to proclaim as his goal "the creation of a cliché [*poncif*]."[91] He saw in this the condition for any future lyric poetry, and had a low opinion of those poets who were not equal to the task. "Do you drink beef tea made of ambrosia? Do you eat cutlets from Paros? How much can you get for a lyre, at the pawnshop?"[92] To Baudelaire, the lyric poet with his halo is antiquated. In a prose piece entitled "Perte d'auréole" [Loss of a Halo], which came to light at a late date, Baudelaire presents such a poet as a supernumerary. When Baudelaire's literary remains were first examined, this piece was rejected as "unsuitable for publication"; to this day, it has been neglected by Baudelaire scholars.

"What do I see, my dear fellow? *You—here?* I find *you* in a place of ill repute—a man who sips quintessences, who consumes ambrosia? Really! I couldn't be more surprised!"

"You know, my dear fellow, how afraid I am of horses and carriages. A short while ago I was hurrying across the boulevard, and amid that churning chaos in which death comes galloping at you from all sides at once I must have made an awkward movement, for the halo slipped off my head and fell into the mire of the macadam. I didn't have the courage to pick it up, and decided that it hurts less to lose one's insignia than to have one's bones broken. Furthermore, I said to myself, every cloud has a silver lining. Now I can go about incognito, do bad things, and indulge in vulgar behavior like ordinary mortals. So here I am, just like you!"

"But you ought to report the loss of your halo or inquire at the lost-and-found office."

"I wouldn't dream of it. I like it here. You're the only person who has recognized me. Besides, dignity bores me. And it amuses me to think that some bad poet will pick up the halo and straightway adorn himself with it. There's nothing I like better than to make someone happy—especially if the happy fellow is someone I can laugh at. Just picture X wearing it, or Y! Won't that be funny?"[93]

The same scene is found in Baudelaire's diaries, except that the ending is different. The poet quickly picks up his halo—but now he is troubled by the feeling that the incident may be a bad omen.[94]

The man who wrote these pieces was no flâneur. They embody, in ironic form, the same experience that Baudelaire put into the following sentence without any embellishment: "Perdu dans ce vilain monde, *coudoyé par les foules,* je suis comme un homme lassé dont l'oeil ne voit en arrière, dans les années profondes, que désabusement et amertume, et, devant lui, qu'un orage où rien de neuf n'est contenu, ni enseignement ni douleur."[95] ["Lost in this base world, jostled by the crowd, I am like a weary man whose eye, looking backward into the depths of the years, sees only disillusion and bitterness, and looking ahead sees only a tempest which contains nothing new, neither instruction nor pain."] Of all the experiences which made his life what it was, Baudelaire singled out being jostled by the crowd as the decisive, unmistakable experience. The semblance [*Schein*] of a crowd with a soul and movement all its own, the luster that had dazzled the flâneur, had faded for him. To heighten the impression of the crowd's baseness, he envisioned the day on which even the fallen women, the outcasts, would readily espouse a well-ordered life, condemn libertinism, and reject everything except money. Betrayed by these last allies of his, Baudelaire battled the crowd—with the impotent rage of someone fighting the rain or the wind. This is the nature of the immediate experience [*Erlebnis*] to which Baudelaire has given the weight of long experience [*Erfahrung*]. He named the price for which the sensation of modernity could be had: the disintegration of the aura in immediate shock experience [*Chockerlebnis*]. He paid dearly for consenting to this disintegration—but it is the law of his poetry. This poetry appears in the sky of the Second Empire as "a star without atmosphere."[96]

Written February–July 1939; published in the *Zeitschrift für Sozialforschung*, January 1940. *Gesammelte Schriften*, I, 605–653. Translated by Harry Zohn.

Notes

Index

Notes

Introduction, by Michael W. Jennings

1. I am indebted to Lindsay Waters for insights into a number of the issues addressed in this essay. He remains one of the most original readers of Walter Benjamin. See especially Waters, "'The Cameraman and Machine Are Now One': Walter Benjamin's Frankenstein," in Hans Ulrich Gumbrecht and Michael J. Marrinan, eds., *Mapping Benjamin: The Work of Art in the Digital Age* (Stanford: Stanford University Press, 2003), pp. 133–141; and idem, "The Machine Takes Command: 1936, February 27—Walter Benjamin Sends Theodor W. Adorno the Second of Four Versions of the Theses on the Development of Art in the Contemporary World," in David Wellbery, ed., *A New History of German Literature* (Cambridge, Mass.: Harvard University Press, 2004), pp. 790–795. I would also like to thank Howard Eiland, who worked on the versions of several of the essays here that originally appeared in Benjamin's *Selected Writings,* and Margareta Ingrid Christian, whose work on the apparatus to this volume made it a much better text than it would otherwise have been.

2. T. S. Eliot, "Charles Baudelaire," in Eliot, *Selected Essays* (New York: Harcourt, Brace, 1932).

3. Stefan George's translation appeared in the journal he edited, *Blätter für die Kunst,* in 1914 under the German title *Die Blumen des Bösen;* rather than "translations," George called his versions *Umdichtungen,* or rewritings. George (1868–1933) published a widely influential body of high-modernist verse in such volumes as *Das Jahr der Seele* (The Year of the Soul; 1898). His charismatic personality, in combination with his attempt to "purify" the German language and culture, led to the cre-

ation of a school—the "George Circle"—made up of conservative and radical rightist intellectuals. George and his circle are often associated with the protofascism that played a role in the prehistory of the Third Reich.

4. Benjamin, Eliot, and George distinguished themselves from a number of important contemporaries who ignored or belittled Baudelaire's role in the rise of literary modernism. Ezra Pound wrote: "Neither [Verlaine nor Baudelaire] is of the least use, pedagogically, I mean. They beget imitations and one can learn nothing from them." Pound to Harriet Monroe, September 1913, in *The Letters of Ezra Pound, 1907–1941* (London: Faber and Faber, 1951), p. 60.

5. Benjamin was not alone in his recognition of the fundamental contradictions in Baudelaire's work. Benjamin's great contemporary Erich Auerbach—really the only German critical voice of the era that bears comparison to Benjamin's—wrote movingly about the tension between the traditional dignity of Baudelaire's diction and the degraded nature of the emotions and subject matter depicted in the poetry. See Auerbach, "The Aesthetic Dignity of the *Fleurs du mal*," in *Scenes from the Drama of European Literature,* trans. Ralph Manheim, Catherine Garvin, and Erich Auerbach (Minneapolis: University of Minnesota Press, 1984; orig. pub. New York: Meridian Books, 1959), pp. 201–249. The essay first appeared in German in 1951.

6. *Tableaux parisiens: Deutsche Übertragung mit einem Vorwort über die Aufgabe des Übersetzers, von Walter Benjamin* (Heidelberg: Verlag von Richard Weissbach), 67 pp.; Benjamin, "Baudelaire-Übertragungen," *Vers und Prosa,* 8 (1924): 269–272.

7. Benjamin, "The Task of the Translator," trans. Harry Zohn, in Benjamin, *Selected Writings, Volume 1: 1913–1926,* ed. Marcus Bullock and Michael W. Jennings (Cambridge, Mass.: Harvard University Press, 1996), pp. 253–263.

8. Charles Baudelaire, *Les Fleurs du mal* (1857), ed. Antoine Adam (Paris: Garnier Frères, 1961). English versions from *Les Fleurs du mal,* trans. Richard Howard (Boston: Godine, 1982), pp. 74, 251, 76, 253.

9. *Les Fleurs du mal,* trans. Richard Howard, pp. 58, 235.

10. Ibid., pp. 266, 88, 268, 90, 36, 214.

11. See Walter Benjamin, "Franz Kafka," in Benjamin, *Selected Writings, Volume 2: 1927–1934,* ed. Michael W. Jennings, Howard Eiland, and

Gary Smith (Cambridge, Mass.: Harvard University Press, 1999), pp. 794–818.

12. Walter Benjamin, *Gesammelte Schriften,* ed. Rolf Tiedemann and Hermann Schweppenhäuser (Frankfurt: Suhrkamp Verlag, 1972–), vol. 5, pp. 1256–58.

13. *The Arcades Project* includes a section, Convolute J, on Baudelaire; this is the original source from which Benjamin quarried many of the ideas and nearly all of the Baudelaire quotations for the essays he wrote over the next several years. See Benjamin, *The Arcades Project,* trans. Howard Eiland and Kevin McLaughlin (Cambridge, Mass.: Harvard University Press, 1999), pp. 228–387.

14. For a more detailed discussion of the philological relationship between *The Arcades Project* and the never-completed book on Baudelaire, see Michael W. Jennings, *Dialectical Images* (Ithaca: Cornell University Press, 1987), pp. 215–219.

15. Baudelaire, *Les Fleurs du mal,* trans. Richard Howard, p. 143.

16. Benjamin, *Gesammelte Schriften,* vol. 1, p. 1161.

17. Benjamin, *The Arcades Project,* N9a,5.

18. On Benjaminian montage, see Brigid Doherty, *Montage* (Berkeley: University of California Press, 2007).

19. Benjamin, *The Arcades Project,* J77,1. On the theoretical model behind the Baudelaire project, see ibid., Convolute N.

20. For Adorno's understanding and critique of Benjamin's method, see "Exchange with Theodor W. Adorno on 'The Paris of the Second Empire in Baudelaire,' in Benjamin, *Selected Writings, Volume 4: 1938–1940,* ed. Michael W. Jennings and Howard Eiland (Cambridge, Mass.: Harvard University Press, 1999). For Fredric Jameson's critique of Benjamin's dialectics, see Jameson, *The Political Unconscious* (Ithaca: Cornell University Press, 1981), pp. 23–30.

21. Benjamin, *The Arcades Project,* K2,5.

22. On the dialectical image, and especially on Benjamin's theory of knowledge, as they relate to photography, see Eduardo Cadava, *Words of Light: Theses on the Photography of History* (Princeton: Princeton University Press, 1997).

23. On this concept from "The Paris of the Second Empire in Baudelaire," see Tom Gunning, "The Exterior as *Intérieur:* Benjamin's Optical Detective," in *boundary 2,* 30, no. 1 (Spring 2003).

24. Benjamin, *The Arcades Project*, J59a,4.

25. Benjamin, *The Origin of German Tragic Drama*, trans. John Osborne (London: NLB/Verso, 1977), pp. 233, 175. There is virtually no scholarly work on the problem of allegory in Benjamin's reading of Baudelaire. On the problem of phantasmagoria, see Michael W. Jennings, "On the Banks of a New Lethe: Commodification and Experience in Walter Benjamin's Late Work," *boundary 2*, 30, no. 1 (2003): 89–104.

26. Benjamin, *Gesammelte Briefe*, ed. Christoph Gödde and Henri Lonitz (Frankfurt: Suhrkamp Verlag, 1995–), vol. 5, p. 168.

27. See Benjamin, "Exchange with Theodor W. Adorno on 'The Paris of the Second Empire in Baudelaire'" and "Exchange with Theodor W. Adorno on 'The Flâneur' Section of 'The Paris of the Second Empire in Baudelaire,'" both in Benjamin, *Selected Writings*, vol. 4, pp. 98–115 and 200–214.

28. Jugendstil was a style of art and architecture—allied to Art Nouveau—that flourished in the last decade of the nineteenth century and the early years of the twentieth century. Jugendstil products tend to mix aspects of "high" and "low" art in an attempt to restructure the human-built environment.

29. Walter Benjamin, "Little History of Photography," in Benjamin, *Selected Writings*, vol. 2, pp. 507–530; "The Work of Art in the Age of Its Technological Reproducibility," Benjamin, *Selected Writings, Volume 3: 1935–1938* (Cambridge, Mass.: Harvard University Press, 2002), pp. 104–105.

30. Benjamin, "The Work of Art in the Age of Its Technological Reproducibility," p. 105.

31. Charles Baudelaire, "The Painter of Modern Life," in Baudelaire, *The Painter of Modern Life and Other Essays*, ed. and trans. Jonathan Mayne (London: Phaidon, 1964), p. 13.

32. Ibid., p. 7.

33. Ibid., p. 9.

34. Ibid., p. 8.

35. Ibid., p. 1.

36. Ibid., p. 2.

37. Benjamin, "Literary History and the Study of Literature," in *Selected Writings*, vol. 2, p. 464.

Paris, the Capital of the Nineteenth Century

This translation was prepared in consultation with previous renderings by Quintin Hoare (1968) and Edmund Jephcott (1978).

1. The *magasin de nouveautés* offered a complete selection of goods in one or another specialized line of business; it had many rooms and several stories, with a large staff of employees. The first such store, Pygmalion, opened in Paris in 1793. The word *nouveauté* means "newness" or "novelty"; in the plural, it means "fancy goods." On the *magasins de nouveautés*, see Walter Benjamin, *Das Passagen-Werk*, vol. 5 of Benjamin, *Gesammelte Schriften* (Frankfurt: Suhrkamp, 1982), pp. 83–109; in English, *The Arcades Project*, trans. Howard Eiland and Kevin McLaughlin (Cambridge, Mass.: Harvard University Press, 1999), pp. 31–61 (Convolute A). Benjamin wrote the essay "Paris, die Hauptstadt des XIX. Jahrhunderts" (Paris, the Capital of the Nineteenth Century) at the suggestion of Friedrich Pollock, codirector of the Institute of Social Research in New York, as an exposé, or synopsis, of the *Passagen-Werk*. Hence its highly concentrated, almost stenographic style. See Benjamin's letter to Theodor W. Adorno dated May 31, 1935, in this volume. The essay appears at the beginning of *The Arcades Project*.

2. Honoré de Balzac, "Histoire et physiologie des boulevards de Paris," in George Sand, Honoré de Balzac, Eugène Sue, et al., *Le Diable à Paris* (The Devil in Paris), vol. 2 (Paris, 1846), p. 91.

3. Karl Boetticher, "Das Prinzip der Hellenischen und Germanischen Bauweise hinsichtlich der Übertragung in die Bauweise unserer Tage" (The Principle of Hellenic and Germanic Building Methods in Light of Their Incorporation into the Building Methods of Today; address of March 13, 1846), in *Zum hundertjährigen Geburtstag Karl Böttichers* (Berlin, 1906), p. 46. The address is cited at more length in *The Arcades Project*, p. 150 (Convolute F1,1). Karl Heinrich von Boetticher (1833–1907), author of *Tektonik der Hellenen* (Hellenic Tectonics; 1844–1852), was an adviser to the German chancellor Bismarck.

4. Sigfried Giedion, *Bauen in Frankreich* [Architecture in France] (Leipzig, 1928), p. 3.

5. See Paul Scheerbart, *Glass Architecture*, trans. James Palmes (New York: Praeger, 1972). In this work, the German author Paul Scheerbart (1863–1915) announces the advent of a "new glass-culture." See Benja-

min's discussion of Scheerbart in his essay "Experience and Poverty," in Benjamin, *Selected Writings, Volume 2: 1927–1934* (Cambridge, Mass.: Harvard University Press, 1999), pp. 733–734; and the short essay "Zur Scheerbart" (1940), in Benjamin, *Gesammelte Schriften,* vol. 2 (Frankfurt: Suhrkamp, 1977), pp. 630–632, English version "On Scheerbart," in Benjamin, *Selected Writings, Volume 4: 1938–1940* (Cambridge, Mass.: Harvard University Press, 2003).

6. Jules Michelet, "Avenir! Avenir!" (Future! Future!), in *Europe,* 19, no. 73 (January 15, 1929): 6.

7. Charles Fourier (1772–1837), French social theorist and reformer, urged that society be reorganized into self-contained agrarian cooperatives which he called "phalansteries." Among his works are *Théorie des quatre mouvements* (1808) and *Le Nouveau Monde industriel* (1829–1830). See *The Arcades Project,* pp. 620–650 (Convolute W, "Fourier").

8. Emile Zola published *Travail* (Labor) in 1901 and *Thérèse Raquin* in 1867. See *The Arcades Project,* pp. 203–204, 627–628. The period style known today as Biedermeier was popular in most of northern Europe between 1815 and 1848. In furniture and interior design, painting and literature, it was characterized by a simplification of neoclassical forms and by motifs drawn from nature. Home furnishings in this style often displayed bold color combinations and lively patterns.

9. See Karl Marx and Friedrich Engels, *Die deutsche Ideologie* (The German Ideology), part 2; translated into English by C. P. Magill in Marx and Engels, *Collected Works,* vol. 5 (New York: International Publishers, 1976). The passage in question is on pp. 513–514. Carl Grün (1817–1887) was a German writer and publicist, a member of the Prussian national Diet, and a follower of Feuerbach.

10. *Levana, oder Erziehungslehre* (1807) is a classic work on pedagogy. See Jean Paul, *Levana, or Doctrine of Education,* trans. Erika Casey, in *Jean Paul: A Reader* (Baltimore: Johns Hopkins University Press, 1992), pp. 269–274. Jean Paul is the pen name of Jean Paul Friedrich Richter (1763–1825), German prose writer and humorist, whose other works include *Titan* (1800–1803) and *Vorschule der Ästhetik* (Elementary Course in Aesthetics; 1804).

11. Panoramas were large circular tableaux, usually displaying scenes of battles and cities, painted in trompe l'oeil and originally designed to

be viewed from the center of a rotunda. They were introduced in France in 1799 by the American engineer Robert Fulton. Subsequent forms included the Diorama (opened by Louis Daguerre and Charles Bouton in 1822 in Paris), in which pictures were painted on cloth transparencies that, by 1831, were being used with various lighting effects; it was this installation that burned down in 1839.

12. That is, Jacques-Louis David (1748–1825), the neoclassical French painter.

13. Emile de Girardin (1806–1881), a member of the Chamber of Deputies, inaugurated the low-priced, mass-circulation newspaper with his editorship of *La Presse* (1836–1856, 1862–1866), at an annual subscription rate of forty francs.

14. Louis Jacques Daguerre (1787–1851), French painter and inventor, helped develop the Diorama in Paris (1822), and collaborated with J. N. Niépce (1829–1833) on work leading to the discovery of the daguerreotype process, communicated to the Academy of Sciences in 1839. Pierre Prévost (1764–1823) was a French painter.

15. François Arago (1786–1853), a scientist who investigated the theory of light and electricity, was director of the Paris Observatory. He presented his expert report in favor of photography in 1838.

16. Nadar is the pseudonym of Félix Tournachon (1820–1910), French photographer, journalist, and caricaturist. His photographs of the Paris sewers, in which he employed his patented new process of photography by electric light, were taken in 1864–1865.

17. A. J. Wiertz, "La Photographie," in *Oeuvres littéraires* (Paris, 1870), pp. 309ff. Antoine-Joseph Wiertz (1806–1865) was a Belgian painter of colossal historical scenes, lampooned by Baudelaire. His article on photography is excerpted in *The Arcades Project*, p. 671 (Convolute Y1,1).

18. Ferdinand Langlé and Emile Vanderburch, *Louis-Bronze et le Saint-Simonien: Parodie de Louis XI* (Théâtre du Palais-Royal, February 27, 1832), cited in Théodore Muret, *L'Histoire par le théâtre, 1789–1851* (Paris, 1865), vol. 3, p. 191.

19. Actually, it was the French philologist and historian Ernest Renan (1823–1892), author of *La Vie de Jésus* (The Life of Jesus; 1863) and many other works, who made this statement. See *The Arcades Project*, pp. 180 (Convolute G4,5) and 197 (Convolute G13a,3).

20. Sigmund Engländer, *Geschichte der französischen Arbeiter-Associationen* [History of French Workers' Associations] (Hamburg, 1864), vol. 4, p. 52.

21. Jean-Antoine, Comte de Chaptal (1756–1832), a French physicist and chemist, served as Minister of the Interior (1800–1804). He was the founder of the first Ecole des Arts et des Métiers.

22. The Saint-Simonians were followers of the philosopher and social reformer Henri de Saint-Simon (1760–1825), considered the founder of French socialism. His works include *Du Système industriel* (1820–1823) and *Le Nouveau Christianisme* (1825). After helping to organize the constitutional monarchy of Louis Philippe (1830–1848), Saint-Simonians came to occupy important positions in nineteenth-century French industry and finance. Michel Chevalier (1806–1879), an economist and advocate of free trade, was coeditor of *Le Globe* (1830–1832) and later, under Napoleon III, a councillor of state and professor at the Collège de France. Barthélemy-Prosper Enfantin (1796–1864), a Saint-Simonian leader known as "Père Enfantin," established in 1832, on his estate at Ménilmontant, a model community characterized by fantastic sacerdotalism and by freedom between the sexes. He later became the first director of the Lyons Railroad Company (1845). See *The Arcades Project*, pp. 571–602 (Convolute U, "Saint-Simon, Railroads").

23. Grandville is the pseudonym of Jean Ignace Isidore Gérard (1803–1847), a caricaturist and illustrator whose work appeared in the periodicals *Le Charivari* and *La Caricature*. His drawings, especially as conceived for the volume *Un Autre Monde* (1844), anticipated Surrealism. See *The Arcades Project*, pp. 171–202 (Convolute G, "Exhibitions, Advertising, Grandville").

24. Karl Marx, *Das Kapital*, vol. 1 (1867); in English, *Capital*, vol. 1, trans. Samuel Moore and Edward Aveling (1887; rpt. New York: International Publishers, 1967), p. 76.

25. Giacomo Leopardi, "Dialogo della moda e della morte" (1827); in English in *Essays and Dialogues*, trans. Giovanni Cecchetti (Berkeley: University of California Press, 1982), p. 67.

26. Benjamin refers to an illustration in Grandville's *Un Autre Monde*, reproduced in *The Arcades Project*, p. 65. See also *Fantastic Illustrations of Grandville* (New York: Dover, 1974), p. 49; this volume contains illustrations from *Un Autre Monde* and *Les Animaux*.

27. Alphonse Toussenel (1803–1885), a French naturalist and follower of Fourier, was editor of *La Paix* and author of *L'Esprit des bêtes* (Spirit of the Beasts; 1856) and other works in a droll mode.

28. The International Workingmen's Association (the First International), whose General Council had its seat in London, was founded in September 1864.

29. Jacques Offenbach (1819–1880), German-born musician and composer, produced many successful operettas and *opéras bouffes* in Paris, where he managed the Gaîté-Lyrique (1872–1876). His famous *Contes d'Hoffmann* (Tales of Hoffmann) was produced after his death.

30. From Charles Baudelaire, *Les Fleurs du Mal* (1857); in English, "A Martyr," in Baudelaire, *Flowers of Evil,* trans. Wallace Fowlie (1964; rpt. New York: Dover, 1992), p. 85.

31. Louis Philippe (1773–1850), a descendant of the Bourbon-Orléans royal line, was proclaimed "Citizen King" in the July Revolution of July 27–29, 1830, against Charles X, and was soon after elected by the Chamber of Deputies as a constitutional monarch. His reign, which sought to portray itself as middle-of-the-road, was marked by the bourgeoisie's rise to power, especially through its domination of industry and finance. He was overthrown by the February Revolution of 1848.

32. François Guizot (1787–1874), a historian and statesman, was premier of France from 1840 to 1848. He was forced out of office by the 1848 revolution.

33. Jugendstil, in the strict sense, was a style of architectural, figurative, and applied art that flourished in the last decade of the nineteenth century and the early years of the twentieth century, and that was allied to Art Nouveau. In Germany, it was led by the architect and craftsman Henry van de Velde (1863–1957), author of *Vom neuen Stil* (The Modern Style; 1907). After 1896, it was associated with the periodical *Die Jugend* (Youth). Benjamin uses the term more broadly to include literature as well. It signifies not only a crossing of the cultural barrier separating "higher" from "lower" arts, but an educational movement intent on restructuring the human environment.

34. Henrik Ibsen's play *The Master Builder* was produced in 1892. See *The Arcades Project,* pp. 221 (Convolute I4,4) and 551 (Convolute S4,6).

35. On the figure of the Parisian apache, who "abjures virtue and laws" and "terminates the *contrat social* forever," and on the "poetry of

apachedom," see "The Paris of the Second Empire in Baudelaire," trans. Harry Zohn, in Benjamin, *Selected Writings, Volume 4*.

36. Baudelaire, "The Swan," in *Flowers of Evil*, p. 75.

37. See the passages from Engels' *Die Lage der arbeitenden Klasse in England* (The Condition of the Working Class in England) and from Poe's story "The Man of the Crowd" cited in *The Arcades Project*, pp. 427–428 (Convolute M5a,1) and 445 (Convolute M15a,2), respectively.

38. *The Aeneid of Virgil*, trans. Allen Mandelbaum (New York: Bantam, 1971), p. 137 (book 6, 1ine 126). Benjamin quotes the Latin.

39. "Spleen et idéal" (Spleen and Ideal) is the title of the first section of Baudelaire's collection of poems *Les Fleurs du Mal* (Flowers of Evil), first published in 1857.

40. "The Voyage," in Baudelaire, *Les Fleurs du Mal*, trans. Richard Howard (Boston: David R. Godine, 1982), pp. 156–157.

41. Baudelaire, "Pierre Dupont," in *Baudelaire as a Literary Critic*, trans. Lois B. Hyslop and Francis E. Hyslop, Jr. (University Park: Pennsylvania State University Press, 1964), p. 53.

42. Applying Kant's idea of the pure and disinterested existence of the work of art, the French philosopher Victor Cousin made use of the phrase *l'art pour l'art* ("art for art's sake") in his 1818 lecture "Du Vrai, du beau, et du bien" (On the True, the Beautiful, and the Good). The idea was later given currency by writers like Théophile Gautier, Edgar Allan Poe, and Charles Baudelaire.

43. Baudelaire's enthusiasm for Wagner's music, which he describes as a "revelation" and as specifically "modern," is expressed in a letter of February 17, 1860, to Wagner, after the composer had come to Paris to direct three concerts of his music, and in an essay, "Richard Wagner et Tannhäuser à Paris" (Richard Wagner and Tannhäuser in Paris), published in 1861. See *The Selected Letters of Charles Baudelaire*, trans. Rosemary Lloyd (Chicago: University of Chicago Press, 1986), pp. 145–146; and Baudelaire, *The Painter of Modern Life and Other Essays*, trans. Jonathan Mayne (1964; rpt. New York: Da Capo, 1986), pp. 111–146.

44. *Confession d'un lion devenu vieux* [Confession of a Lion Grown Old] (Paris, 1888), 4 pp., was published anonymously, without year or place, by Baron Georges Eugène Haussmann (1809–1891). As Prefect of the Seine (1853–1870) under Napoleon III, Haussmann inau-

gurated and carried through a large-scale renovation of Paris, which included the modernization of sanitation, public utilities, and transportation facilities, and which necessitated the demolition of many old Parisian neighborhoods and many arcades built in the first half of the century.

45. Charles Louis Napoleon Bonaparte, known as Louis Napoleon (1808–1873), was a nephew of Napoleon I. After being elected president of the Republic at the end of 1848, he made himself dictator by a coup d'état on December 2, 1851; a year later, he proclaimed himself emperor as Napoleon III. His reign, the Second Empire, was marked by economic expansion, militant foreign intervention, and a wavering authoritarian tone. He was deposed by the National Assembly in 1871, following his capture at the Battle of Sedan during the Franco-Prussian War (1870–1871).

46. Paul Lafargue (1842–1911) was a French radical socialist and writer who was closely associated with Marx and Engels. For his comparison between the market and the gambling house, see *The Arcades Project*, p. 497 (Convolute O4,1).

47. The Court of Cassation was established in 1790 as the highest court of appeals in the French legal system. During the Second Empire, it tended to serve the interests of the bourgeoisie, which had come to power under Louis Philippe. It thus represented a check on the power of Napoleon III and Baron Haussmann.

48. The "red belt" was a name for the suburbs immediately surrounding Paris proper in the later nineteenth century. These districts were populated by many of the working class who had been displaced by Haussmann's urban renewal.

49. The writer Maxime Du Camp (1822–1894) was a friend of Flaubert and Baudelaire. He is the author of *Paris: Ses organes, ses fonctions et sa vie dans la seconde moitié du XIXe siècle*, a six-volume account of nineteenth-century Paris (1869–1875). See *The Arcades Project*, pp. 90–91 (Convolute C,4), on Du Camp's conception of this work.

50. Anonymous, *Paris désert: Lamentations d'un Jérémie haussmannisé* [Deserted Paris: Jeremiads of a Man Haussmannized] (Paris, 1868).

51. The "February Revolution" refers to the overthrow of Louis Philippe's constitutional monarchy in February 1848.

52. Engels' critique of barricade tactics is excerpted in *The Arcades Project*, p. 123 (Convolute E1a,5).

53. The verse derives from the popular lyric poet and songwriter Pierre Dupont (1821–1870). See *The Arcades Project*, p. 710 (Convolute a7,3).

54. The Commune of Paris was the revolutionary government established in Paris on March 18, 1871, in the aftermath of the Franco-Prussian War. It was suppressed in bloody street-fighting that ended May 28, 1871, leaving 20,000 Communards dead.

55. Frédéric Le Play, *Les Ouvriers européens: Etudes sur les travaux, la vie domestique et la condition morale des populations ouvrières de l'Europe, précédées d'un exposé de la méthode d'observation* [European Workers: Studies of the Work, Domestic Life, and Moral Condition of the Laboring Populations of Europe, Prefaced by a Statement on Observational Method] (Paris, 1855). Frédéric Le Play (1806–1882) was an engineer and economist who, as senator (1867–1870), represented a paternalistic "social Catholicism."

56. In his second exposé to the *Passagen-Werk*, written in French in 1939, Benjamin apparently corrects this assertion: "Side by side with the overt position of philanthropy, the bourgeoisie has always maintained the covert position of class struggle" (*The Arcades Project*, p. 24).

57. At the age of eighteen, the French poet Rimbaud wrote from his home in northern France, in a letter of May 13, 1871: "I will be a worker. This idea holds me back when mad anger drives me toward the battle of Paris—where so many workers are dying as I write. . . . Work now?—Never, never. I am on strike." Arthur Rimbaud, *Complete Works: Selected Letters*, trans. Wallace Fowlie (Chicago: University of Chicago Press, 1966), p. 303. Gustave Courbet (1819–1877), leading French realist painter, presided over the Committee of Fine Arts during the Commune. He was imprisoned six months for helping to destroy the column in the Place Vendôme during the uprising of 1871, and in 1875 was ordered to pay for the restoration of the column.

58. In the course of "Bloody Week" (May 21–28, 1871), the desperate Communards set fire to many public buildings, including the Tuileries Palace and the Hôtel de Ville (City Hall).

59. Balzac's comment, from 1845, is cited in *The Arcades Project*, p. 87 (Convolute C2a,8).

The Paris of the Second Empire in Baudelaire

In 1937 Benjamin agreed, at the urging of Max Horkheimer and his associates at the Institute for Social Research, to prepare some part of his work on the Paris arcades for publication. Drawing on the mass of material and ideas he had assembled beginning in the late 1920s, Benjamin set about writing a book-length study of Paris after 1848, organized around the figure of Baudelaire. He produced a detailed outline, which grouped excerpts from *The Arcades Project* under section and chapter headings. The book, which bore the working title *Charles Baudelaire: Ein Lyriker im Zeitalter des Hochkapitalismus* (Charles Baudelaire: A Lyric Poet in the Era of High Capitalism) but which was never completed, would have had three parts: (1) "Baudelaire as Allegorist"; (2) "The Paris of the Second Empire in Baudelaire"; (3) "The Commodity as Poetic Object." Benjamin completed the second part—the present essay—and submitted it for publication to the *Zeitschrift für Sozialforschung* (Journal for Social Research) in 1938.

Benjamin's references to Baudelaire's *Oeuvres* have here been fleshed out with the titles of Baudelaire's works.

1. "A capital is not absolutely necessary for man." Etienne Pivert de Senancour (1770–1846), French author, is best known for *Obermann* (1804), a novel that describes the sufferings of a hero who is tormented by a Rousseau-like sensitivity to the inroads of civilization upon human nature.

2. Lucien de La Hodde (1808–1865), French journalist, poet, historian, and police agent. His works include, aside from the eight volumes of memoirs mentioned here (*Histoires des sociétés secrètes et du parti républicain de 1830 à 1848;* 1850), numerous articles in the journals *Charivari* and *La Réforme,* several volumes of poetry, and a history of the Revolution of 1848.

3. Karl Marx and Friedrich Engels, Review of Adolphe Chenu, *Les Conspirateurs* (Paris, 1850), and of Lucien de La Hodde, *La Naissance de la République en février 1848* (Paris, 1850); quoted from *Die neue Zeit,* 4 (1886): 555. Proudhon, who wanted to dissociate himself from the professional conspirators, occasionally called himself a "new man—a man whose style is not the barricades but discussion, a man who could sit at a table with the chief of police every evening and could take all the de La Hoddes of the world into his confidence." Quoted in Gustave Geffroy, *L'Enfermé* (Paris, 1897), pp. 180ff. [Benjamin's note. Pierre-Joseph Proudhon (1809–1865), a political thinker regarded today as the father of anarchism, advocated a localized mutualist world federation to be achieved through economic action rather than violent revolution. He

was the author of *Qu'est-ce que la propriété?* (1840) and other works.—
Ed.]

4. Karl Marx, *Der achtzehnte Brumaire des Louis Bonaparte* (The Eighteenth Brumaire of Louis Bonaparte), ed. David Riazanov (Vienna, 1917), p. 73. [Benjamin's note. Napoleon III (Charles Louis Napoléon Bonaparte; 1808–1873), nephew of Napoleon Bonaparte, was president of the Second Republic from 1850 to 1852 and thereafter emperor of France. His reign combined authoritarianism and economic liberalism; it ended with France's defeat in the Franco–Prussian War of 1870–1871.

The text by Marx that Benjamin is quoting from throws a revealing light on the subject of the *bohème*. The full passage runs as follows: "Alongside decayed roués with doubtful means of subsistence and of doubtful origin, alongside ruined and adventurous offshoots of the bourgeoisie, were vagabonds, discharged soldiers, discharged jail-birds, escaped galley slaves, swindlers, mountebanks, *lazzaroni* [idlers], pickpockets, tricksters, gamblers, *maquereaux* [pimps], brothel-keepers, porters, literati, organ-grinders, rag-pickers, knife-grinders, tinkers, beggars—in short, the whole indeterminate, disintegrated, fluctuating mass which the French call the *bohème.*" Marx, *The Eighteenth Brumaire of Louis Napoleon,* trans. Joseph Weydemeyer (New York: International Publishers, 1963), section V, paragraph 4.—*Ed.*]

5. Charles Baudelaire, *Oeuvres,* ed. Yves-Gérard Le Dantec, 2 vols., Bibliothèque de la Pléiade, nos. 1 and 7 (Paris, 1931–1932), vol. 2, p. 415: *L'Art romantique,* "Les Drames et les romans honnêtes." [Benjamin's note]

6. The idea that the work of art is autonomous and self-sufficient can be traced back to Kant's emphasis on the "pure" and disinterested existence of the artwork. In France, the phrase *l'art pour l'art* was used by the philosopher Victor Cousin in his 1818 lecture "Du vrai, du beau, et du bien" (On the True, the Beautiful, and the Good), and the idea of "art for art's sake" was taken up by the writers Victor Hugo and Théophile Gautier. It was from Gautier, together with Edgar Allan Poe, that Baudelaire derived his own doctrine of aesthetic experience and the sovereignty of the creative imagination.

7. Jules Lemaître (1853–1914) was a French author and critic whose highly influential evaluations of his contemporaries led to his election to

the Académie Française in 1895. In later years he adopted the right-wing stance of the monarchist, anti-Semitic political group Action Française.

8. Marx and Engels, Review of Chenu and of de La Hodde, p. 556. [Benjamin's note]

9. Jacques Aupick (1789–1857), Baudelaire's stepfather, was a career soldier who rose to the rank of general. He later served as French ambassador to the Ottoman Empire and Spain, before becoming a senator under the Second Empire.

The phrase "February days" refers to the overthrow of Louis Philippe's constitutional monarchy in February 1848 (also known as the February Revolution).

10. Baudelaire, *Oeuvres,* vol. 2, p. 728: "Argument du livre sur la Belgique," last page ("Note detachée"). [Benjamin's note]

11. Baudelaire, *Lettres à sa mère* (Paris: Calmann-Lévy, 1932), p. 83. [Benjamin's note]

12. Victor Hugo (1802–1885), French dramatist, novelist, and poet, was the leading figure among the Romantic writers. Though his novels (such as *Les Misérables,* 1862; and *Notre-Dame de Paris,* 1831) remain his best-known works, his legacy to the nineteenth century was his lyric poetry.

13. Georges-Eugène Sorel (1847–1922), French socialist and revolutionary syndicalist, developed an original and provocative theory on the positive, even creative, role of myth and violence in the historical process. Turning to history and politics rather late in life, he discovered Marxism in 1893. His best-known work, *Réflexions sur la violence* (Reflections on Violence; 1908), exerted an important influence on Benjamin, whose essay of 1921, "Critique of Violence," is in part a response to Sorel. *Culte de la blague* means "cult of the joke." The origin of the phrase is obscure.

14. Baudelaire, *Oeuvres,* vol. 2, p. 666 ("Mon coeur mis à nu"). [Benjamin's note. Céline (pseudonym of Louis-Ferdinand Destouches; 1894–1961), French author best known for the novel *Voyage au bout de la nuit* (Journey to the End of Night; 1932), remained to the end of his life a notorious anti-Semite and nationalist. His *Bagatelles pour un massacre* (Bagatelles for a Massacre), a diatribe that blends anti-Semitism and pacifism, appeared in 1937.—Ed.]

15. Raoul Georges Adolphe Rigault (1846–1871), an official in the Paris Commune, was executed following the recapture of the city by government forces. Blanquists were followers of Louis-Auguste Blanqui (1805–1881), French revolutionary socialist and militant anticlerical. Blanqui was active in all three major upheavals in nineteenth-century France—the revolutions of 1830 and 1848 and the Paris Commune of 1871—and was imprisoned following each series of events. Quotations from Blanqui and Benjamin's commentary on him play a key role in *The Arcades Project*.

16. Charles Prolès, *Les Hommes de la Révolution de 1871: Raoul Rigault* (Paris, 1898), p. 9. [Benjamin's note. For more on Rigault, see Benjamin, *The Arcades Project*, trans. Howard Eiland and Kevin McLaughlin (Cambridge, Mass.: Harvard University Press, 1999), p. 618 (Convolute V9a,2.)—*Ed.*]

17. Baudelaire, *Lettres à sa mere*, p. 278. [Benjamin's note]

18. Marx and Engels, Review of Chenu and of de La Hodde, p. 556. [Benjamin's note]

19. See Ajasson de Grandsagne and Maurice Plaut, *Révolution de 1830: Plan des combats de Paris aux 27, 28 et 29 juillet* (Paris, n.d.). [Benjamin's note. The July Revolution, directed against the regime of Charles X, led to the accession of Louis Philippe. He was dubbed the Citizen King and his reign became known as the July Monarchy.—*Ed.*]

20. The French phrase means "unpaid but impassioned work." Charles Fourier (1772–1837), French social theorist and reformer, called for a reorganization of society based on communal agrarian associations which he termed "phalansteries." In each community, the members would continually change roles within different systems of production. Like Blanqui, Fourier figures crucially in *The Arcades Project* (see Convolute W).

21. Victor Hugo, *Oeuvres complètes: Edition définitive*, novels, vol. 8, *Les Misérables* (Paris, 1881), pp. 522ff. [Benjamin's note]

22. Baudelaire, *Oeuvres*, vol. 1, p. 229. [Benjamin's note. The quotation is line 25 from the poem that begins, "Tranquille comme un sage et doux comme un maudit," and ends, "Tu m'as donné ta boue et j'en ai fait de l'or."—*Ed.*]

23. Quoted in Charles Benoist, "Le 'Mythe' de la classe ouvrière," in *Revue des Deux Mondes*, March 1, 1914, p. 105. [Benjamin's note. "O force,

queen of the barricades, you who shine in lightning and in riots, . . . it is toward you that prisoners stretch out their shackled hands." Gustave Tridon (1841–1871) was a French socialist and a supporter of the Republic.—Ed.]

24. Adolphe Thiers (1797–1877), historian and journalist, was a leading politician and minister during Louis Philippe's reign (1830–1848). He was an opponent of the Second Empire, and subsequently served as president of France from 1871 to 1873.

25. Georges Laronze, Histoire de la Commune de 1871 (Paris, 1928), p. 532. [Benjamin's note]

26. On Louis Auguste Blanqui, see note 15 above.

27. Marx, Der achtzehnte Brumaire des Louis Bonaparte, p. 28. [Benjamin's note. During the insurrection of June 23–26, 1848, workers in Paris were joined by students and artisans in spontaneous demonstrations against the newly elected conservative majority. The insurgents were suppressed in bloody battles on the barricades.—Ed.]

28. Marx and Engels, Review of Chenu and of de La Hodde, p. 556. [Benjamin's note]

29. Report by J.-J. Weiss, quoted in Gustave Geffroy, L'Enfermé (Paris, 1897), pp. 346ff. [Benjamin's note. The passage is quoted at greater length in The Arcades Project, pp. 616–617 (Convolute V8a).— Ed.]

30. Baudelaire appreciated such details. "Why," he wrote, "don't the poor put on gloves when they go begging? They would make a fortune" (Oeuvres, vol. 2, p. 424: L'Art romantique, "L'Ecole païenne," last page). He attributes this statement to an unnamed person, but it bears the stamp of Baudelaire himself. [Benjamin's note]

31. Marx and Engels, Review of Chenu and of de La Hodde, p. 556. [Benjamin's note]

32. Karl Marx, Die Klassenkämpfe in Frankreich, 1848 bis 1850 (Berlin, 1895), p. 87. [Benjamin's note]

33. H. A. Frégier, Des Classes dangereuses de la population dans les grandes villes et des moyens de les rendre meilleures (Paris, 1840), vol. 1, p. 86. [Benjamin's note]

34. Edouard Foucaud, Paris inventeur: Physologie de l'industrie française (Paris, 1844), p. 10. [Benjamin's note]

35. Baudelaire, Oeuvres, vol. 1, p. 120. [Benjamin's note]

36. This budget is a social document not only because it investigates a particular family but also because it attempts to make abject misery appear less objectionable by neatly arranging it under rubrics. With the intent of leaving no inhumanity undocumented by the law whose observance it indicates, the totalitarian states have fostered the flowering of a seed which, as one may surmise, was already present in an earlier stage of capitalism. The fourth section of this budget of a ragpicker— cultural needs, entertainment, and hygiene—looks as follows: "Education of the children: tuition (paid by the employer), 48 francs; book purchases, 1.45 francs. Charitable contributions: workers of this class usually make none. Feasts and holidays—meals taken by the entire family at one of the *barrières* of Paris (eight excursions a year): wine, bread, and roast potatoes, 8 francs. Meals consisting of macaroni prepared with butter and cheese, plus wine on Christmas Day, Shrove Tuesday, Easter, and Whitsun: these expenses are given in the first section. Chewing tobacco for the husband (cigar stubs collected by the workingman himself), representing 5 to 34 francs. Snuff for the wife (bought), 18.66 francs. Toys and other presents for the child, 1 franc. Correspondence with relatives: letters from the workingman's brothers who live in Italy, one per year on the average . . ." "Addendum: The family's most important resource in case of accident is private charity. . . ." "Annual savings (the worker makes no provision whatever; he is primarily concerned with giving his wife and his little daughter all the comforts that are compatible with their situation; he amasses no savings, but every day spends whatever he earns)." (Frédéric Le Play, *Les Ouvriers européens* [Paris, 1855], pp. 274ff.) A sarcastic remark by Buret serves to illustrate the spirit of such an investigation: "Since humaneness, even plain decency, forbids one to let human beings die like animals, one cannot deny them the charity of a coffin." (Eugène Buret, *De la misère des classes laborieuses en Angleterre et en France: De la nature de la misère, de son existence, de ses effets, de ses causes, et de l'insuffisance des remèdes qu'on lui a opposés jusqu'ici; avec l'indication des moyens propres à en affranchir les sociétés* [Paris, 1840], vol. 1, p. 266.) [Benjamin's note]

37. It is fascinating to observe how the rebellion gradually comes to the fore in the various versions of the poem's concluding stanzas. In the first version, these read as follows:

C'est ainsi que le vin règne par ses bienfaits,
Et chante ses exploits par le gosier de l'homme.
Grandeur de la bonté de Celui que tout nomme,
Qui nous avait déjà donné le doux sommeil,
Et voulut ajouter le Vin, fils du Soleil,
Pour réchauffer le coeur et calmer la souffrance
De tous les malheureux qui meurent en silence.

       (*Oeuvres*, vol. 1, p. 605)

[Thus, wine reigns by virtue of its benefits
And sings of its exploits through the throats of men.
How great is the kindness of Him whom all things name,
Who had already given us sweet sleep
And who wished to add Wine, the son of the Sun,
To warm the heart and alleviate the suffering
Of all the unfortunates who die in silence.]

The 1852 version reads as follows:

Pour apaiser le coeur et calmer la souffrance
De tous ces innocents qui meurent en silence,
Dieu leur avait déjà donné le doux sommeil;
Il ajouta le vin, fils sacré du Soleil.

       (*Oeuvres*, vol. 1, p. 606)

[To ease the heart and alleviate the suffering
Of all those innocents who die in silence,
God had already given them sweet sleep;
He added wine, sacred son of the Sun.]

The final version of 1857 shows a radical change of meaning, and reads as follows:

Pour noyer la rancoeur et bercer l'indolence
De tous ces vieux maudits qui meurent en silence,
Dieu, touché de remords, avait fait le sommeil;
L'Homme ajouta le Vin, fils sacré du Soleil!

       (*Oeuvres*, vol. 1, p. 121)

[To drown the bitterness and lull the indolence
Of all those old wretches who die in silence,
God, in remorse, created sleep;
Man added wine, sacred son of the Sun!]

One may clearly observe how the stanza receives its definite form only as the sense becomes blasphemous. [Benjamin's note]

38. Charles-Augustin Sainte-Beuve, *Les Consolations; Pensées d'août* (Paris, 1863), p. 193. [Benjamin's note. Charles-Augustin Sainte-Beuve (1804–1869), French critic and writer, developed a literary critical method based on insight into psychology and biography. His criticism, which originally appeared in major reviews, is collected in *Causeries du lundi* (15 vols., 1851–1862; translated as *Monday Chats,* 1877). He considered his great work to be *Port-Royal* (1840–1859), a history of Jansenism and, more generally, of France in the seventeenth century. He was elected to the Académie Française in 1844, taught at the Ecole Normale Supérieure from 1857, and became a senator in 1865.—*Ed.*]

39. Baudelaire, *Oeuvres,* vol. 1, p. 136. [Benjamin's note]

40. "History of the Working Classes and the Bourgeois Classes." Adolphe Granier de Cassagnac (1806–1880) was a legislative deputy and semi-autonomous journalist; he was a prominent adherent of conservative Bonapartism in the Second Empire.

41. Marx, *Das Kapital,* ed. Karl Korsch (Berlin, 1932), p. 173. [Benjamin's note. For an English version, see *Capital,* vol. 1 (London, 1967), p. 172.—*Ed.*]

42. The title is followed by a prefatory note which was suppressed in the later editions. This note claims that the poems of the group are a highly literary simulation of "the sophisms of ignorance and anger." In truth, it is not a simulation at all. The public prosecutors of the Second Empire understood this, and so do their successors. Baron Seillière indicates this quite casually in his interpretation of the first poem in the series "Révolte." It is entitled "Le Reniement de Saint Pierre" [The Denial of Saint Peter] and includes the following lines:

Rêvais-tu de ces jours. . .
Où, le coeur tout gonflé d'espoir et de vaillance,
Tu fouettais tous ces vils marchands à tour de bras,

Où tu fus maître enfin? Le remords n'a-t-il pas
Pénétré dans ton flanc plus avant que la lance?
(*Oeuvres*, vol. 1, p. 136)

[Did you dream of those days . . .
When, your heart swelling with hope and courage,
You used to drive out all those abject moneylenders with your
    blows—
When you were finally master? Has not remorse
Pierced your side deeper than the spear?]

In this remorse, the ironic interpreter sees self-reproaches for "having missed such a good opportunity to establish the dictatorship of the proletariat" (Ernest Seillière, *Baudelaire* [Paris, 1931], p. 193). [Benjamin's note. Compare *The Arcades Project,* Convolute J21,4.—*Ed.*]

43. Baudelaire, *Oeuvres,* vol. 1, p. 138. [Benjamin's note]

44. Jules Lemaître, *Les Contemporains,* 4th series (Paris, 1895), p. 30. [Benjamin's note]

45. On the June Insurrection of 1848, see note 27 above.

46. *Les Châtiments* (The Chastisements; 1853) consists of a series of satirical poems that Hugo wrote in heated response to the coup d'état of Napoleon III, whom he saw as the archetypal tyrant.

47. Mimi and Schaunard are two characters in Puccini's opera *La Bohème,* which is based on Henri Murger's book *Scènes de la vie de Bohème* (1848).

48. Alfred-Victor, comte de Vigny (1797–1863) was a French Romantic poet, dramatist, and novelist. He introduced the French to poetry in a Byronic mode and novels in the style of Walter Scott.

49. See Auguste-Marseille Barthélemy, *Némésis: Satire hebdomadaire* (Paris, 1834), vol. 1, p. 225 ("L'Archevêché et la bourse"). [Benjamin's note. Auguste-Marseille Barthélemy (1796–1867) was a liberal poet and satirist who wrote in collaboration with J. P. A. Méry in opposition to the Bourbons and Louis Philippe. In 1831 the two poets started *Némésis,* a satirical weekly opposing the new regime. A year later Louis Philippe purchased Barthélemy's silence with a generous pension. Loosely translated, *Messe des agios* means "Mass of the Profits." The word "agio," from the Italian, technically refers to the pre-

mium (profit) made from currency exchange and stock speculation.—
Ed.]

50. Marx, *Der achtzehnte Brumaire des Louis Bonaparte*, p. 124. [Benjamin's note]

51. Pierre-Antoine Dupont (1821–1870) was a popular poet and republican song-writer whose socialist humanism stopped short of full political opposition. Until 1852 he associated with Hugo, Gautier, and Baudelaire. Baudelaire in particular praised Dupont's devotion to liberty. After the coup d'état of December 2, 1851, Dupont—who had avoided arrest by leaving for Savoy—was condemned in absentia to seven years of exile. Impoverished without the support of his Parisian audience, Dupont pledged allegiance to the regime in 1852 and lived quietly thereafter in Paris.

52. Jules-Amédée Barbey d'Aurevilly, *Le XIXe siècle: Les Oeuvres et les hommes,* 1st series, part 3: *Les Poètes* (Paris, 1862), p. 242. [Benjamin's note. Jules-Amédée Barbey d'Aurevilly (1808–1889), French novelist and critic, was a principal arbiter of social fashion and literary taste. His reviews alternated with those of Saint-Beuve in *Le Constitutionnel,* and on Saint-Beuve's death in 1869 he became sole critic. He was known for his attacks on Zola and the Naturalists, and for his defense of Balzac, Stendhal, and Baudelaire.—*Ed.*]

53. Pierre Larousse, *Grand Dictionnaire universel du XIX siècle,* vol. 6 (Paris, 1870), p. 1413 (article on Dupont). [Benjamin's note]

54. Marx, *Dem Andenken der Junikämpfer;* see also D. Riazanov, ed., *Karl Marx als Denker, Mensch und Revolutionär* (Vienna, 1928), p. 40. [Benjamin's note]

55. Pierre Dupont, "Le Chant du vote" (Paris, 1850; unpaginated). [Benjamin's note]

56. Baudelaire, *Oeuvres,* vol. 2, pp. 403ff.: *L'Art romantique,* "Pierre Dupont." [Benjamin's note. The French poet Auguste Barbier (1805–1882), became famous after the Revolution of 1830 for his satirical poems directed against moral decay and the cult of Napoleon. He was elected to the Académie Française in 1869.—*Ed.*]

57. Paul Desjardins, "Charles Baudelaire," in *La Revue Bleue* (Paris, 1887), p. 19. [Benjamin's note]

58. Baudelaire, *Oeuvres,* vol. 2, p. 659: "Mon coeur mis à nu," sec. 59. [Benjamin's note]

59. Ibid., p. 555: *L'Art romantique,* "Pierre Dupont." [Benjamin's note]

60. On the July Revolution (July 27–29, 1830), see note 19 above.

61. Emile de Girardin (1806–1881), French journalist, launched France's first mass-circulation newspaper, *La Presse,* in 1836. *La Presse* brought a number of innovations: it mixed traditional coverage of politics and the arts with elements of fashion, gossip, and scandal, and, above all, introduced the *roman-feuilleton,* the serial novel, which supplied a new mass readership with escapism, adventure, and sentimentality.

62. Sainte-Beuve, "De la littérature industrielle," in *Revue des Deux Mondes* (1839), pp. 682ff. [Benjamin's note]

63. Madame Emile de Girardin (née Delphine Gay), *Oeuvres complètes,* vol. 4: *Lettres parisiennes, 1836–1840* (Paris, 1860), pp. 289ff. [Benjamin's note. Madame de Girardin (1804–1855) published novels, comedies, and verse under the pseudonym Charles de Launay. Louis Jacques Mandé Daguerre (1787–1851), French painter and physicist, contributed significantly to the invention of the photographic process. He refined the work of his partner, Joseph Nicéphore Niépce (1765–1833), reducing the exposure time of the photographic plate from eight hours to twenty minutes. His work was recognized by the French government in 1839, at which time he was declared the inventor of photography.—*Ed.*]

64. *Bévues parisiennes* (Parisian Blunders) was a book that collected and published the errors found in the Parisian press.

65. Gabriel Guillemot, *La Bohème* (Paris, 1868), p. 72. [Benjamin's note]

66. "It does not take much acuteness to perceive that a girl who at eight o'clock may be seen sumptuously dressed in an elegant costume is the same who appears as a shopgirl at nine o'clock and as a peasant girl at ten." F.-F.-A. Béraud, *Les Filles publiques de Paris et la police qui les régit* (Paris and Leipzig, 1839), vol. 1, pp. 51ff. [Benjamin's note]

67. Alfred Nettement, *Histoire de la littérature française sous le Gouvernement de Juillet* (Paris, 1859), vol. 1, pp. 301ff. [Benjamin's note]

68. See S. Charléty, "La Monarchie de Juillet," in Ernest Lavisse, *Histoire de France contemporaine depuis la Révolution jusqu'à la paix de 1919* (Paris, 1921–1922), vol. 4, p. 352. [Benjamin's note. Alexandre Dumas père (1802–1870), French dramatist and novelist, was best known for *The*

Count of Monte Cristo (1844), *The Three Musketeers* (1844), and *The Man in the Iron Mask* (1848). *Le Constitutionnel,* first published in 1815, was the largest and most successful opposition paper under the Restoration; it declined under the July Monarchy but was revived in 1847.—*Ed.*]

69. Eugène Sue (1804–1857), French novelist, found enormous success with the ten volumes of *Les Mystères de Paris* (1842–1843), melodramatic tales of the sufferings and daily lives of the city's underclass during the July Monarchy.

70. Alphonse Marie Louis de Lamartine (1790–1869), French Romantic poet, novelist, and statesman, was best known for his *Méditations poétiques* (1820), which included the famous poem "Le Lac." He served as foreign minister in the Provisional Government following the Revolution of 1848. His *Histoire des Girondins* (History of the Girondists) appeared in 1847.

71. See Eugène de (Jacquot) Mirecourt, *Fabrique de romans: Maison Alexandre Dumas et Cie* [Factory of Novels: The Firm of Alexandre Dumas and Co.] (Paris, 1845). [Benjamin's note]

72. Paulin Limayrac, "Du roman actuel et de nos romanciers," in *Revue des Deux Mondes* (1845), pp. 953ff. [Benjamin's note]

73. Paul Saulnier, "Du roman en général et du romancier moderne en particulier," in *La Bohème* (1855), vol. 1, p. 3. The use of ghostwriters was not confined to serial novels. Eugène Scribe employed a number of anonymous collaborators for the dialogue of his plays. [Benjamin's note]

74. Narcisse-Achille de Salvandy (1795–1856), journalist, historian, and politician, also served for a time as minister of public instruction. He was best known for the caustic political pamphlets he wrote early in his career.

75. Marx, *Der achtzehnte Brumaire des Louis Bonaparte,* p. 68. [Benjamin's note]

76. Alphonse Karr (1808–1890), French journalist and novelist, was best known for his satirical monthly pamphlets, *Les Guêpes* (1839–1876). In later life, he moved to Nice and took up flower farming.

77. Alphonse de Lamartine, "Lettre à Alphonse Karr, Jardinier" in *Oeuvres poétiques complètes,* ed. Guyard (Paris, 1963), p. 1506.

78. In an open letter to Lamartine, the Ultramontane Louis Veuillot wrote: "Could it be that you really don't know that 'to be free' means to

despise gold? And in order to obtain the kind of freedom that is bought with gold, you produce your books in the same commercial fashion as you produce your vegetables or your wine!" Louis Veuillot, *Pages choisies*, ed. Albalat (Lyons, 1906), p. 31. [Benjamin's note. An Ultramontane was a supporter of papal policy in ecclesiastical and political matters.—*Ed.*]

79. Marx, *Der achtzehnte Brumaire*, p. 123. [Benjamin's note]

80. Ibid., p. 122. [Benjamin's note]

81. Sainte-Beuve, *Vie, poésies et pensées de Joseph Delorme* (Paris, 1863), p. 170. [Benjamin's note. André-Marie de Chénier (1762–1794), French poet and journalist, sought to revitalize French poetry through the imitation of Greek lyric forms.—*Ed.*]

82. On the basis of reports from Kisselyev, who at that time was Russia's ambassador in Paris, Pokrewski has demonstrated that things happened as Marx had outlined them in his *Klassenkämpfe in Frankreich*. On April 6, 1849, Lamartine had assured the ambassador that he would concentrate troops in the capital—a measure which the bourgeoisie later attempted to justify by pointing to the workers' demonstrations of April 16. Lamartine's remark that it would take him about ten days to concentrate the troops indeed puts those demonstrations in an ambiguous light. See Mikhail N. Pokrewski, *Historische Aufsätze* (Vienna, 1928), pp. 108ff. [Benjamin's note. For an excerpt from Pokrewski's account, see *The Arcades Project*, p. 767 (Convolute d12,2).—*Ed.*]

83. Sainte-Beuve, *Les Consolations*, p. 118. [Benjamin's note]

84. Quoted in Françoise Porché, *La Vie douloureuse de Charles Baudelaire* (Paris, 1926), p. 248. [Benjamin's note]

85. Ibid., p. 156. [Benjamin's note]

86. Ernest Raynaud, *Charles Baudelaire* (Paris, 1922), p. 319. [Benjamin's note]

87. Baudelaire, *Oeuvres*, vol. 2, p. 385: *L'Art romantique*, "Conseils aux jeunes littérateurs" ("Des salaires"). [Benjamin's note]

88. Quoted in Eugène Crépet, *Charles Baudelaire* (Paris, 1906), pp. 196ff. [Benjamin's note]

89. Baudelaire, *Oeuvres*, vol. 1, p. 209. [Benjamin's note. This poem, which begins "Je n'ai pas pour maîtresse une lionne illustre," first appeared in *Paris à l'eau forte* (Paris in Etchings) on October 17, 1875. In editions of Baudelaire's works, it is included under "Poèmes divers."

See *Les Fleurs du mal,* ed. Antoine Adam (Paris: Garnier Frères, 1961), pp. 224–226, 464.—*Ed.*]

90. Panoramas were large circular tableaux, usually displaying scenes of battles and cities, painted in trompe l'oeil and designed to be viewed from the center of a rotunda. They were introduced in France in 1799 by the American engineer Robert Fulton. Subsequent forms included the Diorama (opened by Louis Daguerre and Charles Bouton in 1822 in Paris), in which pictures were painted on cloth transparencies that, by 1831, were being used with various lighting effects.

91. *Le Livre des cent-et-un,* 15 vols. (Paris: Ladvocat, 1831–1834); *Les Français peints par eux-mêmes,* 8 vols. (Paris: L. Curmer, 1839–1842); *Le Diable à Paris,* 2 vols. (Paris: Hetzel, 1845–1846); *La Grande Ville,* 2 vols. (Paris: Bureau Central des Publications Nouvelles, 1842–1844).

92. Charles Louandre, "Statistique littéraire de la production intellectuelle en France depuis quinze ans," in *Revue des Deux Mondes* (November 15, 1847), pp. 686ff. [Benjamin's note]

93. Henri Monnier (1799–1877), French satirist, was known for his *Scènes populaires* (1830), which introduced the character of Joseph Prudhomme, the typical bourgeois: well-meaning but stupid, pretentious, and verbose. In *Les Bourgeois de Paris* (1834) and *Mémoires de Joseph Prudhomme* (1857), Monnier extended his satirical portrait of the middle class.

94. Paris at Night, Dining in Paris, Paris by Water, Paris by Horseback, Picturesque Paris, Marriage in Paris.

95. On the history of caricature by Eduard Fuchs, see the essay "Eduard Fuchs, Collector and Historian," in Walter Benjamin, *Selected Writings, Volume 3: 1935–1938,* ed. Howard Eiland and Michael W. Jennings (Cambridge, Mass.: Harvard University Press, 2002). The September Laws mandated a significantly more vigilant censorship and led to the virtual elimination of the opposition press. The laws were enacted in 1835, not 1836 as Benjamin indicates.

96. Eduard Fuchs, *Die Karikatur der europäischen Völker* (Munich, 1921), vol. 1, p. 362. [Benjamin's note. Honoré Daumier (1808–1879), French caricaturist, painter, and sculptor, was initially a political caricaturist. After the September Laws eliminated most venues for publishing his political work, he turned to the representation of scenes from everyday life.—*Ed.*]

97. Georges-Eugène, Baron Haussmann (1809–1891), French administrator and urban planner, oversaw the transformation of Paris from feudal city to modern metropolis. After studying law, he entered the civil service in 1831 and rose quickly, serving as prefect of the Seine *département* from 1853 to 1870. Working closely with Napoleon III, Haussmann supervised the rapid introduction of many new features: he cut broad, straight avenues through tangles of medieval streets; modernized the city's water supply and drainage system; built large parks in the city center; and supervised the completion of a number of major public buildings, including the Opéra and the marketplace of Les Halles.

98. Ferdinand von Gall, *Paris und seine Salons* (Oldenburg, 1845), vol. 2, pp. 22ff. [Benjamin's note]

99. Baudelaire, *Oeuvres,* vol. 2, p. 333: "Le Peintre de la vie moderne," sec. 3. [Benjamin's note. Constantin Guys (1805–1892), French painter and the subject of Baudelaire's essay "Le Peintre de la vie moderne" (The Painter of Modern Life; 1859), produced watercolors, engravings, and drawings of café life, military scenes, and the fashionable Parisian society of the Second Empire. For Baudelaire, Guys became the representative modern artist by virtue of his ability to capture and combine the ephemeral and the eternal in the modern world.—*Ed.*]

100. Georg Simmel (1858–1918), German sociologist and neo-Kantian philosopher, developed a theory of modernity, starting with his *Philosophie des Geldes* (Philosophy of Money; 1900) and continuing through classic essays such as "Die Gro¼stadt und das Geistesleben" (The Metropolis and Mental Life; 1903). His work exerted an enormous influence on the next generation of social philosophers, some of whom were his students: Georg Lukács, Ernst Cassirer, Ernst Bloch, Siegfried Kracauer, and Benjamin.

101. Georg Simmel, *Soziologie,* 4th ed. (Berlin, 1958), p. 486. [Benjamin's note]

102. See Bulwer-Lytton, *Eugene Aram: A Tale* (Paris, 1832), p. 314. [Benjamin's note. Edward George Earle Bulwer-Lytton (1803–1873), British novelist, produced a series of reform-minded moral tales. *Eugene Aram* is the story of a repentant murderer.—*Ed.*]

103. Marx and Engels on Feuerbach, in *Marx-Engels-Archiv: Zeitschrift des Marx-Engels-Instituts,* ed. David Riazanov (Frankfurt, 1926), vol. 1, pp. 271ff. [Benjamin's note]

104. Edouard Foucaud, *Paris inventeur: Physiologie de l'industrie française* (Paris, 1844), pp. 222ff. [Benjamin's note]

105. Johann Kaspar Lavater (1741–1801) was a Swiss writer and Protestant pastor whose theories of physiognomy were widely influential in the late eighteenth century. His *Physiognomische Fragmente zur Beförderung der Menschenkenntnis und Menschenliebe* (4 vols., 1775–1778; translated as *Essays on Physiognomy*, 1789–1798) were founded on the conviction that a person's mental faculties and character leave their mark on his or her physical features. Franz Joseph Gall (1758–1828), German physician, founded an institute in Vienna for the study of the brain and skull. His doctrines, which were later dubbed "phrenology" by one of his students, were enormously controversial in their day, and were in fact banned in Germany in 1802. His vast collection of skulls and plaster casts is now at the Musée de l'Homme in Paris.

106. Honoré de Balzac, *Le Cousin Pons* (Paris, 1914), p. 130. [Benjamin's note]

107. Baudelaire, *Oeuvres*, vol. 2, p. 637: *Journaux intimes*, "Fusées," sec. 21. [Benjamin's note]

108. Joseph de Maistre (1753–1821), French essayist and diplomat, combined a vast store of knowledge and a potent style in a series of invectives against Enlightenment rationalism. In his principal works *Du pape* (On the Pope; 1819) and *Les Soirées de Saint-Pétersbourg* (Discussions in St. Petersburg; 1821), he put forth his arguments for a world united under the spiritual rule of the pope. His *Examen de la philosophie de Bacon* appeared posthumously, in 1845. Francis Bacon (1561–1626), English philosopher and writer, sought, in his chief work *Novum Organum* (1620), to replace the deductive logic of Aristotle with an inductive method for interpreting nature.

109. Quoted in Adolphe Schmidt, *Tableaux de la révolution française, publiées sur les papers inédits du département et de la police secrète de Paris*, vol. 3 (Leipzig, 1870), p. 337. [Benjamin's note]

110. Baudelaire, *Oeuvres*, vol. 2, p. 333: "Le Peintre de la vie moderne," sec. 3. [Benjamin's note]

111. In his novel *Séraphita*, Balzac speaks of "a quick look whose perceptions in rapid succession placed the most antithetical landscapes of the earth at the disposal of the imagination." [Benjamin's note]

112. See Régis Messac, Le *"Detective Novel" et l'influence de la pensée*

scientifique (Paris, 1929). [Benjamin's note. James Fenimore Cooper (1789–1851), American novelist, was best known for his Leatherstocking Tales, featuring the wilderness scout called Natty Bumppo, or Hawkeye. They include *The Pioneers* (1823), *The Last of the Mohicans* (1826), *The Prairie* (1827), *The Pathfinder* (1840), and *The Deerslayer* (1841).—Ed.]

113. Paul Féval (1817–1887), French novelist, was the author of serial novels that rivaled those of Dumas in popularity. His most successful novel was *Le Bossu* (The Hunchback; 1857).

114. See Honoré de Balzac, *Splendeurs et misères des courtisanes,* part 2, in *Oeuvres complètes,* vol. 15 (Paris, 1913), pp. 310–311. In English, *A Harlot High and Low,* trans. Rayner Heppenstall (Harmondsworth: Penguin, 1970), p. 270.

115. See André Le Breton, *Balzac* (Paris, 1905), p. 83. [Benjamin's note]

116. Hippolyte Babou, *La Vérité sur le cas de M. Champfleury* (Paris, 1857), p. 30. [Benjamin's note]

117. See Baudelaire, *Les Fleurs du mal* (Paris, 1928), introduction by Paul Valéry. [Benjamin's note. Paul Valéry (1871–1945), French poet and essayist, is best known for essayistic fictions such as *La Soirée avec Monsieur Teste* (1896) and major poems of the Symbolist and post-Symbolist period.—Ed.]

118. Baudelaire, *Oeuvres,* vol. 2, p. 424: *L'Art romantique,* "L'Ecole païenne," last paragraph. [Benjamin's note]

119. "One always has to go back to Sade . . . to explain evil" (ibid., p. 694: "Fragments"—*Le Fou raisonnable et la belle aventurière*). [Benjamin's note. Count Donatien Alphonse François de Sade, better known as the Marquis de Sade (1740–1814), was the author of erotic writings that affirm the liberation of instincts even to the point of crime. In the course of a life that scandalized his contemporaries, he lived out many forms of his compulsions.—Ed.]

120. Ibid., vol. 1, p. 106. [Benjamin's note]

121. Albert Thibaudet, *Intérieurs* (Paris, 1924), p. 22. [Benjamin's note. Albert Thibaudet (1874–1946), French critic, was a principal contributor to the *Nouvelle Revue Française.* His range and discernment made him one of the leading critical voices of the interwar years.—Ed.]

122. The motif of love for a woman passing by is taken up in an early poem by Stefan George. But George misses the important thing: the

stream in which the woman moves past, borne along by the crowd. The result is a self-conscious elegy. The poet's glances—so he must confess to his lady—have "moved away, moist with longing / before they dared mingle with yours" ["feucht vor sehnen fortgezogen / eh sie in deine sich zu tauchen trauten"] (Stefan George, *Hymnen; Pilgerfahrten; Algabal,* 7th ed. [Berlin, 1922], p. 23). Baudelaire leaves no doubt that he looked deep into the eyes of the passer-by. [Benjamin's note]

123. Hans Makart (1840–1884) was an Austrian painter who made his reputation with vast historical and allegorical canvases. His name became a byword for empty monumentality.

124. The *Journal Officiel* was founded in 1869 by Eugène Rouher (1814–1884), minister, senator, and key political figure in the last years of the Second Empire. The journal, though semi-autonomous, followed a rigorous government line.

125. Balzac, *Modeste Mignon,* Editions du Siècle (Paris, 1850), p. 99. [Benjamin's note]

126. Sigmund Engländer, *Geschichte der französischen Arbeiter-Associationen,* 4 vols. (Hamburg, 1863–1864), vol. 3, p. 126. [Benjamin's note]

127. Baudelaire, *Oeuvres,* vol. 1, p. 115. [Benjamin's note. The phrase is from the poem "Brumes et pluies" (Mists and Showers), in the "Tableaux parisiens" section of *Les Fleurs du mal.—Ed.*]

128. Alphonse Bertillon (1853–1914), who became chief of criminal identification for the Paris police in 1880, developed an identification system known as anthropometry, or "the Bertillon system." The system is based on precise bodily measurements, physical descriptions, and photographs.

129. Hoffmann's story "Des Vetters Eckfenster" (1822) has been translated by Ritchie Robertson as "My Cousin's Corner Window," in Hoffmann, *"The Golden Pot" and Other Tales* (New York: Oxford University Press, 1992), pp. 377–401.

130. E. T. A. Hoffmann, *Ausgewählte Schriften,* vol. 15: *Leben und Nachlass,* ed. and with biographical notes by Julius Eduard Hitzig, vol. 3 (Stuttgart, 1839), pp. 32ff. [Benjamin's note]

131. Franz Mehring, "Charles Dickens," in *Die neue Zeit,* 30, no. 1 (1911–1912): 621ff. [Benjamin's note. See *The Letters of Charles Dickens,* ed. Walter Dexter, vol. 1: 1832–1846 (London, 1938), p. 782.—*Ed.*]

132. Baudelaire, *Oeuvres,* vol. 2, p. 710: "Argument du livre sur la Belgique," sec. 2. [Benjamin's note]

133. See *La Transformation de Paris sous le Second Empire: Exposition de la Bibliothèque et des travaux historiques de la ville de Paris,* ed. Marcel Poëte, E. Clouzot, and G. Henriot (Paris, 1910), p. 65. [Benjamin's note]

134. Julien Lemer, *Paris au gaz* (Paris, 1861), p. 10. The same image is found in "Le Crépuscule du soir": the sky "slowly closes like an enormous alcove" (see Baudelaire, *Oeuvres,* vol. 1, p. 108). [Benjamin's note]

135. Alfred Delvau, *Les Heures parisiennes* (Paris, 1866), p. 206. [Benjamin's note]

136. See Louis Veuillot, *Les Odeurs de Paris* (Paris, 1914), p. 182. [Benjamin's note]

137. Robert Louis Stevenson, "A Plea for Gas Lamps," in *Virginibus Puerisque and Other Papers,* in Stevenson, *Works,* Tusitala Edition, vol. 25 (London, 1924), p. 132. [Benjamin's note]

138. There is a parallel to this passage in "Un Jour de pluie." Even though this poem bears another man's name, it can be ascribed to Baudelaire (see Charles Baudelaire, *Vers retrouvés,* ed. Julius Mouquet [Paris, 1929]). The analogy between the last stanza and Poe's mention of Tertullian is all the more remarkable because the poem was written in 1843 at the latest, at a time when Baudelaire did not know Poe.

> Chacun, nous coudoyant sur le trottoir glissant,
> Egoïste et brutal, passe et nous éclabousse,
> Ou, pour courir plus vite, en s'éloignant nous pousse.
> Partout fange, déluge, obscurité du ciel:
> Noir tableau qu'eût rêvé le noir Ezéchiel!
> (Baudelaire, *Oeuvres,* vol. 1, p. 211)

[Benjamin's note. The verse translates as: "Each one, elbowing us on the slippery sidewalk, / Selfish and savage, goes by and splashes us, / Or, to run the faster, gives us a push as he makes off. / Everywhere mud, deluge, darkness in the sky. / A somber scene that Ezekiel the somber might have dreamed." Quintus Septimus Florens Tertullianus (ca. 155/160 A.D.–ca. 220 A.D.) was an early Christian theologian and polemicist who, as the first practitioner of ecclesiastical Latin, exerted a profound influence on the ideas and rhetoric of Western Christianity.—*Ed.*]

139. Edgar Allan Poe, *Nouvelles histoires extraordinaires,* trans.

Charles Baudelaire (Paris: Lévy Frères, 1857), p. 89. [Benjamin's note. The volume that Benjamin cites, first published in 1857, contains a number of Poe's tales, selected, ordered, and translated by Baudelaire; it also contains Baudelaire's important essay "Notes nouvelles sur Edgar Poe."—Ed.]

140. Ibid., pp. 89–90. [Benjamin's note]

141. The image of America that Marx had seems to be of the same stuff as Poe's description. He emphasizes the "feverishly youthful pace of material production" in the States and blames this very pace for the fact that there was "neither time nor opportunity . . . to abolish the old spirit world" (Marx, *Der achtzehnte Brumaire des Louis Bonaparte*, p. 30). In Poe, there is something demonic even about the physiognomy of the businessmen. Baudelaire describes how, as darkness descends, "baleful demons awaken sluggishly" in the air "like a bunch of businessmen" (*Oeuvres*, vol. 1, p. 108). This passage in "Le Crépuscule du soir" may have been inspired by Poe's text. [Benjamin's note]

142. Alois Senefelder (1771–1834) was the German inventor of the lithographic process.

143. See Georges Friedmann, *La Crise du progrès* (Paris, 1936), p. 76. [Benjamin's note. Frederick Winslow Taylor (1856–1915) established the discipline of business administration and pioneered in the study of rationalization and management efficiency. "Taylorism" and "Taylorization" were slogans, particularly in Europe, for a more general industrial modernization.—Ed.]

144. Paul Ernest de Rattier, *Paris n'existe plus* (Paris, 1857), pp. 74ff. [Benjamin's note]

145. Jules Laforgue, *Mélanges posthumes* (Paris, 1903), p. 111. [Benjamin's note. Jules Laforgue (1860–1887), French poet and critic, was a Symbolist master of lyrical irony.]

146. See Marx, *Das Kapital*, ed. Karl Korsch (Berlin, 1932), p. 95. [Benjamin's note. In English in *Capital*, vol. 1 (London, 1967), p. 84.—Ed.]

147. Baudelaire, *Oeuvres*, vol. 1, pp. 420–421: *Le Spleen de Paris*, "Les Foules." [Benjamin's note]

148. On this point, the second "Spleen" poem is the most important addition to the documentation assembled in the first part of this essay.

There is scarcely a single poet before Baudelaire who wrote a verse anything like "Je suis un vieux boudoir plein de roses fanées" (*Oeuvres*, vol. 1, p. 86) ["I am an old boudoir full of faded roses"]. The poem is entirely based on empathy with the material, which is dead in a dual sense. It is inorganic matter, matter that has been eliminated from the circulation process.

> Désormais tu n'es plus, ô matière vivante!
> Qu'un granit entouré d'une vague épouvante,
> Assoupi dans le fond d'un Sahara brumeux;
> Un vieux sphinx ignoré du monde insoucieux,
> Oublié sur la carte, et dont l'humeur farouche
> Ne chante qu'aux rayons du soleil qui se couche.
> (Baudelaire, *Oeuvres*, vol. 1, p. 86: "Spleen [II]")

> [Henceforth you are nothing more, O living matter,
> Than a piece of granite enveloped in a vague sense of horror,
> Slumbering in the depths of some misty Sahara—
> An old sphinx ignored by the careless world,
> Erased from the map, and whose fierce nature
> Sings only to the rays of the setting sun.]

The image of the Sphinx which concludes the poem has the gloomy beauty of the white elephants that are still found in some arcades. [Benjamin's note]

149. Baudelaire, *Oeuvres*, vol. 2, p. 627: *Journaux intimes*, "Fusées," sec. 2. [Benjamin's note]

150. Ibid., vol. 1, p. 421. [Benjamin's note. The phrases are from the prose poem "Les Foules," in *Le Spleen de Paris.—Ed.*]

151. Ibid. [Benjamin's note. "That holy prostitution of the soul which gives itself completely, poetry and charity, to the unexpected that appears, to the unknown that passes."—*Ed.*]

152. Ibid., p. 108. [Benjamin's note]

153. Engels, *Die Lage der arbeitenden Klasse in England* (Leipzig, 1848), pp. 36ff. [Benjamin's note. English translation: *The Condition of the Working-Class in England in 1844* (orig. pub. 1887), in Karl Marx and Friedrich Engels, *On Britain* (Moscow, 1962), pp. 56–57.—*Ed.*]

154. Baudelaire, *Oeuvres*, vol. 2, p. 626: *Journaux intimes*, "Fusées," sec. 1. [Benjamin's note]

155. Percy Bysshe Shelley, "Peter Bell the Third Part," *Complete Poetical Works* (London, 1932), p. 346. [Benjamin's note. Benjamin quotes this verse in a German translation by Brecht; see, on this point, the February 1939 exchange of letters between Benjamin and Theodor Adorno, in this volume. The whole of Shelley's poem is quoted in Convolute M18 in *The Arcades Project* (pp. 449–450).—*Ed.*]

156. Baudelaire, *Oeuvres*, vol. 1, p. 102. [Benjamin's note. This is the first line of "Les Petites Vieilles."—*Ed.*]

157. Ibid. [Benjamin's note]

158. Ibid., vol. 2, p. 193: *Curiosités esthétiques*, "Quelques caricaturistes français*," sec. 1. [Benjamin's note]

159. Ibid., p. 522: *L'Art romantique*, sec. 19.1, "Victor Hugo." [Benjamin's note]

160. Ibid., vol. 1, p. 100. [Benjamin's note. The poem is "Les Sept Vieillards."—*Ed.*]

161. Ibid., p. 103. [Benjamin's note. The phrase is from "Les Petites Vieilles."—*Ed.*]

162. The third poem in the cycle devoted to Hugo, "Les Petites Vieilles," underlines the rivalry by following verbatim the third poem in Hugo's cycle "Fantômes." Thus, there is a correspondence between one of Baudelaire's most perfect poems and one of Hugo's weakest. [Benjamin's note]

163. Sainte-Beuve, *Les Consolations; Pensées d'août* (Paris, 1863), p. 125. The remark, published by Sainte-Beuve from the manuscript, is by Farcy. [Benjamin's note]

164. Hugo von Hofmannsthal, *Versuch über Victor Hugo* (Munich, 1925), p. 49. [Benjamin's note]

165. "The ocean itself got bored with him."

166. Quoted in Gabriel Bounoure, "Abîmes de Victor Hugo," in *Mesures* (July 15, 1936), p. 39. [Benjamin's note. The French translates as "The depths are crowds."—*Ed.*]

167. Victor Hugo, *Oeuvres complètes: Edition définitive,* poetry, vol. 2, *Les Orientales; Les Feuilles d'automne* (Paris, 1880), pp. 365ff. [Benjamin's note]

168. Ibid., p. 363. [Benjamin's note]

169. Hugo, *Oeuvres complètes*, novels, vol. 8, *Les Misérables* (Paris, 1881). [Benjamin's note]

170. "To go to the many," "to join the multitude"—i.e., "to die."

171. Gustave Simon, *Chez Victor Hugo: Les Tables tournantes de Jersey* (Paris, 1923), pp. 306ff. [Benjamin's note]

172. Hugo, *Oeuvres complètes*, poetry, vol. 4, *Les Châtiments* (Paris, 1882), "La Caravane IV." [Benjamin's note]

173. Louis-Eugène Cavaignac (1802–1857), French army general, crushed the insurrection of the Paris workers during the June Days of 1848 and remained chief executive of France until the election of Louis-Napoleon Bonaparte as president in December 1848.

174. Pélin, a typical representative of the lower *bohème*, wrote about this speech in his paper "Les Boulets rouges: Feuille du Club Pacifique des Droits de l'Homme": "*Citoyen* Hugo has made his debut in the National Assembly. As had been expected, he turned out to be a declaimer, a gesticulator, and a phrase-monger. In the vein of his latest crafty and defamatory poster, he spoke of the idlers, the poor, the loafers, the *lazzaroni*, the praetorians of the revolution, and the condottieri—in a word, he exhausted the stock of metaphors and ended with an attack on the *ateliers nationaux*" (*Les Boulets rouges*, First year, June 22–24). In his *Histoire parlementaire de la Seconde République* (Paris, 1891), Eugène Spuller writes: "Victor Hugo had been elected with reactionary votes. . . . He had always voted with the rightists, except for one or two occasions when politics did not matter" (pp. 111 and 266). [Benjamin's note. The *ateliers nationaux*, or "national workshops," provided relief from the deepening economic crisis of 1848. The workshops were closed following the failure of the June Insurrection.—*Ed.*]

175. Hugo, *Les Misérables*, p. 306. [Benjamin's note]

176. Since the days of the French Revolution, the word *citoyen* ("citizen") has carried distinctly revolutionary connotations.

177. Baudelaire, *Oeuvres*, vol. 2, p. 26: "Salon de 1845," sec. 2 ("Robert Fleury"). [Benjamin's note]

178. Ibid., p. 388: *L'Art romantique*, "Conseils aux jeunes littérateurs," sec. 6. [Benjamin's note. The French phrase translates as "the stubborn contemplation of tomorrow's work" (*Advice to Young Men of Letters*).—*Ed.*]

179. Ibid., p. 531: *L'Art romantique*, sec. 19.2 ("Auguste Barbier").

[Benjamin's note. The French translates as "the natural indolence of those who live in a state of inspiration."—*Ed.*]

180. Albert Thibaudet, *Intérieurs* (Paris, 1924), p. 15. [Benjamin's note. Louis Charles Alfred de Musset (1810–1857), French poet, playwright, and translator, ranks alongside Hugo, Lamartine, and Vigny as one of the great Romantic poets. He combined an intense lyricism with a propensity to shock through revelation of his vices: laziness, self-indulgence, a facile talent, and an attraction to opium.—*Ed.*]

181. Quoted in André Gide, "Baudelaire et M. Faguet," in *Nouvelle Revue Française* (November 1, 1910), p. 513. [Benjamin's note. Maurice Barrès (1862–1923) was a French writer and politician whose fervent individualism and nationalism made his ideas a rallying point for the Right.—*Ed.*]

182. Rémy de Gourmont, *Promenades littéraires,* 2nd series (Paris, 1906), pp. 85ff. [Benjamin's note]

183. Preface by Gustave Kahn in Baudelaire, *Mon Coeur mis à nu; Fusées* (Paris, 1909), p. 6. [Benjamin's note. The French poet Gustave Kahn (1859–1936) played a significant role in the early days of the Symbolist movement. Cofounder of the journal *Le Symboliste,* he emerged as an important theorist of poetry.—*Ed.*]

184. Baudelaire, *Oeuvres,* vol. 2, p. 334: "Le Peintre de la vie moderne," sec. 3 (last para.). [Benjamin's note]

185. Quoted in Ernest Raynaud, *Charles Baudelaire* (Paris, 1922), pp. 317ff. [Benjamin's note]

186. Baudelaire, *Oeuvres,* vol. 1, p. 96. [Benjamin's note]

187. François-Arsène Houssaye (1815–1897), French journalist, was befriended by Théophile Gautier and met, through him, the leading writers of his day. His criticism appeared in virtually every leading newspaper and journal.

188. Baudelaire, *Oeuvres,* vol. 1, pp. 405–406. [Benjamin's note. The passage is from the dedicatory essay "A Arsène Houssaye," in *Le Spleen de Paris.*—*Ed.*]

189. "The flâneur must not be confused with the *badaud* [onlooker; rubberneck]; a nuance should be noted here. . . . The simple flâneur is always in full possession of his individuality, whereas the individuality of the *badaud* disappears. It is absorbed by the outside world, . . . which in-

toxicates him to the point where he forgets himself. Under the influence of the spectacle which appears before him, the *badaud* becomes an impersonal creature. He is no longer a human being; he is part of the public, of the crowd." Victor Fournel, *Ce qu'on voit dans les rues de Paris* (Paris, 1858), p. 263. [Benjamin's note]

190. G. K. Chesterton (1874–1936), English novelist, is best known for his "Father Brown" novels, which use the figure of the sleuthing priest to mix detective fiction and social analysis.

191. G. K. Chesterton, *Dickens* [in French] (Paris, 1927), p. 30. [Benjamin's note. Benjamin translates the passage into German from the French version. The extract cited here is the original English from Chesterton, *Charles Dickens* (1906; rpt. New York: Schocken, 1965), pp. 45–46.—*Ed.*]

192. Recalling the period around 1845, Prarond, a friend of Baudelaire's from their youth, wrote: "We seldom used desks at which to reflect and write." Referring to Baudelaire, he continues: "I for my part was more likely to see him composing his verses in a hurry, rushing up and down the street; I never saw him sitting before a ream of paper." (Quoted in Alphonse Séché, *La Vie des Fleurs du mal* [Paris, 1928], p. 84.) Banville makes a similar report about the Hotel Pimodan: "When I visited there for the first time, I found neither encyclopedias nor a study nor a writing desk. Nor was there a sideboard, a dining room, or anything resembling the furnishings of a middle-class apartment." (Théodore de Banville, *Mes souvenirs* [Paris, 1882], p. 82.) [Benjamin's note]

193. Maxime Du Camp, *Souvenirs littéraires,* vol. 2 (Paris, 1906), p. 65. [Benjamin's note]

194. See Georges Rency, *Physiognomies littéraires* (Brussels, 1907), p. 288. [Benjamin's note]

195. Marx, *Randglossen zum Programm der Deutschen Arbeiterpartei,* ed. Karl Korsch (Berlin, 1922), p. 22. [Benjamin's note. See, in English, *Marginal Notes on the Programme of the German Workers' Party,* trans. Peter Ross and Betty Ross, in Karl Marx and Friedrich Engels, *Collected Works,* vol. 24 (New York: International Publishers, 1989), p. 81. In 1875, Gotha, a city in the east-central German province of Thuringia, was the scene of the congress that united the Eisenach and the Lassalle politi-

cal groups into the Socialist Labor Party of Germany. The new party adopted the Gotha Program, which was sharply criticized by Karl Marx for its reformism and moderation.—*Ed.*]

196. Baudelaire, *Dernières lettres inédites à sa mère* (Paris: Crépet, 1926), pp. 44–45. [Benjamin's note]

197. Marx, *Der achtzehnte Brumaire des Louis Bonaparte,* pp. 122ff. [Benjamin's note]

198. See "Pour toi, vieux maraudeur, / L'amour n'a plus de goût, non plus que la dispute" ["For you, old marauder / Love has lost its savor, and quarreling as well"] (Baudelaire, *Oeuvres,* vol. 1, p. 89 ["Le Goût du néant"]).—One of the few repulsive phenomena in the extensive, mostly colorless literature about Baudelaire is a book by one Peter Klassen. This book, which is written in the depraved terminology of the George circle and, as it were, presents Baudelaire under a steel helmet, typically claims that the center of his life was the Ultramontane restoration—that is, the day "when, in the spirit of the restored divine right of kings, the Holy of Holies was carried through the streets of Paris surrounded by gleaming armaments. This may have been one of the decisive moments of his life, because it involved his very essence" (Peter Klassen, *Baudelaire* [Weimar, 1931], p. 9). Baudelaire was six years old at the time. [Benjamin's note]

199. Marcel Proust, "A propos de Baudelaire," in *Nouvelle Revue Française* (June 1, 1921), p. 646. [Benjamin's note. Proust's remark translates as, "It seems impossible to go beyond this."—*Ed.*]

200. Baudelaire, *Oeuvres,* vol. 1, p. 104. [Benjamin's note]

201. Ibid., vol. 2, p. 408: *L'Art romantique,* "Pierre Dupont." [Benjamin's note. The italics are Baudelaire's.—*Ed.*]

202. Balzac, *L'Illustre Gaudissart* (Paris: Calmann-Lévy, 1892), p. 5. [Benjamin's note]

203. Baudelaire, *Oeuvres,* vol. 1, p. 119. [Benjamin's note]

204. Ibid., vol. 2, p. 239: "Salon de 1859," sec. 5. [Benjamin's note]

205. Nietzsche later took a similar view of suicide. "One cannot condemn Christianity enough, because it devalued the *value* of a . . . great *purging* nihilistic movement which may have been in train, . . . and always devalued it by opposing the *deed of nihilism,* suicide." Cited in Karl Löwith, *Nietzsches Philosophie der ewigen Wiederkunft des Gleichen* (Berlin, 1935), p. 108. [Benjamin's note. See Friedrich Nietzsche, *Werke,* ed. Karl Schlechta (Munich: Ullstein, 1956), vol. 3, pp. 792–793. In Eng-

lish as *The Will to Power,* trans. Walter Kaufmann and R. J. Hollingdale (New York: Random House, 1967), p. 143 (March–June 1888).—*Ed.*]

206. Baudelaire, *Oeuvres,* vol. 2, pp. 133–134: "Salon de 1846," sec. 18 ("De l'héroïsme de la vie moderne"). [Benjamin's note. Heracles built his own funeral pyre and threw himself on it in order to relieve the anguish caused by the poisoned garment sent to him by his wife. Marcus Porcius Cato (Cato the Younger; 95 B.C.–46 B.C.) was a Roman patriot and Stoic philosopher who sided with Pompey against Caesar in the civil war in 49 B.C. He committed suicide on receiving news of Caesar's victory at Thapsus. Although there are several suicides named Cleopatra in the ancient world, Benjamin presumably refers to Cleopatra VII (69 B.C.–30 B.C.), last Macedonian queen of Egypt and lover of Mark Antony. Following the defeat of their fleet at the hands of Octavian, Antony killed himself on hearing a false report of her death. She followed him rather than be displayed in Octavian's triumphal procession in Rome.—*Ed.*]

207. Charles Benoist, "L'Homme de 1848, II: Comment il s'est développé le communisme, l'organisation du travail, la réforme," *Revue des Deux Mondes* (February 1914), p. 667. [Benjamin's note]

208. Alfred Rethel (1816–1859), German painter, was inspired by the Revolution of 1848 to do a series of highly original and moving woodcuts in the tradition of the late medieval Dance of Death. The series was titled *Auch ein Totentanz* (1849).

209. Baudelaire, *Oeuvres,* vol. 2, pp. 54–55: "Salon de 1845," last paragraph. [Benjamin's note]

210. Ibid., p. 134: "Salon de 1846" ("De l'héroïsme de la vie moderne"). [Benjamin's note]

211. Ibid., p. 136: "De l'héroïsme de la vie moderne," last paragraph. [Benjamin's note. Vautrin and Rastignac are characters in Balzac's novel *Le Père Goriot* (1834–1835); Birotteau, a character in *Histoire de la grandeur et de la décadence de César Birotteau* (1838). Fontanarès is the hero of Balzac's play *Les Ressources de Quinola* (1842), set in the sixteenth century.—*Ed.*]

212. Friedrich Theodor Vischer (1807–1887) was a leading liberal politician who is best remembered for his championing of literary realism at midcentury.

213. Friedrich Theodor Vischer, *Vernünftige Gedanken über die jetzige*

Mode: Kritische Gänge, new series, book 3 (Stuttgart, 1861), p. 117. [Benjamin's note]

214. Baudelaire, *Oeuvres,* vol. 1, p. 22. [Benjamin's note]

215. Vischer, *Vernünftige Gedanken,* p. 111. [Benjamin's note]

216. Baudelaire, *Oeuvres,* vol. 2, pp. 134ff. [Benjamin's note. *La Gazette des Tribunaux* was a semi-official daily paper founded in 1825; it covered trials and legal matters, often with verbatim accounts. *Le Moniteur,* founded in 1789 and later published under a variety of names, was the official government organ for edicts, laws, and the presentation of policy.—*Ed.*]

217. Gabriel Bounoure, "Abîmes de Victor Hugo," in *Mesures* (July 15, 1936), p. 40. [Benjamin's note]

218. Ferragus is the main character in Balzac's novel of the same name. The Carbonari were an Italian revolutionary group organized in about 1811 to establish a united republican Italy. French Carbonarism, directed against the Bourbon Restoration, was initiated in 1820 by young republican militants.

219. The French phrase means "Passer-by, be modern!" It was inscribed over the door of the old Chat Noir café, located in Montmartre. See *The Arcades Project,* Convolute S5a,4; S5a,1; and J55a,7.

220. Baudelaire, *Oeuvres,* vol. 1, pp. 249ff. [Benjamin's note]

221. Quoted in Firmin Maillard, *La Cité des intellectuels: Scènes cruelles et plaisantes de la vie littéraires des gens de lettres au XIXe siècle* (Paris, 1905), p. 362. [Benjamin's note. "Pas saccadé" translates as "jerky gait." Benjamin says here that poet and ragpicker share the same "gestus," borrowing a term from Brecht. Nadar (pseudonym of Gaspard-Félix Tournachon; 1820–1910), French writer, caricaturist, and photographer, emerged from a large group of Parisian studio portraitists as one of the great portraitists of the century. Among his many innovations are his natural posing of his subjects, a patent on the use of photographs in mapmaking and surveying, the first aerial photograph (from a balloon), and the first photographic interview: twenty-one images of the scientist Eugène Chevreul, accompanied by text.—*Ed.*]

222. Guillaume Apollinaire (pseudonym of Wilhelm Apollinaris de Kostrowitzki; 1880–1918), French poet and critic, was the driving force in the French avant-garde until his early death. His most important works include the pioneering essay "Peintures cubistes" (Cubist Painters;

1913), the poem collections *Alcools* (1913) and *Calligrammes* (1918), the story "Le Poète assassiné" (The Poet Assassinated; 1916), and the play *Les Mamelles de Tirésias* (The Breasts of Tiresias; staged in 1917). Croniamantal is the poet-protagonist in *Le Poète assassiné.*

223. Baudelaire long planned to write novels set in this milieu. His posthumous papers contain the vestiges of such projects, in the form of titles: *Les Enseignements d'un monstre* (The Teachings of a Monster); *L'Entreteneur* (The Keeper); *La Femme malhonnête* (The Dishonest Woman). [Benjamin's note. See *The Arcades Project*, p. 283 (Convolute J30,12).—*Ed.*]

224. Baudelaire, *Oeuvres*, vol. 1, p. 193. [Benjamin's note]

225. Three-quarters of a century later, the antagonism between the pimp and the man of letters was revived. When the writers were driven out of Germany, a Horst Wessel legend entered German literature. [Benjamin's note. Horst Wessel (1907–1930), a pimp who lived in a Berlin slum with a former prostitute, joined the Nazi party in 1926 and became a storm trooper. After he was killed in a fight in his apartment, he was glorified as a martyr for the Nazi cause. A poem he had published in Joseph Goebbels' *Der Angriff* was set to the tune of a cabaret song and became the official Nazi anthem.—*Ed.*]

226. Baudelaire, *Oeuvres*, vol. 2, p. 336 ("Le Peintre de la vie moderne"). [Benjamin's note. See Baudelaire, *The Painter of Modern Life and Other Essays*, trans. Jonathan Mayne (1964; rpt. New York: Da Capo, 1986), pp. 13–14. See also *The Arcades Project*, Convolute J6a,2 and J6a,3.—*Ed.*]

227. Kahn, Preface in Baudelaire, *Mon coeur mis à nu; Fusées* (Paris, 1909), p. 15. [Benjamin's note. The French phrase translates as "a refusal to take the opportunity offered by the nature of the lyric pretext."—*Ed.*]

228. Baudelaire, *Oeuvres*, vol. 2, p. 580: *L'Art romantique*, "Les Misérables," sec. 3. [Benjamin's note]

229. Ibid., p. 508: *L'Art romantique*, "Richard Wagner et Tannhäuser," sec. 4, para. 1. [Benjamin's note]

230. Ibid., p. 337: "Le Peintre de la vie moderne," sec. 4. [Benjamin's note]

231. Ibid., p. 363: "Le Peintre de la vie moderne," sec. 13. [Benjamin's note]

232. Ibid., p. 326: "Le Peintre de la vie moderne," sec. 1. [Benjamin's note]

233. The term "Alexandrism" was originally applied to a soft and sentimental tendency in Hellenistic sculpture. Abel-François Villemain (1790–1870) was a French politician and literary critic. Victor Cousin (1792–1867) was a politician and philosopher who attempted to integrate a number of philosophical doctrines in a movement called "eclecticism." He introduced Hegel's thought to France.

234. Baudelaire, *Oeuvres*, vol. 1, p. 99. [Benjamin's note. "The form of a city, alas, changes more quickly than a mortal's heart."—*Ed.*]

235. Emile Verhaeren, *Les Villes tentaculaires* (Paris, 1904), p. 119, "L'Ame de la ville." [Benjamin's note. Verhaeren (1855–1916), a Belgian poet who wrote in French, created a body of work noted for its range. His collections include *Les Flamandes* (1883), *Les Moines* (1886), *Les Soirs* (1887), *Les Debâcles* (1888), *Les Flambeaux noirs* (1890), *Au Bord de la route* (1891), and *Les Campagnes hallucinées* (1893).—*Ed.*]

236. Charles Péguy, *Oeuvres de prose* (Paris, 1916), pp. 388ff. [Benjamin's note. Charles Péguy (1873–1914) was a French poet and philosopher whose work brought together Christianity, socialism, and French nationalism.—*Ed.*]

237. Victor Hugo, *Les Misérables* (Paris, 1881), p. 55ff. [Benjamin's note. The sibyl at Delphi sat on a golden tripod when she made her prophecies.—*Ed.*]

238. Friedrich von Raumer, *Briefe aus Paris und Frankreich im Jahre 1830* (Leipzig, 1831), vol. 2, p. 127. [Benjamin's note. Friedrich von Raumer (1781–1873), German historian, is best known for his *Geschichte der Hohenstaufen und ihrer Zeit* (History of the Hohenstaufens and Their Time; 6 volumes, 1924).—*Ed.*]

239. Hugo, *Oeuvres complètes*, poetry, vol. 3 (Paris, 1880). [Benjamin's note]

240. Ibid. [Benjamin's note]

241. Léon Daudet, *Paris vécu* (Paris, 1929), vol. 1, p. 220ff. [Benjamin's note. Léon Daudet (1867–1942) edited the right-wing Catholic journal *L'Action Française,* organ of the eponymous nationalist political movement that he founded with Charles Maurras in 1898. The journal was noted for its antidemocratic and anti-Semitic views.—*Ed.*]

242. Maxime Du Camp (1822–1894), French writer and photogra-

pher, first became known for *Egypte, Nubie, Palestine et Syrie* (1852), based on his travels with Gustave Flaubert and one of the first travel books illustrated with photographs. He subsequently forged a career as a publisher and produced work in virtually every genre. His *Paris: Ses organes, ses fonctions et sa vie dans la seconde moitié du XIXe siècle* (6 vols., 1869–1875) mixes a vivid account of everyday life in Paris with technical details of urban administration.

243. Paul Bourget, "Discours académique du 13 juin 1895: Succession à Maxime Du Camp," in *L'Anthologie de l'Académie Française* (Paris, 1921), vol. 2, pp. 191ff. [Benjamin's note]

244. Maxime Du Camp, *Paris: Ses organes, ses functions et sa vie dans la seconde moitié du XIX siècle,* vol. 6 (Paris, 1886), p. 253. [Benjamin's note]

245. Joseph Joubert, *Pensées, précédées de sa correspondance* (Paris, 1883), vol. 2, p. 267. [Benjamin's note. "Poets are inspired more by the image than by the actual presence of objects." The French writer Joseph Joubert (1754–1824) is best known for his brilliant private journals, which were not originally intended for publication. Chateaubriand published them in 1838 under the title *Pensées.—Ed.*]

246. Charles Meryon (1821–1868), French engraver and painter, turned to engraving in part because of his color-blindness. He is best known for his series of highly detailed city views which have a kind of hallucinatory clarity, especially the series *Eaux-fortes sur Paris* (Etchings of Paris; 1852–1854, reworked 1861). After 1858 he suffered from symptoms of madness.

247. In the twentieth century, Meryon found a biographer in Gustave Geffroy. It is no accident that Geffroy's masterpiece is a biography of Blanqui. [Benjamin's note. Gustave Geffroy (1830–1896), French writer and critic, was a contributor to Georges Clemenceau's newspaper *La Justice;* his essays championed the Impressionists and the Naturalists. His biography of Blanqui is entitled *L'Enfermé* (1897).—*Ed.*]

248. Quoted in Gustave Geffroy, *Charles Meryon* (Paris, 1926), p. 2. Meryon began as a naval officer. His last etching depicts the naval ministry on the Place de la Concorde. A procession of horses, carriages, and dolphins is shown in the clouds, rushing toward the ministry. There are ships and sea serpents, too, and some human-like forms can be seen in the crowd. Geffroy easily finds the "meaning" of this image without

dwelling on the form or the allegory: "His dreams hastened to this building, which was as solid as a fortress. This is where the record of his career had been entered in his youth, when he was still engaging in far-flung travels. And now he bids farewell to this city and this building, which have caused him so much suffering." Ibid., p. 161. [Benjamin's note. "Le Squelette laboureur" (The Laborer-Skeleton) is a poem in *Les Fleurs du mal.—Ed.*]

249. Ibid. The will to preserve "traces" is most decisively involved in this art. Meryon's title page for his series of etchings shows a split rock bearing the imprinted traces of ancient plant forms. [Benjamin's note]

250. See Pierre Hamp's reproachful remark: "The artist . . . admires the column of a Babylonian temple and despises the factory chimney." Pierre Hamp, "La Littérature, image de la société," *Encyclopédie française,* vol. 16: *Arts et littératures dans la société contemporaine,* I (Paris, 1935), fasc. 16.64–1. [Benjamin's note]

251. Baudelaire, *Oeuvres,* vol. 2, p. 293: *Curiosités esthétiques,* sec. 11, "Peintres et aqua-fortistes." [Benjamin's note]

252. Proust, "A propos de Baudelaire," *Nouvelle Revue Française* (June 1, 1921), p. 656. [Benjamin's note]

253. Charles Marie Leconte de Lisle (pseudonym of Charles Marie Lecomte; 1818–1894), French poet and a leading figure among the group of writers called the Parnassians, is renowned for his translations of Homer, Aeschylus, and Euripides. He was elected to the Académie Française in 1886.

254. Giovanni Battista Piranesi (1720–1778) was an Italian etcher, archaeologist, and architect. His *Vedute di Roma* (Views of Rome; published in stages after 1745), consisting of 137 etchings of ancient and modern Rome, with their poetic treatment of ruins, had a great effect on the Romantic idea of Rome.

255. Baudelaire, *Oeuvres,* vol. 1, p. 53. [Benjamin's note]

256. Barbey d'Aurevilly, "Du dandysme et de G. Brummel," in *Memoranda* (Paris, 1887), p. 30. [Benjamin's note]

257. Baudelaire, *Oeuvres,* vol. 2, p. 162: *Curiosités esthétiques,* "Exposition universelle, 1855" ("Eugène Delacroix"). [Benjamin's note. Eugène Delacroix (1798–1863), foremost French Romantic painter, had his most profound effect as a colorist. Théophile Gautier (1811–1872), French man of letters, was a leader of the Parnassians and a friend of Baudelaire's.

He published the novel *Mademoiselle de Maupin* in 1835. Hyacinthe Delatouche (1785–1851) published his novel *Fragoletta*, which concerns a hermaphrodite, in 1829.—*Ed.*]

258. Henri de Saint-Simon (1760–1825), French social theorist, is credited with founding Christian socialism. His most important work, *Le Nouveau Christianisme* (The New Christianity; 1825), insisted that human fraternity must accompany any scientific restructuring of society. Charles Duveyrier (1803–1866) was the editor of *L'Organisateur*, a weekly journal published by the Saint-Simonians between 1829 and 1831. Duveyrier's "Ville Nouvelle" (New City) appeared in *Le Livre des Cent-et-un* in 1832; it attempts to reanimate a moribund Paris through the vision of Paris as global metropolis combining the populations and best features of all continents.

259. Henry-René d'Allemagne, *Les Saint-Simoniens, 1827–1837* (Paris, 1930), p. 310. [Benjamin's note]

260. Claire Démar (ca. 1800–1833), French woman of letters, was a passionate advocate of Saint-Simonianism. She committed suicide. See *The Arcades Project,* Convolute U14,5 and p2,4ff. Barthélemy Prosper Enfantin (1796–1864), eccentric French social, political, and economic theorist, was a leading member of the Saint-Simonian movement.

261. Claire Démar, *Ma loi d'avenir: Ouvrage posthume publié par Suzanne* (Paris, 1834), pp. 58ff. [Benjamin's note]

262. Quoted in Maillard, *La Légende de la femme émancipée* (Paris, n.d.), p. 65. [Benjamin's note]

263. Baudelaire, *Oeuvres,* vol. 2, p. 445: *L'Art romantique,* "Madame Bovary," sec. 3, last paragraph. [Benjamin's note]

264. Ibid., p. 448: *L'Art romantique,* "Madame Bovary," sec. 5. [Benjamin's note]

265. Ibid., vol. 1, p. 157. [Benjamin's note]

266. Ibid., p. 161. [Benjamin's note]

267. This may be an allusion to Claire Démar's *Ma loi d'avenir.* [Benjamin's note. On Fourier, see note 20 above.—*Ed.*]

268. Baudelaire, *Oeuvres,* vol. 2, p. 534: *L'Art romantique,* sec. 19.3 ("Marceline Desbordes-Valmore"). [Benjamin's note]

269. *Paris sous la République de 1848: Exposition de la Bibliothèque et des travaux historiques de la ville de Paris* (Paris, 1909), p. 28. [Benjamin's note. "Les Vésuviennes" was the name given to a group of women of un-

conventional morals who formed a political association in 1848. See *The Arcades Project*, Convolute V9,3; p5,1; and p2,2.—*Ed.*]

270. A fragment from 1844 (*Oeuvres*, vol. 1, p. 213) seems pertinent here. Baudelaire's well-known drawing of his mistress shows her walking in a way that bears a striking resemblance to the gait of a pregnant woman. This does not disprove his antipathy. [Benjamin's note. The 1844 fragment begins, "Noble femme au bras fort," and ends, "Tant tu crains et tu fuis le stigmate alarmant / Que la vertu creusa de son sec infamant / Au flanc des matrones enceintes."—*Ed.*]

271. George Sand (pen name of Aurore Dupin, Baronne Dudevant; 1804–1876), French writer, published more than eighty novels. A Romantic early in her career, she later developed a concern for social issues. Her liaisons with Jules Sandeau, Alfred de Musset, and Frédéric Chopin were open and notorious.

272. Jules Lemaître, *Les Contemporains* (Paris, 1895), pp. 29ff. [Benjamin's note. On Lemaître, see note 7 above.—*Ed.*]

273. Baudelaire, *Oeuvres*, vol. 1, p. 67 ("L'Invitation au voyage"). [Benjamin's note]

274. Ibid., vol. 2, p. 630: *Journaux intimes*, "Fusées," sec. 11. [Benjamin's note]

275. Ibid., p. 352: "Le Peintre de la vie moderne," sec. 9 ("Le Dandy"). [Benjamin's note]

276. Ibid., p. 351. [Benjamin's note]

277. François-René, Vicomte de Chateaubriand (1768–1848), French writer and statesman, was the foremost French Romantic author. His great stylistic gift, and especially his musical prose, produced a series of masterly essays, histories, and apologies for Christianity.

278. Taxile Delord et al., *Les Petits-Paris: Par les auteurs des "Mémoires de Bilboquet"* (Paris, 1854), vol. 10: *Paris, viveur*, pp. 25ff. [Benjamin's note]

279. The term *Trauerspiel*, which means literally "mourning play," "play of sorrow," designates in particular a genre of royal martyr drama popular in sixteenth- and seventeenth-century Europe, a genre analyzed by Benjamin in his book *Ursprung des deutschen Trauerspiels* (Origin of the German Trauerspiel; written 1924–1925). According to Benjamin, Shakespeare's *Hamlet* is a supreme example of Trauerspiel.

280. Baudelaire, *Oeuvres*, vol. 1, p. 101. [Benjamin's note]

281. See Champfleury, *Souvenirs et portraits de jeunesse* (Paris, 1872), p. 135. [Benjamin's note. Champfleury (pen name of Jules Husson; 1821–1889) was a prominent theorist and practitioner of French literary realism.—*Ed.*]

282. Reprinted from *La Situation,* in André Billy, *Les Ecrivains de combat* (Paris, 1931), p. 189. [Benjamin's note. A *cabotin* is a ham actor. Jules Vallès (1832–1885), French novelist and journalist, is remembered above all as the author of autobiographical novels.—*Ed.*]

283. See Gide, "Baudelaire et M. Faguet," in *Nouvelle Revue Française* (November 1, 1910), p. 29. [Benjamin's note. André Gide (1869–1951), French writer, humanist, and moralist, produced a series of remarkable novels, including *L'Immoraliste* (The Immoralist; 1902) and *Les Faux Monnayeurs* (The Counterfeiters; 1926). A cofounder of the *Nouvelle Revue Française,* he received the Nobel Prize for literature in 1947. See "André Gide and Germany" and "Conversation with André Gide" in Benjamin, *Selected Writings, Volume 2: 1927–1934,* ed. Michael W. Jennings, Howard Eiland, and Gary Smith [Cambridge, Mass.: Harvard University Press, 1999].—*Ed.*]

284. See Jacques Rivière, *Etudes* (Paris, 1948), p. 15. [Benjamin's note. Jacques Rivière (1886–1925), French man of letters, edited the *Nouvelle Revue Française* from 1919 until his death.—*Ed.*]

285. See Lemaître, *Les Contemporains,* p. 29. [Benjamin's note]

286. Jules Laforgue, *Mélanges posthumes* (Paris, 1903), p. 113. [Benjamin's note. The line is from Baudelaire's poem "Le Balcon": "The night would thicken, as if it were a wall." On Laforgue, see note 145 above.—*Ed.*]

287. From this wealth, the following may be cited: "Nous volons au passage un plaisir clandestin / Que nous pressons bien fort comme une vieille orange [We hastily steal a clandestine pleasure, / Which we squeeze very hard like an old orange]" (Baudelaire, *Oeuvres,* vol. 1, p. 17: "Au Lecteur").

"Ta gorge triomphante est une belle armoire [Your triumphant bosom is a fine wardrobe]" (Ibid., p. 65: "Le Beau Navire").

"Comme un sanglot coupé par un sang écumeux / Le chant du coq au loin déchirait l'air brumeux [Like a sob stifled by frothy blood, / The distant cockcrow was rending the hazy air]" (ibid., p. 118: "Le Crépuscule du matin").

"La tête, avec l'amas de sa crinière sombre / Et de ses bijoux précieux, / Sur la table de nuit, comme une renoncule, / Repose [The head, with the mass of its dark mane / And its precious jewels, / Rests on the night-table / Like a ranunculus]" (ibid., p. 126: "Une Martyre"). [Benjamin's note]

288. Pierre Antoine Lebrun (1785–1873), French classicist tragedian and poet, wrote *Le Cid d'Andalousie* (1825). *Chambre* ("bedroom") and *mouchoir* ("handkerchief") were words deemed inappropriate to the elevated language of tragic drama.

289. Charles-Augustin Sainte-Beuve, *Vie, poésies et pensées de Joseph Delorme* (Paris, 1863), vol. 1, p. 170. [Benjamin's note. "Joseph Delorme" is Sainte-Beuve's pseudonym.—*Ed.*]

290. Baudelaire, *Oeuvres*, vol. 1, p. 57. [Benjamin's note. "The vague terrors of those frightful nights which compress the heart the way one crumples a piece of paper." These lines are from the poem "Réversibilité," in *Les Fleurs du mal* ("Spleen et idéal").—*Ed.*]

291. Népomucène Lemercier (1771–1840), French neoclassical dramatist and novelist, is considered a forerunner of Romanticism.

292. Quoted in Rivière, *Etudes* (Paris, 1948), p. 15. [Benjamin's note. Paul Claudel (1868–1955), poet, playwright, and essayist, was an important force in French letters at the turn of the century. The tone and lyricism of his work owe much to his deeply felt Catholicism.—*Ed.*]

293. On January 10, 1870, Prince Pierre Bonaparte, Napoleon III's rather unstable cousin, killed a young journalist in the heat of a quarrel concerning alleged published insults. The journalist, Yvan Salmon, went by the name Victor Noir. The prince was acquitted of murder by a special high court of justice at Tours. The affair and its outcome contributed significantly to the unpopularity of the imperial family and to the growth of a revolutionary party.

294. Ernest Henri Granger (1844–1914), a wealthy French lawyer, allied himself with Blanqui in 1865 and rose to become a trusted deputy.

295. Gustave Geffroy, *L'Enfermé* (Paris, 1897), pp. 276ff. [Benjamin's note]

296. Quoted in Eugène Crépet, *Charles Baudelaire* (Paris, 1906), p. 81. [Benjamin's note. *Le Salut Public* was a short-lived newspaper founded by Baudelaire, Champfleury, and Charles Toubin. Two issues appeared, in February and March 1848. The name, recalling the infa-

mous Committee of Public Safety formed under the Terror in 1793, came from Baudelaire. Its brief, unsigned articles were full of revolutionary enthusiasm for "the people," its republic, and a socialist Christ.—*Ed.*]

297. Baudelaire, *Oeuvres*, vol. 1, p. 136. [Benjamin's note. "Un monde où l'action n'est pas la soeur du rêve": the line is from the poem "Le Reniement de Saint Pierre," in *Les Fleurs du mal.*—*Ed.*]

298. The following three paragraphs on method, as well as the section entitled "Taste" which follows them, were evidently composed as portions of an introduction to the book—tentatively titled *Charles Baudelaire: A Lyric Poet in the Era of High Capitalism*—that Benjamin intended to write but never completed. See the first note to this essay.

299. *Doxa* is Greek for "opinion," "false judgment." In *The Republic,* Plato posits an intermediate stage between true knowledge and ignorance. This quasi-knowledge of quasi-being is *doxa;* its objects are the data of sense perception and the commonly held opinions of human beings.

300. The incalculable consequences of the more resolute procedure are rather forbidding in other respects as well. There is little point in trying to include the position of a Baudelaire in the fabric of the most advanced position in mankind's struggle for liberation. From the outset, it seems more promising to investigate his machinations where he was undoubtedly at home: in the enemy camp. Very rarely are they a blessing for the other side. Baudelaire was a secret agent—an agent of the secret discontent of his class with its own rule. [Benjamin's note. The quotation to which this note is appended comes from Benjamin's own essay "Eduard Fuchs, Collector and Historian," in Benjamin, *Selected Writings,* vol. 3.—*Ed.*]

301. This is Marx's description of the commodity in the section of *Capital* entitled "The Fetishism of Commodities and Its Secret." The sentence reads: "At first sight, a commodity appears a very trivial thing, easily understood. Analysis shows that it is, in reality, a very queer thing, abounding in metaphysical subtleties and theological niceties."

302. Jean Antoine Claude Chaptal, Comte de Chanteloup (1756–1832), was a French chemist, physician, and politician. He played a significant role in the development of the chemical industry in France, and in European industrial expansion in general.

303. On *l'art pour l'art,* see note 6 above.

304. "Pierre Louÿs écrit: le throne; on trouve partout des abymes, des ymages, ennuy des fleurs, etc. . . . Triomphe de l'*y*." [Benjamin's note. "Pierre Louÿs writes 'le throne' [with the older Latinate spelling]; everywhere one finds abysses, ymages, ennuy of flowers, and the like. . . . The triumph of the *y*." Benjamin is quoting from Paul Morand, *1900* (Paris, 1931), pp. 180–181.—*Ed.*]

Central Park

1. These passages on Baudelaire were composed in part as preparatory studies for Benjamin's planned book on Baudelaire, tentatively titled *Charles Baudelaire: Ein Lyriker im Zeitalter des Hochkapitalismus* (Charles Baudelaire: A Lyric Poet in the Era of High Capitalism). They are closely linked to the material developed in "The Paris of the Second Empire in Baudelaire" and "On Some Motifs in Baudelaire" (both included in this volume), and they give some idea of the tenor of the unwritten parts of the Baudelaire book: "Baudelaire as Allegorist" (the first section) and "The Commodity as Poetic Object" (the third section).

The source of most of the reflections and commentaries in "Central Park" is Benjamin's *Arcades Project*, particularly Convolute J, "Baudelaire," from which Benjamin extracted numerous passages, often only slightly revising them. The arrangement of the forty-six loose-leaf sheets on which the fragments of "Central Park" were originally written—that is, the arrangement reproduced here and in the German edition of Benjamin's works—may or may not derive from Benjamin himself. Benjamin's title points to the central importance he ascribed to these fragments in the context of his work on Baudelaire, as well as to his hopes for resettling in America, where his friends spoke of finding an apartment for him in proximity to Central Park in New York.

In the opening passage of "Central Park," he refers to René Laforgue, *L'Echec de Baudelaire: Etude psychoanalytique sur la névrose de Charles Baudelaire* (Paris, 1931); in English as *The Defeat of Baudelaire: A Psycho-Analytical Study.*

This translation was prepared in consultation with a previous rendering of "Central Park" by Lloyd Spencer in *New German Critique*, 34 (Winter 1985), pp. 28–58.

2. Stefan George (1868–1933) was a German lyric poet and the editor of the influential *Blätter für die Kunst,* a periodical that ran from 1892 to 1918 and aimed at revitalizing the German literary language, which George felt was in decline. He founded a literary school, the "George circle," which was held together by his authoritarian personality and a Symbolist aesthetic. His translation of Baudelaire's *Fleurs du mal* appeared in 1901. "Spleen et idéal," or, in George's rendering, "Trübsinn und Vergeistigung" (Melancholy and Spiritualization), is the title of the first section of *Les Fleurs du mal;* in the first edition of 1857, it contained seventy-seven poems, and in the second, enlarged edition of 1861, eighty-five poems. On the tense interplay of melancholy and the ideal in Baudelaire, see the brief essay "Baudelaire" in Benjamin, *Selected Writings, Volume 1: 1913–1926,* ed. Marcus Bullock and Michael W. Jennings (Cambridge, Mass.: Harvard University Press, 1996), p. 362.

3. For Baudelaire's concept of modern heroism, see section 3 of "The Paris of the Second Empire in Baudelaire," printed above in this volume. See also sections 14, 20, 22, 27, 35, and 44 of "Central Park," below. On Baudelaire's monadological conception (referred to immediately below in the text), see Walter Benjamin, *The Arcades Project,* trans. Howard Eiland and Kevin McLaughlin (Cambridge, Mass.: Harvard University Press, 1999), Convolute J38a,7 and J44,5; also Convolute N10,3.

4. Victor Hugo (1802–1885), French dramatist, novelist, and poet, was the most important of the Romantic writers. While his novels (such as *Les Misérables,* 1862; and *Notre-Dame de Paris,* 1831) remain his best-known works, his legacy to the nineteenth century was his lyric poetry.

5. The line "Dans le coeur immortel qui toujours veut fleurir" ("In the immortal heart that always wants to flower") occurs in Baudelaire's poem "Le Soleil" (The Sun). The word *vendanges* ("grape harvest") is found in the poem "Semper Eadem" (Always the Same), in the lines "Quand notre coeur a fait une fois sa vendange, / Vivre est un mal" ("When once our heart has harvested its fruit, / Then living is an evil"); and in "L'Imprévu" (The Unforeseen), in the line "Dans ces soirs solennels de célestes vendanges" ("In those solemn evenings of heaven's harvests").

6. Baudelaire's idea of natural correspondences—reflected in his poem "Correspondances"—derives mainly from the Swedish mystic

Emanuel Swedenborg (1688–1772), who envisioned a universal language in which everything outward and visible in nature was a symbol pointing to an inward spiritual cause.

7. Louis-Napoléon Bonaparte (1808–1873), nephew of Napoleon Bonaparte, was president of the Second Republic from 1850 to 1852 and thereafter, as Napoleon III, was emperor in the Second Empire. His reign combined authoritarianism and economic liberalism; it ended with France's defeat in the Franco-Prussian War of 1870–1871.

8. Benjamin cites Baudelaire's poem "L'Irrémédiable" (The Irremediable), in the "Spleen et idéal" section of *Les Fleurs du mal:* "Tête-à-tête sombre et limpide / Qu'un coeur devenu son miroir!" ("Tête-à-tête as somber and lucid / As a heart that has become its own mirror!"). On Benjamin's theory of Baroque allegory, which emphasizes the dissociative and estranging character of allegorical perception, as well as the fragmentary character of the allegorical emblem, see his *Ursprung des deutschen Trauerspiels* (published 1928), in Benjamin *Gesammelte Schriften*, vol. 1 (Frankfurt: Suhrkamp, 1974), pp. 203–430; in English, *The Origin of German Tragic Drama*, trans. John Osborne (London: NLB/Verso, 1977).

9. Henri Monnier (1805–1877), French caricaturist and playwright, created the popular character Joseph Prudhomme, the typical bourgeois (1830). He is discussed in Baudelaire's essay "Quelques caricaturistes français" (Some French Caricaturists).

10. Jugendstil was the German and Austrian variant of the Art Nouveau style of the 1890s. The movement took its name from the Munich journal *Die Jugend* (Youth). It typically represented organic forms, fluid curving lines, and stylized nature motifs—often in the most modern, technologically advanced materials.

11. Convolute S8a,1 in *The Arcades Project* gives the continuation of the sentence: ". . . to sterilize them ornamentally."

12. Maurice Rollinat (1846–1903) was a French poet known for his recitations at the Chat Noir café in Paris. His collection of poems *Névroses* (1883) shows the influence of Baudelaire.

13. Title of prose poem 46 in Baudelaire's *Spleen de Paris* (published posthumously in 1869). It means "loss of halo" or "loss of aura." See *The Arcades Project*, Convolute J59,7.

14. An allusion to a concept in the later philosophy of Edmund Husserl (1859–1938).

15. "Fidus" was the pseudonym of Hugo Höppener (1868–1948), German architect and painter in the Jugendstil movement.

16. Charles Meryon (1821–1868), French etcher and engraver, was a friend of Baudelaire's. His highly detailed portraits of the city of Paris are discussed in Baudelaire's essay "Salon de 1859" (excerpted in *The Arcades Project,* Convolute J2,1).

17. Jules Laforgue (1860–1887), French poet and critic, was a Symbolist master of lyrical irony. For his comment on Baudelaire's "Americanism," see *The Arcades Project,* Convolute J9,4. It is a question of "crude comparisons which suddenly, in the midst of a harmonious period, cause him to put his foot in his plate; . . . disconcerting purplish flash and dazzle. . . . This is Americanism superimposed on the metaphorical language of the 'Song of Songs'" (trans. William Jay Smith).

18. Alphonse de Lamartine (1790–1869), French Romantic poet, novelist, and statesman, is best known for his *Méditations poétiques* (1820), which includes the famous poem "Le Lac." He briefly led the provisional government following the revolution of 1848. His history of the Girondists appeared in 1847.

19. Alfred de Musset (1810–1857), French poet, playwright, and translator, ranks alongside Hugo, Lamartine, and Vigny as one of the great Romantic poets. He combined an intense lyricism with a propensity to shock through revelation of his vices: laziness, self-indulgence, a facile talent, and an attraction to opium.

20. Théophile Gautier (1811–1872), French poet and man of letters, was a leader of the Parnassians, a poetic school that strove for detachment, technical perfection, and precise description in its verse. The school derives its name from its anthology, *Le Parnasse contemporain* (1866–1876). Charles-Marie Leconte de Lisle (pseudonym of Charles-Marie Lecomte; 1818–1894), French poet and leading figure among the Parnassians, is renowned for his translations of Homer, Aeschylus, and Euripides. He was elected to the Académie Française in 1886.

21. Paul Verlaine (1844–1896) is generally considered to be one of the major French poets of the second half of the nineteenth century. With Baudelaire, Rimbaud, and Mallarmé, he is sometimes seen as a precur-

sor of the French Symbolist poets of the 1880s. His main works include *Poèmes saturniens* (1866), *Fêtes galantes* (1869), *Romances sans paroles* (1873–1874), *Sagesse* (1880–1881), and *Les Poètes maudits* (1884). Arthur Rimbaud (1854–1891) was a French Symbolist poet and adventurer whose poetry had a profound influence on modern literature. His major works include *Une Saison en enfer* (1873), a hallucinatory work of autobiography, and *Les Illuminations*, prose poems.

22. Honoré Daumier (1808–1879), French caricaturist, painter, and sculptor, was initially a resolutely political caricaturist. The September Laws eliminated most venues for publishing his political work, and he turned for the remainder of his life to the representation of scenes from everyday life.

23. Louis-Auguste Blanqui (1805–1881), French revolutionary socialist and militant anticlerical, was active in all three major upheavals in nineteenth-century France—the revolutions of 1830 and 1848 and the Paris Commune—and was imprisoned following each series of events. Quotations from Blanqui and Benjamin's commentary on him play a key role in *The Arcades Project*.

24. Nietzsche says this in the fourth book of *Die fröhliche Wissenschaft* (The Gay Science), aphorism 295.

25. "The nameless elegance of the human frame." The line is from Baudelaire's poem "Danse Macabre," in the second section of *Les Fleurs du mal*, "Tableaux parisiens" (Parisian Scenes), which was added in the second edition of 1861.

26. Gottfried Keller (1819–1890), Swiss writer, was one of the great German-language prose stylists of the nineteenth century. After failing to establish himself as a painter in Munich, he returned to Zurich and inaugurated a career in literature. *Der grüne Heinrich* (Green Henry; 1854–1855, revised version 1879–1880) and the story collection *Die Leute von Seldwyla* (The People of Seldwyla; first volume 1856, second volume 1874) are his best-known works.

27. *Créer un poncif*: to create a stereotype. See Baudelaire's "Fusées," no. 20: "To create a new commonplace [*poncif*]—that's genius. I must create a commonplace."

28. Epinal images were sentimental religious posters. They were named after the town of Epinal in northeastern France, where this art was produced.

29. Sören Kierkegaard (1813–1855), Danish philosopher and theologian, presented his idea of the aesthetic life in volume 1 of *Either-Or* (1843), especially in the famous concluding section, "Diary of the Seducer."

30. Benjamin's phrase comes from Gottfried Keller's poem "Verlorenes Recht, verlorenes Glück" (Lost Right, Lost Happiness): "War wie ein Medusenschild / der erstarrten Unruh Bild" ("Was like a Medusa-shield, / image of petrified unrest"). On Keller, see note 26 above.

31. In *The Arcades Project,* Convolute J56a,7, Benjamin illustrates this point by referring to Poe's portrayal of the crowd.

32. *Croque-morts* are hired mourners. Benjamin refers to a passage at the end of Baudelaire's "Salon de 1846": with their black suits and frock coats, the men of the modern city form "an endless procession of hired mourners" (cited in *The Arcades Project,* Convolute J31a,3). Louis Veuillot (1813–1883), French journalist, was the editor of *L'Univers Religieux* (1843). He was also the author of *Le Pape et la diplomatie* (1861) and *Les Odeurs de Paris* (1866). Convolute D2,2, in *The Arcades Project,* quotes a passage from the latter work complaining that the architecture of the new Paris, despite its eclecticism, is uniformly tedious in its recourse to "the emphatic and the aligned."

33. "George Sand" was the pseudonym of Aurore Dudevant (1804–1876), a Romantic novelist who stood for free association in all social relations, and whose protagonists are generally virtuous peasants or workmen. In Convolute J49a,1 of *The Arcades Project,* Benjamin suggests that Baudelaire could not forgive George Sand for "having profaned, through her humanitarian convictions, this image [of the lesbian or the masculine woman] whose traits she bore."

34. After 1799, the Garde Nationale, which had been formed to support the French Revolution, was a reserve army that was mobilized in times of crisis. During the Revolution of 1848, many of its members defected to the antigovernment side. It was formally dissolved in the summer of 1848.

35. An arcanum is a deep secret, a mystery. The plural "arcana" (Benjamin's term is *Arkana*) refers to specialized knowledge or detail that is mysterious to the average person. See section 41 below.

36. Jules Lemaître (1853–1914) was a French author and critic whose

highly influential evaluations of his contemporaries led to his election to the Académie Française in 1895. In later years he adopted the right-wing stance of Action Française. For his assessment of Baudelaire's intellectual powers, see *The Arcades Project,* Convolute J15,1.

37. The passage comes from section 8 of the "Salon de 1859," and is cited in *The Arcades Project,* Convolute Q4a,4: "I would rather return to the dioramas, whose brutal and enormous magic has the power to impose on me a useful illusion. I would rather go to the theater and feast my eyes on the scenery, in which I find my dearest dreams artistically expressed and tragically concentrated. These things, because they are false, are infinitely closer to the truth" (trans. Jonathan Mayne).

38. "L'Amour du mensonge" (Love of Falsehood) is a poem in the second section of *Les Fleurs du mal,* "Tableaux parisiens." The poem celebrates beauty as mask.

39. "Une Martyre," a poem in the fourth section of *Les Fleurs du mal,* "Fleurs du mal," describes the dead body and severed head of a murdered young woman; the poet imagines her bedroom, with its luxurious décor and morbid hothouse atmosphere, as the scene of necrophiliac love. "La Mort des amants" (The Death of Lovers), from the sixth section of *Les Fleurs du mal,* "La Mort," presents the lovers' vision of their own death in a room furnished with delicately scented beds, divans deep as tombs, and shelves decked with strange flowers. Hans Makart (1840–1884), Austrian painter, gained his reputation with vast historical and allegorical canvases that made his name a byword for empty monumentality. On Jugendstil, see note 10 above.

40. "Madrigal triste" (Sad Madrigal) was written in 1861 and published in *Le Parnasse Contemporain* in 1866, as part of the collection of sixteen new poems entitled "Nouvelles Fleurs du mal." It was incorporated in the first posthumous edition of *Les Fleurs du mal,* issued by the poet's friends Charles Asselineau and Théodore de Banville in 1868.

41. *Fantasque escrime:* "fantastical swordplay" ("Le Soleil").

42. *Lesebuch für Städtebewohner* (A Reader for Those Who Live in Cities) is the title of a group of poems written by Bertolt Brecht in 1926–1927. For an English translation, see Brecht, *Poems, 1913–1956,* ed. John Willett and Ralph Manheim (New York: Methuen, 1987), pp. 131–150. The prostitute poem is the fifth of the series, pp. 135–136.

43. In his essay "A Propos de Baudelaire" (1921), Marcel Proust writes: "The world of Baudelaire is a strange sectioning of time in which only the red-letter days [*rares jours notables*] can appear." Cited by Benjamin in *The Arcades Project,* Convolute J44,5.

44. In 1846, Baudelaire announced, in advertisements, the appearance of a collection of poems to be called *Les Lesbiennes,* a title which primarily denoted the female inhabitants of the island of Lesbos in ancient times (the subject of his poem "Femmes damnées"). Two years later, during the period of revolutionary activity, he announced the forthcoming publication of some twenty-six poems under the title *Les Limbes* (Limbo). Neither of these projected volumes actually appeared. The first use of the title "Les Fleurs du mal" occurred with the publication of eighteen poems in the *Revue des Deux Mondes,* a bastion of conservative Romanticism, in 1855. The new title was suggested to the poet by his friend the critic and novelist Hippolyte Babou.

45. Adrienne Monnier (1892–1955) was a poet, autobiographer, and bookseller. Her bookshop on the rue de l'Odéon in Paris, La Maison des Amis des Livres, was the meeting place for a wide circle of important early twentieth-century writers, including André Gide, Paul Valéry, Rainer Maria Rilke, Paul Claudel, James Joyce, and Ernest Hemingway. *La rogne* means "ill-humor."

46. Léon-Paul Fargue (1876–1947) was a French poet and essayist whose work spanned numerous literary movements. By the age of nineteen, he had published a major poem, "Tancrède," in the magazine *Pan* and had become a member of the Symbolist circle connected with *Le Mercure de France.* After 1930, he devoted himself almost exclusively to journalism, writing newspaper columns and longer, lyrical essays about Parisian life. His best-known work is the prose-poem memoir *Le Piéton de Paris* (The Parisian Pedestrian; 1939).

47. Céline (pseudonym of Louis-Ferdinand Destouches; 1894–1961), French author best known for the novel *Voyage au bout de la nuit* (Journey to the End of Night; 1932), was a lifelong anti-Semite and nationalist. *Gauloiserie* translates as "salaciousness" and "coarse jesting."

48. *Côté ordurier:* "obscene side."

49. Ange Pechméja (1819–1887) was a French poet exiled for his opposition to Napoleon III. He lived in Romania during the Second Em-

pire, and was in correspondence with Flaubert, Gautier, and Baudelaire. He published the first article on Baudelaire to appear beyond the Danube.

50. Maurice Maeterlinck (1862–1949), Belgian poet, dramatist, and essayist, lived in Paris after 1896 and was influenced by the Symbolists. His major works include *Pelléas et Mélisande* (1892), *Le Trésor des humbles* (1896), and *L'Oiseau bleu* (1908). In 1911 he was awarded the Nobel Prize in Literature.

51. *Odeur de futailles* means "odor of wine-casks." The phrase figures in Baudelaire's vivid evocation of the Parisian ragpickers in "Le Vin des chiffonniers" (The Ragpickers' Wine), a poem composed before 1843 and first published in a wine-growers' journal in 1854. It is included in section 3 of *Les Fleurs du mal,* "Le Vin."

52. Gustave Courbet (1819–1877), French realist painter, presided over the Committee of Fine Arts during the Commune (1871). He was imprisoned six months for helping to destroy the column in the Place Vendôme, and had to comply with a court order (1875) to pay for restoration of the column. He painted a portrait of Baudelaire circa 1847.

53. "The bloody apparatus of Destruction": this is the last line of the poem "La Destruction" in *Les Fleurs du mal.*

54. "Men of the nineteenth century, the hour of our apparitions is fixed forever, and always brings us back the very same ones." From Auguste Blanqui, *L'Eternité par les astres* (Paris, 1872), pp. 74–75. This quotation appears as an epigraph at the conclusion of the Exposé of 1939, in *The Arcades Project.*

55. See Convolute N9a,4 in *The Arcades Project.*

56. For Proust's remarks on the Baudelairean *intérieur,* see Convolute I2a,6 in *The Arcades Project.*

57. Michel Leiris (1901–1990), French writer, was a pioneer in modern confessional literature as well as a noted anthropologist, poet, and art critic. For more on the word *familier* in Baudelaire, see *The Arcades Project,* Convolute J60,1.

58. Compare Convolute J60,4 in *The Arcades Project.*

59. Poem 100 in *Les Fleurs du mal* (it is untitled) begins: "La servante au grand coeur dont vous étiez jalouse" ("That good-hearted servant of whom you were jealous"). The poem is addressed to Baudelaire's mother, with whom he lived for a time, along with his nursemaid

Mariette, in a house in Neuilly, just outside Paris, after his father's death in 1827 (when he was six).

60. The phrase *lourds tombereaux* (heavily laden wagons) occurs in the third stanza of "Les Sept Vieillards" (The Seven Old Men), in the "Tableaux parisiens" section of *Les Fleurs du mal.*

61. "Where everything, even horror, turns to magic." From "Les Petites Vieilles" (The Little Old Women) in *Les Fleurs du mal.* Poe's description of the crowd is found in his story "The Man of the Crowd."

62. "La Vie antérieure" (The Previous Life) is the title of a poem in the "Spleen et idéal" section of *Les Fleurs du mal.* The phrase can also be translated as "past life."

63. Convolute D2a,1, in *The Arcades Project,* mentions that a rage for tortoises overcame Paris in 1839. Benjamin comments: "One can well imagine the elegant set mimicking the pace of this creature more easily in the arcades than on the boulevards." See also "The Paris of the Second Empire in Baudelaire," in this volume, for Benjamin's contextualization of this idea.

64. Mayeux is a hunchbacked character of popular farce; described as a "priapic puppet," he personified the patriotic petty bourgeois. Vireloque is a character created by the illustrator Paul Gavarni. Gavroche is a heroic street urchin in Victor Hugo's novel *Les Misérables* (part IV, book 6). Ratapoil is a figure created by Daumier to caricature militarism; he bore a resemblance to Napoleon III.

65. *Joufflu:* "chubby-cheeked." See Baudelaire's "Salon of 1859" in *The Mirror of Art,* trans. Jonathan Mayne (New York: Phaidon, 1955), p. 251 ("Religion, History, Fantasy"). Baudelaire refers to Cupid's *joues rebondissantes* ("fat wobbling cheeks").

66. Pierre Béranger (1780–1857) was an immensely popular lyric poet of liberal political sympathies.

67. "De l'essence du rire" (On the Essence of Laughter) was first published in 1855 in *Le Portefeuille,* and later incorporated in the volume of Baudelaire's critical writings that was titled *Curiosités esthétiques* (1868).

68. Benjamin draws here on the distinction, developed in the essay "On Some Motifs in Baudelaire," between the "isolated experience" [*Erlebnis*] and traditional, cohesive, and cumulative experience [*Erfahrung*]. He plays on the derivation of *Erlebnis* from *leben* ("to live").

69. The name "Ossian" became known throughout Europe in 1762, when the Scottish poet James Macpherson "discovered" and published the poems of Ossian, first with the epic *Fingal* and the following year with *Temora;* both of these works were supposedly translations from third-century Gaelic originals, but were largely composed by Macpherson himself. Heinrich Heine's *Buch der Lieder* (Book of Songs) appeared in 1827.

70. On the "now of recognizability" *(Jetzt der Erkennbarkeit),* see especially Convolute N3,1 in *The Arcades Project;* also Convolute K2,3.

71. Carl Gustav Jochmann (1789–1830), a German writer of Baltic origin, lived in England, France, Switzerland, and Germany. He is known today mainly as the author of *Über die Sprache* (On Language; 1828), though he also produced a wide range of essays, political, sociological, literary, and theological. See Walter Benjamin, "'The Regression of Poetry,' by Carl Gustav Jochmann," and the final section of "Germans of 1789," in Benjamin, *Selected Writings, Volume 4: 1938–1940,* ed. Howard Eiland and Michael W. Jennings (Cambridge, Mass.: Harvard University Press, 2003).

72. "Le Jeu" (Gaming), a poem in the "Tableaux parisiens" section of *Les Fleurs du mal,* evokes a gambling den and its ravaged occupants, as seen in a dream. "Les Deux Bonnes Soeurs" (The Two Kind Sisters), in the section entitled "Fleurs du mal," concerns the "amiable" pair Death and Debauch, the tomb and the brothel.

73. Pierre-Antoine Dupont (1821–1870) was a popular poet and republican songwriter whose socialist humanism stopped short of full political opposition. Until 1852, he associated with Hugo, Gautier, and Baudelaire. Baudelaire in particular praised Dupont's devotion to liberty. After Louis Napoleon's coup d'état of December 2, 1851, Dupont—who had avoided arrest by fleeing to Savoy—was condemned in absentia to seven years of exile. Impoverished without the support of his Parisian audience, Dupont in 1852 pledged support for the regime and lived quietly thereafter in Paris. Baudelaire's first essay on Dupont was written in 1851, at a time when he was imbued with the ideals that had inspired the Revolution of 1848. Within a year, however, he was evincing a more aristocratic conception of literature and society, and his second essay on Dupont, in 1861, is less enthusiastic.

74. In the notes toward a never-completed critical-autobiographical

volume entitled *Mon coeur mis à nu* (My Heart Laid Bare), published posthumously together with other fragments (the so-called *Fusées*)in the *Journaux intimes* (Intimate Journals; 1909), Baudelaire writes: "Glorifier le culte des images (ma grande, mon unique, ma primitive passion)"— "Praise the cult of images (my great, my unique, my primitive passion)." *Primitive passion* can also be translated as "earliest passion." The note could refer to the importance that pictures *(images)* had for Baudelaire when he was a child; his father was an art lover and amateur painter.

75. Valéry's remarks are cited in *The Arcades Project,* Convolute J1,1. "Baudelaire's problem . . . must have . . . posed itself in these terms: 'How to be a great poet, but neither a Lamartine nor a Hugo nor a Musset.' . . . These words . . . must have been . . . his *raison d'état.*" It was partly a matter of gleaning "the impurities, the imprudences" in the work of his predecessors, "everything that might scandalize, and thereby instruct, . . . a pitiless young observer in the way of his own future art."

76. Franz Kafka (1883–1924), born in Prague of Jewish parentage, was the author of startling and haunting works of fiction, such as the short stories "Die Verwandlung" (The Metamorphosis; 1915) and "In der Strafkolonie" (In the Penal Colony; 1919), and the posthumously published novels *Der Prozess* (The Trial; 1925) and *Das Schloss* (The Castle; 1926). Knut Hamsun (1859–1952) was a Norwegian novelist who criticized the American way of life and idealized rural existence. He supported the German invasion of Norway and in 1947 was condemned for treason. His most famous novel—a great popular success—was *Hunger* (1890).

77. See Walter Benjamin, "Goethe's Elective Affinities," in *Selected Writings,* vol. 1, pp. 297–360. On the distinction between "truth content" and "material content," see especially pp. 297–300.

78. The phrase translates as "that heroic melancholy." The German humanist Philip Schwartzerd (1497–1560) used the pseudonym "Melanchthon," a Greek translation of his surname, which means "black earth." A reformer, theologian, and educator, he was a friend of Martin Luther and defended his views. In 1521 he published *Loci communes,* the first systematic treatment of evangelical doctrine. Because of his academic expertise, he was asked to help in establishing schools, and he virtually reorganized the whole educational system of Germany, founding or reforming several of its universities.

79. This is the first line of "Spleen (II)" in *Les Fleurs du mal:* "I have more souvenirs than if I'd lived a thousand years." In French, *souvenir* can mean "souvenir" (keepsake) as well as "memory." See section 32a above and Convolute J53,1 in *The Arcades Project.*

80. Benjamin refers to the grand synthesizing conclusion of his book *Ursprung des deutschen Trauerspiels,* composed in 1924–1925. See note 8 above.

On Some Motifs in Baudelaire

1. Charles Baudelaire, *Oeuvres,* ed. Yves-Gérard Le Dantec (Paris: Bibliothèque de la Pléïade, 1931–1932), vol. 1, p. 18. [Benjamin's note. "Hypocrite reader—my fellow creature—my brother!" The quotation is from "Au lecteur" (To the Reader), the introductory poem of *Les Fleurs du mal* (first edition 1857; second and enlarged edition 1861).—Ed.]

2. Alphonse Prat de Lamartine (1790–1869), popular poet and orator, helped to shape the Romantic movement in French literature. He served as foreign minister in the provisional government of 1848, and was the author of *Méditations poétiques* (Poetic Meditations; 1820), *La Chute d'une ange* (The Fall of an Angel; 1838), and *Histoire des Girondins* (History of the Girondists; 1846).

3. Paul Verlaine (1844–1896) was one of the major French poets of the later nineteenth century. His main works include *Fêtes galantes* (Elegant Diversions; 1869), *Romances sans paroles* (Songs without Words; 1873–1874), *Sagesse* (Wisdom; 1880–1881), and *Les Poètes maudits* (Accursed Poets; 1884). Arthur Rimbaud (1854–1891) was a French poet and adventurer whose poetry had a profound influence on modern literature. His major works include *Une Saison en enfer* (A Season in Hell; 1873), a hallucinatory work of autobiography, and *Les Illuminations* (1886), prose poems.

4. Victor Hugo (1802–1885), poet, novelist, dramatist, and statesman, was the most important of the French Romantic writers. While his novels, such as *Les Misérables* (1862) and *Notre-Dame de Paris* (1831), remain his best-known works, his legacy to the nineteenth century was his lyric poetry. Heinrich Heine (1797–1856), German poet and critic, fled Germany because of his liberal views and lived in Paris after 1831. His best-

known works include *Reisebilder* (Travel Images; 1826–1831), *Buch der Lieder* (Book of Songs; 1827), and *Romanzero* (Ballad Collection; 1851).

5. Wilhelm Dilthey (1833–1911) was a German philosopher and historian of ideas. His book *Das Erlebnis und die Dichtung* (Experience and Poetry; 1906) put forward a hermeneutics based on empathetic understanding as an active, productive process. Ludwig Klages (1872–1956), German philosopher, psychologist, and anthropologist, exerted a wide influence in the first half of the twentieth century. His central thesis—most exhaustively expressed in *Der Geist als Widersacher der Seele* (The Intellect as Opponent of the Soul; 1929–1933, 3 vols.), but also evident in his graphological treatise *Handschrift und Charakter* (Handwriting and Character; 1917)—was that an originary unity of soul and body has been destroyed by the human rational capacity. Strongly influenced by Nietzsche, Bergson, and Bachofen, Klages' ideas have gained notoriety because of their absorption into Nazi ideology, whose anti-Semitism Klages shared. C. G. Jung (1875–1961) was a Swiss psychiatrist who served as president of the International Psychoanalytic Association (1911–1914). He met Freud in 1907 and became his leading collaborator, but grew increasingly critical of his approach. Jung's book *Wandlungen und Symbole der Libido* (1911–1912; translated as *The Psychology of the Unconscious*), which posited the existence of a collective unconscious dominated by archetypes, caused a break between the two men in 1913.

6. Henri Bergson (1859–1941), French philosopher, elaborated what came to be called a process philosophy, which rejected static values in favor of values of motion, change, and evolution. He was also a master literary stylist, of both academic and popular appeal. His *Matière et mémoire: Essai sur la relation du corps à l'esprit* (Matter and Memory: Essay on the Relation of the Body to the Mind) appeared in 1896.

7. Here and elsewhere in this essay, Benjamin distinguishes between two functions of memory, *Gedächtnis* and *Erinnerung*, the former understood as a gathering of often unconscious data, and the latter understood as an isolating of individual "memories" per se. This distinction is roughly paralleled by the one between the terms *Erfahrung* (tradition-bound, long experience) and *Erlebnis* (the isolated experience of the moment.) See note 11 below.

8. Bergson argues that the concrete living present, which consists

in the consciousness one has of one's body as a center of action, necessarily occupies a moment of duration very different from our ideas of chronological time. Every perception fills a certain "depth of duration" *(épaisseur de durée),* prolonging the past into the present and thereby preparing the future. As a constantly varying spatiotemporal "rhythm," a flow of states, duration is the basis of matter, which, insofar as it is extended in space, must be seen as a present which is always beginning again. See Bergson, *Matter and Memory,* trans. N. M. Paul and W. S. Palmer (New York: Zone Books, 1991), pp. 137–139, 186, 205, 244, and passim.

9. Marcel Proust, *A la recherche du temps perdu* (Paris: Pléiade, 1962), vol. 1, p. 44 *(Du côté de chez Swann).*

10. Karl Kraus (1874–1936), Austrian journalist and dramatist, edited and wrote for the journal *Die Fackel* from 1899 to 1936. He is best known for his savage satires of journalistic rhetoric. See Benjamin's essay of 1931, "Karl Kraus," in *Selected Writings, Volume 2: 1927–1934,* ed. Michael W. Jennings, Howard Eiland, and Gary Smith (Cambridge, Mass.: Harvard University Press, 1999), pp. 433–458.

11. This is Benjamin's most concentrated definition of *Erfahrung,* experience over time. In the pages that follow, he will contrast it with *Erlebnis,* the isolated experience of the moment. In notes connected to the composition of "Über einige Motive bei Baudelaire," Benjamin writes that experiences in the sense of *Erlebnisse* are "by nature unsuitable for literary composition," and "work is distinguished by the fact that it begets *Erfahrungen* out of *Erlebnissen.*" See *Gesammelte Schriften,* vol. 1 (Frankfurt: Suhrkamp, 1974), p. 1183. See also Benjamin, *The Arcades Project,* trans. Howard Eiland and Kevin McLaughlin (Cambridge, Mass.: Harvard University Press, 1999), p. 802 (Convolute m2a,4): *Erfahrung* is inseparable from the representation of a continuity.

12. *Eingedenken* is Benjamin's coinage from the preposition *eingedenk* ("mindful of") and the verb *gedenken* ("recollect," "remember"). The resultant term has a more active sense than *erinnern* ("remember") and often verges on the notion of commemoration.

13. Freud's *Jenseits des Lust-Prinzips* (Beyond the Pleasure Principle) first appeared in 1920. Its primary contribution to psychoanalytic theory is a revision of Freud's early insistence that dreams avoid trauma. Based

on his work with war veterans suffering from shell shock, Freud concluded that neurotics are in fact characterized by a compulsion to revisit or relive the traumatic scene.

14. Theodor Reik (1888–1969) was an Austrian psychoanalyst and, after 1911, a collaborator of Freud's.

15. Theodor Reik, *Der überraschte Psychologe* (Leiden, 1935), p. 132. In English, *Surprise and the Psycho-Analyst: On the Conjecture and Comprehension of Unconscious Processes,* trans. Margaret M. Green (New York: Dutton, 1937), p. 131.

16. In the present context, there is no substantial difference between the concepts *Erinnerung* and *Gedächtnis* as used in Freud's essay. [Benjamin's note. Freud's assumption, in the original wording, is that "das Bewu¼tsein entstehe an der Stelle der Erinnerungsspur."—*Ed.*]

17. Paul Valéry (1871–1945), French man of letters, is best known for his prose work *La Soirée avec Monsieur Teste* (An Evening with Monsieur Teste; 1896) and his verse masterpiece, *La Jeune Parque* (1917). His criticism is often cited in Benjamin's later writings. He was elected to the Académie Française in 1925.

18. Paul Valéry, *Analecta* (Paris, 1935), pp. 264–265. [Benjamin's note]

19. Alfred de Musset (1810–1857), French poet, playwright, and translator, ranks alongside Hugo, Lamartine, and Vigny as one of the great Romantic poets. He combined an intense lyricism with a propensity to shock through revelation of his vices: laziness, self-indulgence, a facile talent, and an attraction to opium.

20. Paul Valéry, "The Place of Baudelaire," in Valéry, *Leonardo, Poe, Mallarmé,* trans. Malcolm Cowley and James R. Lawler (Princeton: Princeton University Press, 1972), p. 195. Valéry's introduction dates from 1926.

21. Jules Vallès (1832–1885), French socialist journalist and novelist, was a member of the Paris Commune and founded the revolutionary journal *Le Cri du peuple* (1871). His best-known work is the three-volume autobiographical novel *Jacques Vingtras* (1879–1886). Clara-Agathe Nargeot (née Thénon; 1829–?) was a French painter who did a portrait of Baudelaire. Armand de Pontmartin (1811–1890) was a conservative critic whom Baudelaire called a "drawing-room preacher." Paul Claudel (1868–1955), French poet, dramatist, and diplomat, was associated with

the Symbolist movement. Théophile Gautier (1811–1872), French poet and man of letters, was a leader of the Parnassians, a poetic school that strove for detachment, technical perfection, and precise description in its verse. The school derives its name from its anthology *Le Parnasse Contemporain* (1866–1876). Nadar (pseudonym of Gaspard-Félix Tournachon; 1820–1910), French writer, caricaturist, and photographer, was one of the great portraitists of the nineteenth century. Among his many innovations were his natural posing of his subjects, a patent on the use of photographs in mapmaking and surveying, the first aerial photograph (made from a balloon), and the first photographic interview.

22. Constantin Guys (1805–1892), French painter, is the subject of Baudelaire's essay "Le Peintre de la vie moderne" (1859). Guys produced watercolors, engravings, and drawings of café life, military scenes, and the fashionable Parisian society of the Second Empire. For Baudelaire, Guys became the representative modern artist through his ability to capture and combine the ephemeral and the eternal in the modern world.

23. André Gide, "Baudelaire et M. Faguet," in *Morceaux choisis* (Paris, 1921), p. 128. [Benjamin's note. Gide (1869–1951), French novelist and man of letters, received the Nobel Prize for Literature in 1947. See "André Gide and Germany" and "Conversation with André Gide," in Benjamin, *Selected Writings,* vol. 2, pp. 80–84 and 91–97.—*Ed.*]

24. Jacques Rivière, *Etudes* [18th ed. (Paris, 1948), p. 14]. [Benjamin's note. Rivière (1886–1925), French novelist and critic, edited the *Nouvelle Revue Française* from 1919 until his death. He championed such figures as Proust, Stravinsky, and Nijinsky.—*Ed.*]

25. François-Arsène Houssaye (1815–1897), French journalist, was befriended by Gautier and met, through him, the leading writers of his day. His criticism appeared in virtually every leading newspaper and journal. *La Presse,* the first mass-circulation newspaper, made important innovations. It mixed traditional coverage of politics and the arts with elements of fashion, gossip, and scandal; and it introduced the *feuilleton-roman* (the serial novel), which supplied a new mass readership with sensationalist literature.

26. To endow this crowd with a soul is the very special purpose of the flâneur. His encounters with it are the experience that he never tires

of telling about. Certain reflexes of this illusion are an integral part of Baudelaire's work. It has continued to be an active force to this day. Jules Romains' *unanimisme* is an admirable late flowering of it. [Benjamin's note. Jules Romains (1885–1972), French novelist, poet, and playwright, was the author of *Les Hommes de bonne volonté* (Men of Good Will; 27 vols., 1932–1946) and other works. He moved to the United States in 1940.—*Ed.*]

27. Eugène Sue (1804–1857), French author, is known for his serial novels which attracted a wide readership. His most popular were *Les Mystères de Paris* (The Mysteries of Paris; 1842–1843) and *Le Juif errant* (The Wandering Jew; 1844–1845).

28. Friedrich Engels, *Die Lage der arbeitenden Klasse in England: Nach eigner Anschauung und authentischen Quellen,* 2nd ed. (Leipzig, 1848), pp. 36–37. [Benjamin's note. In English, *The Condition of the Working Class in England,* trans. Florence Wischnewetzky (1886; rpt. London: Penguin, 1987), pp. 68–69. Engels' study was first published in 1845.—*Ed.*]

29. Léon Gozlan (1803–1866) was a journalist, novelist, and playwright. He was the author of *Le Triomphe des omnibus: Poëme héroïcomique* (Triumph of the Omnibuses: Heroic-Comic Poem; 1828) and *Balzac en pantoufles* (Balzac in Slippers; 1865). Alfred Delvau (1825–1867) was a journalist and a friend of Baudelaire's. Among his works is *Les Heures parisiennes* (The Parisian Hours; 1866). Louis Lurine (1816–1860), French writer, was the editor of the anthology *Les Rues de Paris* (The Streets of Paris; 1843–1844).

30. Georg Wilhelm Friedrich Hegel, *Werke,* vol. 19, *Briefe von und an Hegel* (Letters to and from Hegel), ed. Karl Hegel (Leipzig, 1887), part 2, p. 257. [Benjamin's note]

31. Paul Desjardins, "Poètes contemporains: Charles Baudelaire," in *Revue Bleue: Revue Politique et Littéraire* (Paris), 14, no. 1 (July 2, 1887): 23. [Benjamin's note. Paul Desjardins (1859–1940), a literary critic and professor of rhetoric, was the organizer, from 1910 to 1940, of the "Decades of Pontigny," a series of meetings at the abbey in Pontigny attended by intellectuals from across Europe and designed to further the tradition of European humanism. Benjamin directed a meeting on his own writings at the abbey in May 1939. On Benjamin's relationship to

Desjardins and his institution, see the "Chronology" at the end of this volume.—*Ed.*]

32. Characteristic of Barbier's method is his poem "Londres," which in twenty-four lines describes the city, awkwardly closing with the following verses:

> Enfin, dans un amas de choses, sombre, immense,
> Un peuple noir, vivant et mourant en silence.
> Des êtres par milliers, suivant l'instinct fatal,
> Et courant après l'or par le bien et le mal.

> [Finally, within a huge and somber mass of things,
> A blackened people, who live and die in silence.
> Thousands of beings, who follow a fatal instinct,
> Pursuing gold by good and evil means.]

> Auguste Barbier, *Iambes et poèmes* (Paris, 1841)

Barbier's tendentious poems, particularly his London cycle, *Lazare* [Lazarus], influenced Baudelaire more profoundly than people have been willing to admit. Baudelaire's "Crépuscule du soir" [Half-Light of Evening] concludes as follows:

> ils finissent
> Leur destinée et vont vers le gouffre commun;
> L'hôpital se remplit de leurs soupirs.—Plus d'un
> Ne viendra plus chercher la soupe parfumée,
> Au coin du feu, le soir, auprès d'une âme aimée.

> [they accomplish
> Their fate and draw near the common pit;
> Their sighs fill the hospital ward.—More than one
> Will come no more to get his fragrant soup,
> At the fireside, in the evening, by the side of a loved one.]

Compare this with the end of the eighth stanza of Barbier's "Mineurs de Newcastle" [Miners of Newcastle]:

> Et plus d'un qui rêvait dans le fond de son âme
> Aux douceurs du logis, à l'oeil bleu de sa femme,
> Trouve au ventre du gouffre un éternel tombeau.

[And more than one who in his heart of hearts had dreams
Of home, sweet home, and of his wife's blue eyes,
Finds, within the belly of the pit, an everlasting tomb.]

With some masterful retouching, Baudelaire turns a "miner's fate" into the commonplace end of big-city dwellers. [Benjamin's note. Henri Auguste Barbier (1805–1882) was a French poet and satirist whom Baudelaire admired but criticized for moralistic tendencies. His *Iambes* (1831) satirized the monarchy of Louis Philippe.]

33. Albert Thibaudet, *Intérieurs* (Paris, 1924), p. 22. [Benjamin's note. Thibaudet (1874–1936) was an eminent French literary historian.— *Ed.*]

34. Proust, *A la recherche du temps perdu* (Paris, 1923), vol. 6, p. 138 *(La Prisonnière)*. [Benjamin's note]

35. The motif of love for a woman passing by occurs in an early poem by Stefan George. The poet has missed the important thing: the stream in which the woman moves past, borne along by the crowd. The result is a self-conscious elegy. The poet's glances—so he must confess to his lady—have "moved away, moist with longing / before they dared mingle with yours" ("feucht vor sehnen fortgezogen / eh sie in deine sich zu tauchen trauten"). From Stefan George, "Von einer Begegnung" (Encounter), in *Hymnen; Pilgerfahrten; Algabal* (Berlin, 1922). Baudelaire leaves no doubt that *he* looked deep into the eyes of the passer-by. [Benjamin's note]

36. This passage has a parallel in "Un Jour de pluie." Even though it bears the name of another writer, this poem must be ascribed to Baudelaire. The last verse, which gives the poem its extraordinarily somber quality, has an exact counterpart in "The Man of the Crowd." Poe writes: "The rays of the gas lamps, feeble at first in their struggle with the dying day, had now at length gained ascendancy, and threw over everything a fitful and garish luster. All was dark yet splendid—as that ebony to which has been likened the style of Tertullian." The coincidence here is all the more astonishing as the following verses were written in 1843 at the latest, a period when Baudelaire did not know Poe.

Chacun, nous coudoyant sur le trottoir glissant,
Egoïste et brutal, passe et nous éclabousse,
Ou, pour courir plus vite, en s'éloignant nous pousse.

Partout fange, déluge, obscurité du ciel.
Noir tableau qu'eût rêvé le noir Ezéchiel!

[Each one, elbowing us on the slippery sidewalk,
Selfish and savage, goes by and splashes us,
Or, to run the faster, gives us a push as he makes off.
Everywhere mud, deluge, darkness in the sky.
A somber scene that Ezekiel the somber might have dreamed!]

[Benjamin's note]

37. There is something demonic about Poe's businessmen. One is reminded of Marx, who blamed the "feverishly youthful pace of material production" in the United States for the lack of "either time or opportunity . . . to abolish the old world of the spirit." Baudelaire describes how, as darkness descends, "baleful demons" awaken in the air "sluggish as a bunch of businessmen." This passage, from "Crépuscule du soir," may have been inspired by Poe's text. [Benjamin's note]

38. A pedestrian knew how to display his nonchalance provocatively on certain occasions. Around 1840 it was briefly fashionable to take turtles for a walk in the arcades. The flâneurs liked to have the turtles set the pace for them. If they had had their way, progress would have been obliged to accommodate itself to this pace. But this attitude did not prevail. Taylor—who popularized the slogan "Down with dawdling!"—carried the day. [Benjamin's note. Frederick Winslow Taylor (1856–1915), American efficiency engineer, devoted the last fifteen years of his life to developing the so-called Taylor system, expounded in his book *The Principles of Scientific Management* (1911).—*Ed.*]

39. In Glassbrenner's character, the man of leisure appears as a paltry scion of the *citoyen*. Nante, Berlin's street-corner boy, has no reason to bestir himself. He makes himself at home on the street, which naturally does not lead him anywhere, and is as comfortable as the philistine is within his four walls. [Benjamin's note. Adolf Glassbrenner (1810–1876) was a German writer best known for his humorous and satirical sketches of Berlin life.—*Ed.*]

40. Ernst Theodor Amadeus Hoffmann (1776–1822), German writer, composer, and civil servant, is best known for his short tales, many of which combine Romantic and gothic elements. "Des Vetters Eckfenster"

(The Cousin's Corner Window; 1822), one of his late tales, is a dialogue in which a poet attempts to instruct his cousin in the art of seeing.

41. What leads up to this confession is remarkable. The visitor notes that the cousin watches the bustle down below only because he enjoys the changing play of colors; in the long run, he says, this must be tiring. In a similar vein, and probably not much later, Gogol wrote the following line about a fair in the Ukraine: "So many people were on their way there that it made one's eyes swim." The daily sight of a lively crowd may once have constituted a spectacle to which one's eyes needed to adapt. On the basis of this supposition, one may assume that once the eyes had mastered this task, they welcomed opportunities to test their newly acquired ability. This would mean that the technique of Impressionist painting, whereby the image is construed from a riot of dabs of color, would be a reflection of experiences to which the eyes of a big-city dweller have become accustomed. A picture like Monet's *Cathedral of Chartres,* which looks like an image of an anthill of stone, would be an illustration of this hypothesis. [Benjamin's note. Nikolai Gogol (1809–1852) is known as the father of realism in Russian literature. He was the author of *The Inspector General* (1836), *Cossack Tales* (1836), and *Dead Souls* (1842). Benjamin quotes from his story "Propavshaya gramota" (The Lost Letter). Claude Monet (1840–1926) was one of the greatest of the French Impressionist painters.—*Ed.*]

42. In his story, E. T. A. Hoffmann makes some edifying reflections—for instance, on the blind man who turns his face toward the sky. In the last line of "Les Aveugles" [The Blind], Baudelaire, who knew Hoffmann's story, modifies Hoffmann's reflections in such a way as to deny their edifying quality: "Que cherchent-ils au Ciel, tous ces aveugles?" ["What are all those blind people looking for in the heavens?"] [Benjamin's note. Biedermeier refers to a middle-class style of furniture and interior decoration popular in early nineteenth-century Germany; it is similar to Empire style, but simpler and more sober. A *tableau vivant* (literally, "living picture") is a scene presented onstage by costumed actors who remain silent and still as if in a picture.—*Ed.*]

43. Karl Varnhagen von Ense (1785–1858) was a German diplomat and man of letters. His wife, Rahel, was a leading intellectual and salon figure in early nineteenth-century Berlin.

44. Heinrich Heine, *Gespräche: Briefe, Tagebücher, Berichte seiner Zeitgenossen,* ed. Hugo Bieber (Berlin, 1926), p. 163. [Benjamin's note]

45. James Sydney Ensor (1860–1949) was a Belgian painter and printmaker whose works are characterized by their troubling fantasy, explosive colors, and subtle social commentary.

46. Valéry, *Cahier B* (Paris, 1910), pp. 88–89. [Benjamin's note]

47. Baudelaire, *Oeuvres,* vol. 2, p. 333 ("Le Peintre de la vie moderne"). [Benjamin's note]

48. Karl Marx, *Das Kapital,* vol. 1 (Berlin, 1932), p. 404. [Benjamin's note]

49. In English in the original.

50. The shorter the training period of an industrial worker, the longer the basic training of a military man. It may be part of society's preparation for total war that training is shifting from techniques of production to techniques of destruction. [Benjamin's note]

51. Alain, *Les Idées et les âges* (Paris, 1927), vol. 1, p. 183 ("Le Jeu"). [Benjamin's note. Alain (pen name of Emile Chartier; 1868–1951), French essayist, took his pseudonym from a fifteenth-century poet. His collected essays, *Propos,* found a primarily youthful audience.—*Ed.*]

52. Aloys Senefelder (1771–1834), Czech-born inventor, was the first to devise processes of lithography (1796) and color lithography (1826). He served as inspector of maps at the royal Bavarian printing office in Munich.

53. Ludwig Börne, *Gesammelte Schriften,* vol. 3 (Hamburg and Frankfurt, 1862), pp. 38–39. [Benjamin's note. Börne (born Löb Baruch; 1786–1837), writer and social critic, lived in exile in Paris after 1830. A member of the Young Germany movement, he was one of the first writers to use the feuilleton section of the newspaper as a forum for social and political criticism.—*Ed.*]

54. Gambling nullifies the lessons of experience [*Ordnungen der Erfahrung*]. It may be due to an obscure sense of this that the "vulgar appeal to experience" (Kant) has particular currency among gamblers. A gambler says "my number" in the same way a man-about-town says "my type." Toward the end of the Second Empire, this attitude was widespread. "On the boulevards it was customary to attribute everything to chance." This way of thinking is fortified by betting, which is a device for giving events the character of a shock, detaching them from the contexts

of experience. For the bourgeoisie, even political events were apt to assume the form of incidents at a gambling table. [Benjamin's note]

55. Johann Wolfgang Goethe, *Dichtung und Wahrheit*, part 2, book 9. In the sentence preceding, Benjamin writes: "Der Wunsch . . . gehört . . . den Ordnungen der Erfahrung an."

56. Joseph Joubert, *Pensées*, vol. 2 (Paris, 1883), p. 162. [Benjamin's note. Joubert (1754–1824), French thinker and moralist, was an associate of Diderot and Chateaubriand. He took part in the first phase of the Revolution as a justice of the peace in his hometown, Montignac, but withdrew from politics in 1792. His *Pensées*, culled from his journals, were first published in 1838.—*Ed.*]

57. These lines come from Baudelaire's poem "L'Horloge" (The Clock), the last poem in the "Spleen et idéal" section of *Les Fleurs du mal*. The third stanza of the poem begins: "Trois mille six cents fois par heure, la Seconde / Chuchote: *Souviens-toi!*" ("Three thousand six hundred times an hour, the second-hand / Whispers: 'Remember!'")

58. The narcotic effect that is involved here is time-specific, like the malady it is supposed to alleviate. Time is the material into which the phantasmagoria of gambling has been woven. In *Les Faucheurs de nuit* [Reapers by Night; 1860], [Edouard] Gourdon writes: "I assert that the mania for gambling is the noblest of all passions, for it includes all the others. A series of lucky *coups* gives me more pleasure than a non-gambler can have in years. . . . If you think I see only profit in the gold I win, you are mistaken. I see in it the pleasures it procures for me, and I enjoy them to the full. They come too quickly to make me weary, and there are too many of them for me to get bored. I live a hundred lives in one. When I travel, it is the way an electric spark travels. . . . If I am frugal and reserve my banknotes for gambling, it is because I know the value of time too well to invest them as other people do. A certain enjoyment that I might permit myself would cost me a thousand other enjoyments. . . . I have intellectual pleasures, and want no others." In the beautiful observations on gambling in his *Jardin d'Epicure* [Garden of Epicurus; 1895], Anatole France presents a similar view. [Benjamin's note]

59. Benjamin refers to a quintessential work by the fourteenth-century Italian painter Giotto di Bondone—namely, his portrait of "Wrath" *(Iracondia),* one of the seven vices depicted in the frescoes of the Arena

or Scrovegni Chapel in Padua (ca. 1305–1306). The portrait shows a female figure rending her garments in a fit of rage.

60. Proust, "A propos de Baudelaire," *Nouvelle Revue Française,* 16 (June 1, 1921): 652. [Benjamin's note. This is a translation of Benjamin's German translation of Proust. For a more literal translation of the original French, see *The Arcades Project,* p. 309 (Convolute J44,5). Proust speaks of "un étrange sectionnement du temps" ("a strange sectioning of time") in the world of Baudelaire.—*Ed.*]

61. Baudelaire's idea of natural correspondences—reflected in his poem "Correspondances," cited below in the text—derives mainly from the Swedish mystic Emanuel Swedenborg (1688–1772), who envisioned a universal language in which everything outward and visible in nature was a symbol pointing to an inward spiritual cause. Baudelaire develops his idea of modern beauty *(beauté moderne)* at the end of his "Salon de 1846" (section 18).

62. Charles Fourier (1772–1837), French social theorist and reformer, called for a reorganization of society based on communal agrarian associations which he called "phalansteries." In each community, the members would continually change roles within different systems of production. Synaesthesia is a condition in which one type of stimulation evokes the sensation of another, as when the hearing of a sound produces the visualization of a color.

63. Beauty can be defined in two ways: in its relationship to history and in its relationship to nature. Both relationships bring out the role of semblance, the aporetic element in the beautiful. (Let us characterize the first relationship briefly. On the basis of its *historical* existence, beauty is an appeal to join those who admired it in an earlier age. Being moved by beauty means *ad plures ire,* as the Romans called dying. According to this definition, "semblance of beauty" means that the identical object which admiration is courting cannot be found in the work. This admiration gleans what earlier generations admired in it. A line by Goethe expresses the ultimate wisdom here: "Everything that has had a great effect can really no longer be evaluated.") Beauty in relation to *nature* can be defined as "that which remains true to its essential nature only when veiled." (See *Neue deutsche Beiträge,* ed. Hugo von Hofmannsthal [Munich], 2, no. 2 [1925]: 161 [Benjamin, "Goethes Wahlverwandtschaften" (Goethe's Elective Affinities).—*Ed.*].) *Correspondances* help us to think

about such veiling. We may call it, using a somewhat daring abbreviation, the "reproducing aspect" of the work of art. The *correspondances* constitute the court of judgment before which the art object is found to be a faithful reproduction—which, to be sure, makes it entirely aporetic. If one attempted to reproduce this aporia in the material of language, one would define beauty as the object of experience [*Erfahrung*] in the state of resemblance. This definition would probably coincide with Valéry's formulation: "Beauty may require the servile imitation of what is indefinable in things" (*Autres rhumbs* [Paris, 1934], p. 167). If Proust so readily returns to this object of experience (which in his work appears as time recaptured), one cannot say he is revealing any secrets. It is, rather, one of the disconcerting features of his technique that he continually and loquaciously builds his reflections around the concept of a work of art as a copy, the concept of beauty—in short, the hermetic aspect of art. He writes about the origin and intentions of his work with a fluency and an urbanity that would befit a refined amateur. This, to be sure, has its counterpart in Bergson. The following passage, in which the philosopher indicates all that may be expected from a visual actualization of the uninterrupted stream of becoming, has a flavor reminiscent of Proust. "We can let our day-to-day existence be permeated with such vision and thus, thanks to philosophy, enjoy a satisfaction similar to that of art; but this satisfaction would be more frequent, more regular, and more easily accessible to ordinary mortals" (*La Pensée et le mouvant: Essais et conférences* [Paris, 1934], p. 198). Bergson sees within reach what Valéry's better, Goethean understanding visualizes as the "here" in which the inadequate becomes an actuality. [Benjamin's note. The last phrase of this note—"in dem das Unzulängliche Ereignis wird"—is an allusion to the Chorus Mysticus that ends Goethe's *Faust, Part II*. *Ad plures ire* literally means "to go to the many," to join the masses that have passed away— i.e., to die.—*Ed.*]

64. Marceline Desbordes-Valmore (1786–1859), French actress and writer, was the author of children's stories and poetry (collected in *Poésies*, published in 1842). The phrase "hysterical tears" appears in English.

65. Proust, *A la recherche du temps perdu*, vol. 8, pp. 82–83 *(Le Temps retrouvé)*. [Benjamin's note]

66. Jules-Amédée Barbey d'Aurevilly, *Les Oeuvres et les hommes*

(*XIXe siècle*), part 3, *Les Poètes* (Paris, 1862), p. 381. [Benjamin's note. Barbey d'Aurevilly (1808–1889), French critic and novelist, was a longtime friend of Baudelaire. Timon, a misanthropic Athenian, is the hero of Shakespeare's *Timon of Athens* (ca. 1607–1608). Archilochus (6th century B.C.) was a Greek lyric poet and writer of lampoons, in whose work the poetry of heroism yields to that of feeling and reflection.—*Ed.*]

67. In the mystical "Colloquy of Monos and Una," Poe has, so to speak, taken the empty time sequence to which the subject in the mood of spleen is delivered up, and copied it into the *durée;* he seems blissfully happy to have rid himself of its horrors. It is a "sixth sense" acquired by the departed, consisting of an ability to derive harmony even from the empty passage of time. To be sure, it is quite easily disrupted by the rhythm of the second-hand. "There seemed to have sprung up in the brain *that* of which no words could convey to the merely human intelligence even an indistinct conception. Let me term it a mental pendulous pulsation. It was the moral embodiment of man's abstract idea of *Time.* By the absolute equalization of this movement—or of such as this—had the cycles of the firmamental orbs themselves been adjusted. By its aid I measured the irregularities of the clock upon the mantel, and of the watches of the attendants. Their tickings came sonorously to my ears. The slightest deviation from the true proportion . . . affected me just as violations of abstract truth are wont, on earth, to affect the moral sense." [Benjamin's note]

68. Max Horkheimer, "Zu Bergsons Metaphysik der Zeit," *Zeitschrift für Sozialforschung,* 3 (1934): 332. [Benjamin's note]

69. See Bergson, *Matière et mémoire: Essai sur la relation du corps à l'esprit* (Paris, 1933), pp. 166–167. [Benjamin's note. See, in English, *Matter and Memory,* p. 139.—*Ed.*]

70. In Proust, the deterioration of experience manifests itself in the complete realization of his ultimate intention. There is nothing more ingenious or more loyal than the way in which he casually, and continually, tries to convey to the reader: Redemption is my private show. [Benjamin's note]

71. Baudelaire, *Oeuvres,* vol. 2, p. 197 ("Quelques Caricaturistes français"). [Benjamin's note]

72. Ibid., pp. 222–224 ("Salon de 1859: Le Public moderne et la photographie"). [Benjamin's note. The quotations from Baudelaire that im-

mediately follow in the text are likewise from this essay (p. 224). Baudelaire's critique of photography is cited at greater length in *The Arcades Project*, pp. 691–692 (Convolute Y10a,1–Y11,1).—*Ed.*]

73. Valéry, "Avant-propos" [Foreword], *Encyclopédie française*, vol. 16: *Arts et littératures dans la société contemporaine*, I (Paris, 1935), 16.4–5/6. [Benjamin's note]

74. "Ach, du warst in abgelebten Zeiten meine Schwester oder meine Frau!" This is a line from Goethe's poem dedicated to Charlotte von Stein, "Warum gabst Du uns die tiefen Blicke" (Why Did You Give Us Deep Gazes). The poem was discovered in 1864 in a letter of April 14, 1776, to Frau von Stein, Goethe's beloved.

75. The moment of such a success is itself marked as something unique. It is the basis of the structural design of Proust's works. Each situation in which the chronicler is touched by the breath of lost time is thereby rendered incomparable and removed from the sequence of days. [Benjamin's note]

76. Novalis, *Schriften* (Berlin, 1901), part 2 (first half), p. 293. [Benjamin's note. Novalis (pseudonym of Friedrich Leopold, Freiherr von Hardenberg; 1772–1801) was a poet and theorist, and a central figure of the early German Romantic period. His works include the verse collections *Blütenstaub* (Pollen; 1798) and *Hymnen an die Nacht* (Hymns to the Night; 1800), and the unfinished novel *Heinrich von Ofterdingen* (1802).—*Ed.*]

77. This conferred power is a wellspring of poetry. Whenever a human being, an animal, or an inanimate object thus endowed by the poet lifts up its eyes, it draws him into the distance. The gaze of nature, when thus awakened, dreams and pulls the poet after its dream. Words, too, can have an aura of their own. This is how Karl Kraus described it: "The more closely you look at a word, the more distantly it looks back." (Karl Kraus, *Pro domo et mundo* [Munich, 1912], p. 164.) [Benjamin's note]

78. See Walter Benjamin, "L'Oeuvre d'art à l'époque de sa reproduction mécanisée," in *Zeitschrift für Sozialforschung*, 5 (1936): 43. [Benjamin's note. See "The Work of Art in the Age of Its Technological Reproducibility (Third Version)," in Benjamin, *Selected Writings, Volume 4: 1938–1940*, ed. Howard Eiland and Michael W. Jennings (Cambridge, Mass.: Harvard University Press, 2003), sec. 3, pp. 255–256.—*Ed.*]

79. Proust, *A la recherche du temps perdu*, vol. 8, p. 33 *(Le Temps retrouvé)*. [Benjamin's note]

80. Valéry, *Analecta*, pp. 193–194. [Benjamin's note]

81. From "Correspondances," in *Les Fleurs du mal*.

82. Goethe's poem "Selige Sehnsucht" (Blessed Longing) was published in the volume *West-östlicher Divan* (Divan of West and East; 1819).

83. Baudelaire, *Oeuvres*, vol. 1, p. 40. [Benjamin's note. This is the first stanza of Poem XXIV (untitled) of the "Spleen et idéal" section of *Les Fleurs du mal.—Ed.*]

84. Ibid., vol. 1, p. 190 ("L'Avertisseur" [The Lookout]). [Benjamin's note]

85. Ibid., vol. 1, p. 40 ("Tu mettrais l'univers entier dans ta ruelle" [You'd Take the Whole World to Bed]). [Benjamin's note]

86. Ibid., vol. 2, p. 622 ("Choix de maximes consolantes sur l'amour" [Consoling Maxims on Love]). [Benjamin's note]

87. Ibid., vol. 2, p. 359 ("Le Peintre de la vie moderne" [The Painter of Modern Life]). [Benjamin's note]

88. Georg Simmel, *Mélanges de philosophie rélativiste: Contribution à la culture philosophique*, trans. Alix Guillain (Paris, 1912), pp. 26–27. [Benjamin's note. The original title of Simmel's essay is "Exkurs über die Soziologie der Sinne" (On the Sociology of the Senses; 1911).—*Ed.*]

89. Baudelaire, *Oeuvres*, vol. 2, p. 273 ("Salon de 1859," sec. 8, "Le Paysage" [Landscape]). [Benjamin's note]

90. Ibid., vol. 1, p. 94 ("L'Horloge" [The Clock]). [Benjamin's note]

91. See Jules Lemaître, *Les Contemporains: Etudes et portraits littéraires* (Paris, 1897), pp. 31–32. [Benjamin's note. Benjamin refers to a passage from Baudelaire's notebooks: "To create a new commonplace [*poncif*]—that's genius. I must create a commonplace." See *"My Heart Laid Bare" and Other Prose Writings*, trans. Norman Cameron (1950; rpt. New York: Haskell House, 1975), p. 168 ("Fusées," no. 20). See also Baudelaire's "Salon de 1846," sec. 10.—*Ed.*]

92. Baudelaire, *Oeuvres*, vol. 2, p. 422 ("L'Ecole païenne" [The Pagan School]). [Benjamin's note]

93. Ibid., vol. 1, pp. 483–484. [Benjamin's note. "Perte d'auréole" was rejected by the *Revue Nationale et Etrangère* in 1865, two years before Baudelaire's death, and was first published in 1869 in the posthumous

edition of his *Petits poèmes en prose,* also known as *Le Spleen de Paris.*—Ed.]

94. It is not impossible that this diary entry was occasioned by a pathogenic shock. The form the entry takes, which links it to Baudelaire's published work, is thus all the more revealing. [Benjamin's note. For the diary entry in question, see *"My Heart Laid Bare" and Other Prose Writings,* p. 165 ("Fusées," no. 17).—Ed.]

95. Baudelaire, *Oeuvres,* vol. 2, p. 641. [Benjamin's note. He quotes from the conclusion of the final section of "Fusées."—Ed.]

96. This phrase comes from section 8 of Friedrich Nietzsche's uncompleted, posthumously published early work *Die Philosophie im tragischen Zeitalter der Griechen* (Philosophy in the Tragic Age of the Greeks). In its original context, it refers to the Presocratic Greek philosopher Heraclitus, whom Nietzsche presents, in a typically self-reflecting vein, as a proud solitary, flaming inwardly while outwardly looming dead and icy.

Index

Adam and Eve / Garden of Eden, 27–28

Adorno, Theodor, 12, 18, 215n20

Advertising, 148; of commodities, 37; in newspapers, 60, 61–62, 191

Alain (pen name of Emile Chartier), 193, 284n51

Alexandrine, 142

Alienation, 9, 24, 36, 40

Allegory, 42, 116, 137–138, 143, 159, 167, 168, 169; Baroque, 149, 154, 163, 264n8; in Benjamin, 17. *See also* Baudelaire, Charles: allegory in works of

Ambiguity, 8, 41

Androgyny, 119, 120, 139

Antiquity, 17, 110, 112–116, 119, 134, 139, 149, 156, 160

Apaches, 40, 107, 108, 109, 125, 221n35

Apollinaire, Guillaume, 109, 252n222

Arago, François, 34, 219n15

Arcades, 30–33, 33, 41, 45, 223n44; as both street and interior, 8, 41, 68, 81, 85; demise of, 81; flâneurs and, 68–69, 85, 188; gas lighting of, 31, 81

Architecture, 31, 33, 39, 45

Art, 203; for art's sake *(l'art pour l'art)*, 47, 58–59, 131–132, 137, 143, 222n42, 226n6; collectors, 39; commercial, 45; as commodities, 154; as copy of beauty, 287n63; denaturing of, 9; as fetish, 22–23; modern, 110, 111; morality and, 59; as ritual, 22, 198; technology and, 34, 39, 163, 203; utility and, 47, 59

Auerbach, Erich, 214n5

Aupick, Jacques, 49, 227n9

Aura, 148, 152, 156, 202, 204–205, 289n77; Baudelaire and, 23, 205–206; Benjamin and, 22–23; of commodities, 149; experience of, 204–206; shock experience and, 210

Aureole, 138, 208–209

Avant-garde art and artists, 7, 8, 252n222

Babou, Hippolyte, 73, 269n44

Bachofen, Jakob Johann, 275n5

Bacon, Francis, 71, 240n108

Balzac, Honoré de, 30, 45, 70, 72, 73, 104, 106, 108, 240n111; bourgeois characters, 140; gladiator imagery,

Balzac, Honoré de *(continued)*
103. WORKS: *La Fille aux yeux d'or*,
119; *Modeste Mignon*, 78
Barbey d'Aurevilly, Jules-Amédée,
57–58, 200, 234n52, 287n66
Barbier, Auguste, 58, 183, 187, 234n56,
280n32
Barrès, Maurice, 97, 248n180
Barthélemy, Auguste-Marseille.
WORKS: *Némésis*, 57, 233n49
Baudelaire, Charles, 14, 59, 120, 149,
150, 269n44; abyss (theme), 134,
161; as agent of class discontent,
11–12, 15, 40–41, 59, 261n300; allegory in works of, 10, 18, 19, 40, 52,
111, 127–128, 136, 138, 139, 144, 147,
148, 149, 152, 154, 155, 162, 163, 164,
169, 256n48; "Americanism" of, 139,
165, 265n17; as apolitical/asocial
writer, 2, 56, 59, 74, 89, 155; on the
artist, 96–97, 98, 99, 178; *l'art pour
l'art*, break with, 58–59; aura and,
23, 205–206; big city (theme), 99,
111–112, 118, 133, 145, 149, 152, 183;
Blanqui and, 50–51; on the bourgeois class, 145; Catholicism and,
154; on children, 141; classical antiquity (concept), 109–110, 112–113,
117, 118–119, 139, 149, 156; cloud imagery, 158; commodities and, 148–
149; comparison with his contemporaries, 139; competition with
other poets, 142, 167; on conspir-
acy/conspirators, 49, 56, 129;
correspondances doctrine, 152, 168,
197–198, 199, 200, 286n61; creditors
of, 78–79, 99; crowds / the masses
and, 81, 88, 89, 96, 100, 180–181, 183,
184–185, 188, 209–210; on dandies,
124–125; death imagery, 245n148;
death (theme), 41, 48, 112, 145, 162,
196, 209, 268n39, 272n72; death
and the city (theme), 41, 166; death
and the woman (theme), 9, 41, 144,

145, 269n39; death of, 84, 116, 118,
128, 137, 163, 188, 290n93; diaries of,
209; disintegration and desolation
in works of, 200, 205; *dupe*/victim
(theme), 71; Dupont and, 57–59;
earnings from writings, 65; essay
on Dupont, 164, 272n73; essay on
Guys, 110, 178–179; essay on
Meryon, 116–117; exile in Belgium,
16, 48–49, 81; experience of the
public, 167; on eyes and the gaze,
206–207; failure of, 11, 16, 96, 166;
fashion and, 105–107, 110–111; father, influence of, 273n74; fencing
metaphor, 97–98, 99, 103, 179, 194;
as flâneur, 124, 125, 188; on
flâneurs, 72, 79, 98–99, 188; on
Flaubert, 120–121; on gambling
and games of chance, 194, 195–196;
and Gautier, 163–164; heroic imagery, 15–16, 21, 96, 100, 101, 102, 104,
105, 106, 107, 109, 110, 123–124, 125,
129, 134, 135, 140, 144, 149, 154, 161,
168, 183–184; history (concept), 156;
Hugo and, 49, 90, 91, 94, 96, 110,
112, 113, 142, 246n162; ignorance of
the outside world, 100–101; ignorance of working class, 192; imagery in poetry of, 20, 21, 41, 123, 127,
156; imagination of, 147; inspiration, 160; interior, 156; isolation of,
11, 41, 125, 169; on Lamartine, 65;
language and prosody, 17, 18, 21,
99, 126–127, 128, 159; legend of, 28;
life history, 146; literature about,
250n198; love of Rome, 118, 119;
machine imagery, 162–163; male
readers of, 151; melancholy in writings of, 3–4, 11, 29, 40, 136, 141, 147,
161, 163, 168, 200; on men of letters, 65, 66; mental illness and
hospitalization, 97, 99, 116; mistress (Jeanne Duval), 28, 99,
258n270; modernity in works of,

Kierkegaard, Sören, 18, 142, 150, 267n29
Klages, Ludwig, 171, 275n5
Kraus, Karl, 174, 276n10, 289n77

Labyrinth, 85, 145, 146, 166
Lafargue, Paul, 43, 223n46
Laforgue, Jules, 85, 127, 134, 139, 244n145, 265n17
Lamartine, Alphonse de, 63–65, 125, 139, 171, 177, 237n82, 248n180, 265nn18,19, 274n2. WORKS: *Harmonies*, 63; *Histoire des Girondins*, 62, 236n70; *Méditations*, 63
Latin literature and culture, 149, 153, 163, 243n138
Lavater, Johann Kaspar, 70, 240n105
Lebrun, Pierre Antoine. WORKS: *Le Cid d'Andalousie*, 127, 260n288
Leconte de Lisle, Charles Marie, 118, 125, 139, 256n253, 265n20
Leiris, Michel, 156, 270n57
Lemaître, Jules, 47, 56, 123, 127, 147, 267n36
Lemercier, Népomucène, 127–128, 260n291
Lenin, V. I., 50
Le Play, Frédéric, 54, 230n36. WORKS: *Ouvriers européens*, 44
Lesbians, 119, 120, 121–122, 139, 144, 150
London, 80, 89, 99, 280n32; crowds / the masses and, 79, 80–81, 82, 181–182, 188–189; dandies, 125; World Exhibition of 1851, 37. *See also* Poe, Edgar Allan, works: "The Man of the Crowd"
Louis Napoleon. *See* Napoleon III
Louis Philippe, King of France, 9, 38, 43, 67, 77, 221n31, 228n19, 233n49
Lukács, Georg, 239n100. WORKS: *History and Class Consciousness*, 13–14

Lurine, Louis, 182, 279n29
Lyric poetry, 170–171, 271n66; after Baudelaire, 208; of Baudelaire, 2, 23, 40, 128, 139, 147, 170, 205, 208; crowd as subject of, 90; decline of, 54, 154; experience and, 177; of George, 1, 263n2; Greek, 237n81, 288n66; of Hugo, 171, 227n12, 263n4, 274n4; *Les Fleurs du mal* as, 2, 135, 208; Paris as subject of, 40, 54; public reception of, 20, 170, 171; of Valéry, 176

Machinery, 21, 32, 162–163, 191–192, 193
Maeterlinck, Maurice, 152, 162, 270n50
Male sexuality, 148
Mallarmé, Stéphane, 132–133, 165, 265n21, 277n20
Market/marketplace, 8, 15, 35, 40, 42, 45, 59, 63, 64, 65, 66, 67, 71, 80, 86, 92, 93, 131, 132, 142, 143, 163, 167, 189
Marquis de Sade, 14, 74, 241n119
Marx, Karl / Marxism, 8, 33, 36, 38, 57, 58, 63, 85, 130, 181; on city social life, 69; on commodities, 13; on conspiracy/conspirators, 46–47, 49, 51, 52; establishes International Workingmen's Association, 37; image of America, 244n141; on June Insurrection, 50; on labor, 100, 191–192; on production, 32; racial theory, 55–56. WORKS: *Capital*, 13, 55; *Communist Manifesto*, 40; *The Eighteenth Brumaire of Louis Napoleon*, 132; *Class Struggles in France*, 52
Materialist method, 129–131, 169
Melancholy, 29, 161, 162, 202
Melanchthon (pseud. of Philip Schwartzerd), 168, 273n78
Memory, 146, 168, 174–175, 194, 203;

Paris (continued)
of people, 78–79; as subject of lyric poetry, 40, 54; urban development and crowding, 115–116, 117. See also Arcades; Panoramas in Paris

Paris Commune, 44–45, 49, 50, 266n23

Paris world exhibition of 1867, 37

Parnassians (literary group), 256nn253,257, 265n20, 278n21

Passion, aesthetic, 142, 150

Passion, primitive, 164, 273n74

Peasantry, 52–53, 63–65, 102; as Lumpenproletariat, 101

Péguy, Charles, 112, 254n236

Perception, 4, 28, 160, 191, 201–202, 205

Phantasmagoria, 9, 14, 18, 19, 24; of capitalist culture, 37; of the city, 40; commodities and, 15; of gambling and games of chance, 285n58; of happiness from misery, 161; of the interior, 38; of Parisian life, 13, 70, 72; of space and time, 43; urban, 14; world exhibitions and, 36

Photograms, 7

Photography, 9, 35, 45, 60–61, 190–191, 202–203, 204, 235n63; aerial, 278n21; by electric light, 219n16; history of, 34, 35, 79; as metaphor, 5–7, 27; versus painting, 35, 203; as political tool, 35; scientific applications of, 34–35; technology and, 34

Physiognomy, 10–11, 39, 91, 114, 138, 149, 189, 207

Physiologies (writings on personality types), 13, 14, 67, 68, 69–70

Pierre Bonaparte, Prince, 260n293

Piranesi, Giovanni Battista, 118, 256n254

Poe, Edgar Allan, 14, 39, 40, 74–75, 81, 82, 161, 192, 243nn138,139; Baudelaire and, 177; description of businessmen, 244n141, 282n37; description of the crowd, 82–84, 85, 157, 186–188, 189, 190, 191, 194, 271n61; detective stories, 108; on flâneurs, 79; translation of, by Baudelaire, 186. WORKS: "Colloquy of Monos and Una," 288n67; "The Man of the Crowd," 20–21, 79, 186, 189, 271n61, 281n36; "The Murders in the Rue Morgue," 73; "The Mystery of Marie Roget," 73, 74–75; "Philosophy of Furniture," 39–40; "The Purloined Letter," 73

Poetry: la poésie pure, 132–133. See also Lyric poetry

Pontmartin, Armand de, 178, 277n21

Pound, Ezra, 214n4

Pregnancy, 122, 148, 150, 258n270

Prehistory, 7, 28, 198, 202

Presse, La (newspaper), 60, 62, 98, 180, 219n13, 235n61, 278n25

Prévost, Pierre, 34

Primal history, 12, 32

Privacy, 21

Private individual, 38, 39–40

Production, 155; aesthetic, 2; artistic, 7; capitalist, 191; commodity, 8–9, 13, 15; cultural, 7, 8; experience and, 192; laborers as commodities, 88–89; mass, 131, 146, 159, 165; process of, 122, 130–131, 133, 146; rhythm of, 191

Progress, 19, 83–84, 96, 123, 130–131, 161–162, 164–165

Prolès, Charles, 49, 228n16

Proletariat, 36, 40, 43, 44, 48, 50, 52, 78, 103, 181, 233n42; at the barricades, 50; Marx on, 55–56. See also Working class / workers

Prostitutes, 41, 66, 86–87, 207; in big cities, 165, 166; as commodities, 148; crowds / the masses and, 146;

as mass-produced articles, 165; as
seller and sold, 9, 144
Proust, Marcel: on aura, 204–205;
Baudelaire and, 101, 118, 177, 200,
269; memory and experience and,
174–176; obsession with time and
memory, 196–197, 199, 204, 287n63,
289n75; as reader of *Les Fleurs du
mal*, 197. Works: *A la recherche du
temps perdu*, 172–173, 174; "A
propos de Baudelaire," 250n199,
256n252, 269n43, 286n60; "La Parisienne," 185
Psychiatry, 178
Psychic mechanisms, 176–177
Puccini, Giacomo. Works: *La
Bohème*, 233n47

Ragpicker, 11, 52, 53–54, 108–109, 125,
157, 230n36, 252n221
Rattier, Paul Ernest, 84–85
Raumer, Friedrich von, 113, 254n238
Redemption, 17, 28, 151, 155, 160, 161,
162, 288n70
Reik, Theodor, 175, 277n14
Renan, Ernest, 219n19
Reproduction, 203, 204; artistic, 138,
158, 203, 287, 292; of nature as
photography, 45; technology of,
158
Rethel, Alfred. Works: *Dance of
Death*, 105, 251n208
Revolution of 1848, 48, 58, 65, 166,
267n34, 272n73
Rigault, Raoul, 49, 228n15
Rimbaud, Arthur, 45, 139, 150, 171,
265n21, 274n3
Ritual, 21, 22, 37, 174–175, 197, 198,
204
Rivière, Jacques, 179–180, 278n24
Romains, Jules, 279n26
Romanticism, 1, 7, 103, 136, 142,
233n48, 248n180, 256n254, 258n271,
260n291, 269n44, 277n19, 289n76;

Baudelaire and, 1; Hugo and,
227n12, 248n180, 263n4, 277n19
Rousseau, Jean-Jacques, 104, 225n1

Sainte-Beuve, Charles-Augustin, 54–
55, 65, 127, 232n38, 234n52; crowds /
the masses and, 90; on newspa-
pers, 60
Saint-Simon, Henri de, 35, 36,
220n22; utopian ideal, 119–120,
257nn258,260
Sand, George, 122, 144, 258n271,
267n33
Satan/Lucifer, 11, 56, 57, 59, 125, 195;
satanic laughter, 158–159
Scent, 199, 200
Scheerbart, Paul, 8, 32, 217n5.
Works: *Glass Architecture*, 33
Scribe, Eugène, 236n73
Selfsame, the ever-, 137, 140, 150, 151,
159
Semblance, 41, 96, 131, 136, 146, 147,
148, 150, 163, 167, 210, 286n6
Senefelder, Aloys, 193–194, 284n52
Sensorium, 21, 152, 191
September Laws, 67, 238nn95,96,
266n22
Serial novels, 60, 62, 63, 181
Sex / sex appeal / sexuality, 19, 37, 41,
87, 122, 137, 141, 144, 148, 163, 165,
185, 205
Shelley, Percy Bysshe, 89–90, 246n155
Shock experience, 14–15, 176, 185, 210;
in Baudelaire, 23, 148, 178, 179–180;
in crowds, 192; defense against,
178; interception of, 201; photography and, 191; reception of, 177; sexual, 185. *See also* City/metropolis:
shock experience of
Simmel, Georg, 69, 207, 239n100
Social realism, 187
Society of the Tenth of December,
47, 57
Solitude/solitary, 38, 70, 81, 83, 108,

157, 189, 291n96; of Baudelaire, 81, 107, 149
Sorel, Georges, 49, 227n13
Souvenirs, 159, 168, 274n79
Spectacle, 80, 82, 87, 89–92, 102, 107, 129–130, 149, 164, 194, 249n189, 283n41
Sphinx imagery, 245n148
Stevenson, Robert Louis, 82
Storytelling, 12, 20, 174
Strindberg, August, 161
Sue, Eugène, 105, 279n27. WORKS: *Les Mystères de Paris,* 62, 63, 73, 181, 236n69
Suicide, 60, 104, 105, 114, 250n205, 251n206, 257
Supernatural, 91, 93, 100
Surrealism, 8, 17, 45
Symbolism, 97, 195, 198, 241n117, 244n145, 248n183, 263n2, 265n17, 266n21, 269n46, 278n22

Taste, 131–133
Taylor, Frederick Winslow, 84, 244n143
Technology, 19, 21, 23, 137; art and, 34, 39, 163; Jugendstil and, 138; modernity and, 144; photography and, 34; of production, 7; regressive interpretation of, 150; of reproduction, 158, 203, 204
Telegraph, 61
Thibaudet, Albert, 77, 185, 241n121
Thiers, Adolphe, 50, 51, 229n24
Time, 43, 288n67. *See also* Baudelaire, Charles: time (theme); Benjamin, Walter: time (theme); Proust, Marcel: obsession with time and memory
Toussenel, Alphonse, 37, 221n27
Trace, 20, 39, 72, 74, 77–79, 97, 140, 173–176, 256n249
Tradition, 12, 13, 22, 49, 130, 131, 172, 174, 202

Traffic, 21, 84, 92, 115, 191
Training, 21, 125, 177, 191–192, 284
Trains and railroads, 31, 38, 207

Usefulness, 39
Utopia, 32, 33, 36, 37, 39, 41, 58, 84, 119, 141

Valéry, Paul, 74, 167, 176–177, 203, 205, 241n117, 269n45, 277n17; on Baudelaire, 177; isolation of, 190. WORKS: "La Situation de Baudelaire," 177
Vallès, Jules, 126, 178, 259n282, 277n21
Varnhagen von Ense, Karl, 190, 283n43
Veils, 184, 185, 198, 205, 287n63
Verhaeren, Emile, 112, 254n235
Verlaine, Paul, 125, 139, 171, 214n4, 265n21, 274n3
Vésuviennes (political group), 122, 257n269
Veuillot, Louis, 267n32
Viel-Castel, Count, 56–57
Vigny, Alfred de, 127, 248n180, 265n19. WORKS: *Eloa,* 57, 233n48
Vischer, Theodor, 106, 107, 251n212
Vitalism, 171

Wagner, Richard, 42, 110, 222n43
Weissbach, Richard, 2
Wiertz, A. J., 33, 35, 219n17
Wine tax, 52–53
Wish/dream images, 32, 45, 194–195
Women, 122, 144
Working class / workers, 36, 44, 48; at the barricades, 50; skilled and unskilled, 192, 193
World exhibitions, 9, 35–37, 45

Zola, Emile, 218n8. WORKS: *Thérèse Raquin,* 33, 218n8; *Travail,* 33